THE IDEA OF FORM

Cultural Memory

in

the

Present

Mieke Bal and Hent de Vries, Editors

THE IDEA OF FORM
Rethinking Kant's Aesthetics

Rodolphe Gasché

STANFORD UNIVERSITY PRESS

STANFORD, CALIFORNIA 2003

Stanford University Press
Stanford, California

© 2003 by the Board of Trustees of the
Leland Stanford Junior University.
All rights reserved.

Chapter 3 has been adapted from "Of Mere Form:
On Kant's Analytic of the Beautiful" by Rodolphe
Gasché, in *Interrogating the Tradition: Hermeneutics
and the History of Philosophy* by Charles E. Scott
and John Sallis (eds.), by permission of the State
University of New York Press. © 2000, State
University of New York. All rights reserved.

Printed in the United States of America
on acid-free, archival-quality paper.

Library of Congress Cataloging-in-Publication Data

Gasché, Rodolphe.
    The idea of form : rethinking Kant's aesthetics /
Rodolphe Gasché.
        p.   cm. — (Cultural memory in the present)
    Includes bibliographical references and index.
    ISBN 0-8047-4613-3 (cloth : alk. paper) —
ISBN 0-8047-4621-4 (pbk. : alk. paper)
    1. Kant, Immanuel, 1724–1804—Aesthetics.
2. Aesthetics, Modern—18th century.   I. Title.
II. Series.
B2799.A4 G37   2003
111'.85'092—dc21   2002007739

Original Printing 2003
Last figure below indicates year of this printing:
12   11   10   09   08   07   06

Typeset by James P. Brommer in 11/13.5 Garamond

Contents

Acknowledgments	ix
Introduction	1
1. One Principle More	13
2. Transcendentality, in Play	42
3. On Mere Form	60
4. Presenting the Maximum	89
5. Absolutely Great	119
6. Interest and Disinterestedness	155
7. The Arts, in the Nude	179
8. Hypotyposis	202
Notes	221
Bibliography	247
Index	253

Acknowledgments

This book is the labor of several years. It would have taken even longer without the opportunity provided by various invitations to lecture and, especially, to conduct seminars on certain aspects of Kant's aesthetics. I need to single out above all an invitation from Herman Parret to participate in the colloquium on Kant's aesthetics at the Centre Culturel International at Cerisy-la-Salle (Normandy, France) in 1993, which provided the incentive to work on Kant's notion of free play. During a weeklong course entitled "Judgment and the Idea of Nature in Kant's Third Critique," which I taught in 1996 at the Collegium Phenomenologicum in Perugia, I was able sketch out the rudiments of the interpretation of form that I propose in this book. Three seminars on Kant's *Critique of Judgment* that I conducted during a stay at the Zentrum für Literaturwissenschaft in Berlin in spring 1997 made it possible to reshape and finalize my stance on Kant's understanding of form in his aesthetics. I also want to record my gratitude for the three seminars that I was able to devote to the *Critique of Judgment* at the University of Amsterdam in 2000, during which I produced the final draft of my exposition of the relation of the fine arts to the moral in the Third Critique. Finally, I thank the organizers of the conference "Kant's *Critique of Judgment* and Political Thinking," held at Northwestern University at the beginning of 2002, for having given me one last opportunity to test my interpretation before the manuscript of the book went into production.

During the years I wrote this book I discussed its issues with numerous friends and colleagues. Without their valuable comments and criticism it would not have taken its present shape. I am particularly indebted to Jay M. Bernstein, Hent de Vries, Idit Dobbs-Weinstein, Rudolf A. Makkreel, Winfried Menninghaus, Dennis J. Schmidt, Rob van Gerwen, and Linda Zerilli, not only for their encouragement but also for their questions, which were enormously helpful in sharpening my interpretation of Kant's thought.

I would also like to thank Beth Gerwin for her assistance in preparing the manuscript for publication.

Some of the chapters of this book have been published before. Chapter 2 appeared under the same title ("Transcendentality, in Play") in *Kants Ästhetik/Kant's Aesthetics/L'esthétique de Kant*, ed. Herman Parret (Berlin: de Gruyter, 1998). Chapter 3 was adapted from my "Of Mere Form: On Kant's Analytic of the Beautiful," in *Interrogating the Tradition: Hermeneutics and the History of Philosophy*, ed. Charles E. Scott and John Sallis (Albany: State University of New York Press, 2000), and appears here by permission of the publisher. A preliminary draft of a short section of Chapter 4 was published in *Il cannochiale. Rivista di studi filosofici* (Naples), special issue on *Darstellung*, 1, 1998, pp. 179–91. Chapter 6, to which I have made only minor changes, was published as "Linking onto Disinterestedness, or the Moral Law in Kant's *Critique of Judgment*," in *Between Ethics and Aesthetics: Crossing the Boundaries*, ed. Dorota Glowacka and Stephen Boos (Albany: State University of New York Press, 2002), and appears here by permission of the publisher. Finally, Chapter 8 was written for a special issue of *Argumentation* entitled "Rhetoric in the History of Philosophy" (4, no. 1, 1990, pp. 85–100), where it appeared under the title "Some Reflections on the Notion of Hypotyposis in Kant."

THE IDEA OF FORM

Introduction

According to Kant, the ability to judge objects as either beautiful or sublime is not primarily a product of culture. Both types of aesthetic judgments have their roots in human nature. Even though the judgment upon the sublime admittedly requires a basis in culture, it is at bottom a natural capacity. This is even more true of the beautiful, which needs culture to a much lesser degree. Clearly, the ability to judge things as beautiful is a gift of nature to all human beings. But if taste is a disposition rooted in human nature, does this not somehow anticipate the kind of objects with which it might be concerned? Would it not be reasonable to expect these objects to be primarily natural objects? Indeed, Kant's aesthetics is unquestionably an aesthetics of nature. Whereas the beautiful arts are allotted only a very short discussion in the *Critique of Judgment*, natural beauty constitutes the prime object of Kant's "Analytic of the Beautiful." Similarly, in the "Analytic of the Sublime," Kant's prompt dismissal of the artificial sublime strictly limits the judgment of the sublime to phenomena of nature as well. Some commentators on Kant's aesthetics, assuming that an inquiry into aesthetic judgment should inevitably investigate artificial beauty and contribute to our understanding of the fine arts, have expressed deep disappointment with the privilege accorded to natural beauty. But if Kant conceives of beauty and sublimity primarily in view of what is beautiful and sublime in nature, might it not be that his aesthetics pursues an agenda quite distinct from the one commonly attributed to this discipline? Furthermore, if Kant predicates beauty chiefly of wild things of nature (and artifacts that either have something wild about them, like the meandering lines of wall coverings, or originate in cultures that are—so he believed—still in a state of nature, like the canoes or cloths of the Caribs and Iroquois), and if he identifies the sublime where raw nature is at its wildest, this restriction of the realm to which judgments of taste naturally apply orients the task of Kant's aesthetics in an intriguing direction. Given that nature is defined by Kant as the domain of objectivity, and hence of what can possibly be known, nature in the wild stands as cognitively undomesticated nature. Vice versa, things—including artifacts—for which no determined concepts are available, and whose purpose cannot be made out, are similar to things found in uncharted nature. It follows that the beauty or sublimity that wild nature is judged to have, and the pleasure that is felt on the occasion of judging, must refer to an accomplishment of sorts by the aesthetic judgments. The investigation of Kant's aesthetics in the following study therefore concerns aesthetic judgment's singular achievement with respect to the phenomena of nature that have not yet been cognitively mastered, or that would even seem to be absolutely unmasterable.

In the wake of Hegel's disparaging remarks on natural beauty, the philosophical discipline of aesthetics as it emerged in the middle of the eighteenth century has largely been replaced by a philosophy of the fine arts, or an aesthetics whose sole interest is artificial beauty.[1] But the *Critique of Judgment*, whose theoretical potential for the understanding of beauty was historically realized only in projects that radically reoriented and transformed Kant's insights, not only stands apart from post-Kantian attempts to conceptualize beauty but also breaks with prior notions of aesthetics. Kant's critical rejection of the notion of perfection, which was so important in eighteenth-century aesthetics, is just one case in point. However, this rupture with his ancestors does not annul the many points of contact between Kant's attempt to think through aesthetic judgment and eighteenth-century elaborations on taste. First and foremost among such elaborations are those of Alexander Gottlieb Baumgarten, who not only coined the title "Aesthetics" for the new philosophical discipline that emerged with his 1850 publication of the *Aesthetica* but also conceived of this discipline as a distinct branch of epistemology, one devoted to the analysis of sensitive, or aesthetic, cognition. Such cross-references to earlier positions in the history of aesthetics, where natural beauty also plays a dominant role, are no doubt essential to understanding Kant's assessment of taste as judgmental in character; nevertheless, the Third Critique is not superannuated by its overriding concern with the beautiful and the sublime in nature. The very frustration that the *Critique of Judgment* causes in many of its readers, the unrelenting criticism leveled against it, and the unending flow of misinterpretations to which its basic concepts have been subjected since the beginning of the nineteenth century (especially those by Schopenhauer and Nietzsche) all attest, if paradoxically, to its continuing appeal. Indeed, one may even wonder whether it is not precisely because Kant's aesthetics is an aesthetics of natural beauty, rather than of artwork, that it is important for the understanding of the fine arts, and particularly of modern and postmodern art, which are the exclusive concern of post-Kantian aesthetics.

Kant's aesthetics is something of an oddity in the history of aesthetics. It does not establish conceptual rules for the beautiful, to the end of constituting a science of the beautiful (that is, aesthetics in the spirit of the eighteenth century). Rather, Kant's aesthetics—specifically the "Critique of the Aesthetical Judgment" in the Third Critique—inquires into the formal conditions of possibility of aesthetic judgment in general. However, such judgment is pure only when it occurs in the face of objects, such as the wildflower, that are still cognitively unmastered, or objects, such as the wild ocean, that are seemingly beyond all control. Only when faced with wild objects or unbounded nature, for which no determined concepts are available, can radical disinterestedness be achieved. Such objects are also bereft of the possibility of becoming objects of sensory satisfaction. The Kantian investigation into what constitutes aesthetic judgments is an aesthetics because these judgments are grounded in and determined by affects caused within the judging subject. In other words, whenever the subject successfully judges the wild things of nature or nature at its wildest, this judgment is accompanied by an animating feeling of pleasure. Given that I possess no determined concept regarding the species and the purpose of the wildflower, and that no concept is adequate to comprehend the ocean in a state of tumult, the pleasure I feel is the pleasure of having succeeded, against all odds, in making a judgment at all. As is well known, aesthetic judgment is based on the intuition of the form of the object, and of the totality of what is boundlessly formless. If the intuition of form in wild things and the awareness of totality in the face of boundless formlessness are accompanied by pleasure, form and totality obviously fulfill a purpose. Undoubtedly, aesthetic judgments are not cognitive or theoretical judgments; but the awareness of form resulting from aesthetic judgment of the beautiful and the awareness of totality resulting from aesthetic judgment of nature at its wildest indicate that the pleasure felt in both cases is the satisfaction of having secured what Kant calls a "cognition in general." Cognition in general is the purpose or end in view of which the judgment of taste predicates beauty of wild nature or sublimity of nature at its wildest. Aesthetic judgment is thus something of a para-epistemic accomplishment. Where cognition fails, aesthetic judgment ensures a minimal mastery and minimal identification of something for which no determined concepts of the understanding are at hand. Such judgment is not "ante-" or "proto-" epistemic, since these qualifications would suggest, of course, that its achievements precede epistemic accomplishments properly speaking. The achievements of reflective judgment—which comprises both aesthetic and teleological judgment—are in no way foundational for or anterior to those of cognitive judgment. Of course, as Kant explains, reflective judgments can be followed by determinate ones. But the accomplishments of aesthetic reflective judgment stand beside and on a par with cognitive accomplishments; thus aesthetic judgment holds its place as equal to cognition. This para-epistemic dimension of judgments of taste is the hallmark of Kant's aesthetics.

Yet Kant's expression "cognition in general" does not imply that the peculiar achievements of aesthetic judgment are modeled exclusively upon the cognitive realm. "Cognition in general" includes both the state in which the imagination and the understanding agree with each other and the state in which they disagree. The former is demonstrated by the representation of a beautiful object. The latter—that is, the state in which aesthetic judgment achieves a cognition in a broad sense when the powers involved in cognition fail to enter into a harmonious relation—is demonstrated by the representation of the sublime. For, indeed, the cognitive powers' inability to come to grips with an absolutely formless object calls reason, the power of the ideas, onto the scene, which by entering into a relation with the imagination enables a judgment, namely, that this object is sublime. The judgment that something is sublime testifies to the successful securing of a representation in front of an object that is formless to the point of inhibiting all such effort. As the intervention of the idea of totality, and hence of reason, in the judgment upon the sublime shows, aesthetic judgment is thus also involved in a para-ethical task. Indeed, as we will see, the idea of totality that makes a judgment of sublimity possible does not yet constitute that judgment as a moral one. The role of reason is limited here to making a representation possible by invoking the powers of the ideas. However, the judgment of the sublime not only anticipates the regulative use of ideas in cognition properly speaking but also, by making the subject aware of its supersensible power, announces practical reason. Just as the reflective aesthetic judgment is situated apart from and on par with cognitive judgments, it is also distinct from moral judgments.

According to Kant's well-known claim in the section of the *Critique of Pure Reason* entitled "Transcendental Aesthetics," any endeavor "to bring the critical treatment of the beautiful under rational principles, and so to raise its rules to the rank of a science," is a fruitless one. Kant demarcates himself here from Baumgarten—the "admirable analytical thinker"—and argues that the nature of the source from which the rules or criteria of beauty are abstracted dictates that Baumgarten's aesthetics must necessarily remain empirical, and can "never serve as determinate *a priori* laws by which our judgment of taste must be directed."[2] If Kant proposes an aesthetics of his own in the *Critique of Judgment*, he does not thereby withdraw the criticism he leveled, in the First Critique, against what he labeled an "abortive attempt" to account critically and rationally for the beautiful. The part devoted to aesthetics in the Third Critique should not be understood as an effort to establish the rules that constitute beauty (or sublimity) and to organize them into a rational science. Rather, Kant's aesthetics amounts to a critical assessment of the judgment of taste: an assessment that, in distinction from the first two Critiques, does not extend to a positive metaphysics, or a science of the beautiful or the sublime. As Ernst Cassirer has noted, the possibility of developing a transcendentally based aesthetics did not derive from any deepening understanding of the phenomenon of art and artistic creation. On the contrary, this possibility rests on a certain progress made within the critique of theoretical cognition, which assures the realization of such an aesthetics. Cassirer writes: "An extension and deepening of the concept of the a priori in theory first makes possible the a priori in aesthetics and paves the way for its determination and perfection." This refinement of the theoretical notion of the a priori actually broadened the problem of the accessibility of nature to our faculties of cognition—that is, the problem of the purposiveness of nature. It now included not only the question of the conformity of nature in general to the faculties of the mind but also the possible adequacy of contingent and singular phenomena of nature to reason.[3] In particular, the expansion of what is theoretically a priori determinable and cognizable allowed the inclusion of phenomena of nature in the wild, and of nature at its wildest. With this development, a transcendental perspective on aesthetics became both a possibility and a necessity.[4]

The realization that unknown or wild things of nature have form, or that nature even at its wildest still suggests totality, is pleasurable because it reveals the adequacy of nature to the mental faculties. Thus a thing for which no determined concepts of the understanding are available is beautiful if it can be judged to display form, while an absolutely formless thing of nature is sublime if it can be judged to be a totality. Translated into para-epistemological terms: a wild thing is beautiful if it yields to the minimal conditions for the cognition of empirical objects; nature at its wildest is sublime if it meets reason's demand for totality. This para-epistemic (and para-ethical) assessment of the judgment of taste calls for some anticipatory remarks concerning what I will seek to demonstrate in the present study.

It has been suggested that most of the existing interpretations of Kant's aesthetics can be situated on a continuum that stretches between two extremes, one a narrow aestheticist or formalist approach in which beauty and art are separated from questions of truth and moral rectitude, and the other a broader approach that grants the relevance of the aesthetic attitude for a discussion of truth and morality.[5] This divide unfolds along the lines of what has been called Kant's "double aesthetics,"[6] and prioritizes either the problematic of the beautiful or that of the sublime. As this study will argue, both extremes miss the transcendental thrust of Kant's aesthetics and remain caught within an empiricist understanding of what the *Critique of Judgment* seeks to establish. By understanding "form" as a surface phenomenon of things—their shape and the arrangement of their parts into a whole—the aestheticist approach fails to see that in the transcendental perspective of Kant's investigation, form is tied to the formation of a representation of objects of nature that are cognitively unaccounted for. The attempted rapprochement of the aesthetic and the moral dimensions on the other extreme exhibits a similar oblivion to the transcendental nature of the Third Critique's task. Even though Kant concludes his analysis of reflective aesthetic judgment by construing the beautiful as a "symbol of morality," this in no way abolishes the initial distinction between pure judgments of taste and moral judgments, on which rests the possibility of the transcendental (rather than empirical) analysis of aesthetic judgments. Pure judgments of taste are not one category among others of aesthetic judgments. Rather, they are at the very core of Kant's "Critique of the Aesthetical Judgment" insofar as it is a critique. Furthermore, as the term "symbol" suggests, Kant's conclusion makes sense only against the background of the inquiry into those structural traits of the pure judgments of taste that enable and predispose it to relate, a priori, to the morally good. Since Kant conceived of the Third Critique as a bridge between theoretical and practical reason, causality and freedom, nature and morality, which he held to be separated by an abyss, the question of how reflective judgment manages to bridge the chasm in question is central to this study. However, the way in which the analysis of reflective judgment takes place in the "Analytic of the Aesthetical Judgment" in the cases of both the beautiful and the sublime—namely, according to the fundamental categories of the understanding (quantity, quality, relation, modality)—does not warrant the assumption that from the start of his analysis, Kant shows the cognitive and the moral dimensions to be in balance in reflective judgment. To proceed this way is to overlook the technicalities of the "Analytic." More seriously, it is to confuse certain statements in the "Analytic" that concern the relation of the beautiful to the morally good—statements whose nature is empirical, or which imply determining judgments upon the beautiful—with statements that concern the structural nature of the disinterested reflective aesthetic judgment.

This danger of confusing levels of thought is particularly critical in Kant's discussion of the ideal of beauty. Therefore, in conformity with the transcendental quest of the *Critique of Judgment*, the present study will assess how the cognitive and the moral relate to each other in reflective judgments not by recourse to empirical judgments of taste, which are never pure, but by appeal to the pure judgment of taste, in short, in structural terms. I will elaborate in detail upon the role of reason in judgments of taste, and not only in those judgments passed upon the sublime—in which reason is admittedly involved—but, more important, in judgments upon the mere form of objects, that is, upon the beautiful, where Kant makes no explicit reference to reason. Only such an analysis can respond to the question of how the judgment of taste bridges the gap between the theoretical and the moral.

A few remarks about the aestheticist interpretation of Kant's "Analytic of the Beautiful" are in order here. According to the aestheticist and formalist interpretation of Kantian aesthetics, beautiful form consists in the formal and harmonious arrangement of parts into a whole, and has no other end than the pleasure it stirs in the beholder. Form is perceived here as autonomous, and is celebrated for its own sake; it has no further purpose than to be subjectively pleasing. The pleasure that it provides arises from the mere play of its elements, and has no relation to any further end. The main thrust of this book is directed against this interpretation. This is not to say, however, that I would join forces with the representatives of the other extreme—those concerned with truth and morality in the beautiful and in the arts—and that, like them, I would hold "form" in the aestheticist and formalist interpretation to be empty of all content and to give a merely self-complacent pleasure. Kant's relentless effort in the *Critique of Judgment* to separate beautiful form from anything sensible or moral would seem to suggest that his use of form, or more precisely "mere form," in this work breaks with the Aristotelian or scholastic tradition, according to which form is always the form of some matter and hence is understood in its difference from, that is, in relation to, its other. Form is always the form *of* something, and, in principle, cannot be thought independently. This continues to be true despite Kant's claim that the mere form of objects must be kept separate from all matter, such as charm, or any content, such as moral concepts. Undoubtedly, the notion of form in Kant's transcendental idealism no longer concerns the constitution of things themselves. Rather, as the *Critique of Pure Reason* argues, the exclusive concern of form is the constitution of the objects of experience, for which it provides the a priori ordering principles —that is, the forms of sensibility (space and time) and of the understanding (the categories). Form, here, concerns the fundamental syntheses without which no sensible intuition and no cognition would be possible. Nonetheless, form continues to have a material correlate, which is the very matter of the experience.[7] The concept of mere form encountered in the Third Critique, on the basis of which wild objects of nature are found to be beautiful, is anything but a free-floating form. It is a concept that is intelligible from Kant's elaborations on the transcendental concept of form in the First Critique. As we shall see, the mere form found in wild objects of nature concerns the faculties involved in securing a representation. This is also to say that it secures an experience of such "wild" objects, for which no determined concept of the understanding is as yet available. Mere form here is anything but an empty, contentless arrangement. It is the form that the cognitive powers achieve in the face of wild objects whose representation suggests purposiveness, notwithstanding the absence of determinate concepts. Mere form is thus above all a para-epistemic concept.

Kant's analysis of the beautiful was long considered to be the sole part of the Third Critique that merited serious consideration; currently, it is the part on the sublime that enjoys this elevated status. It is important to remark that this shift in privilege from the beautiful to the sublime is largely a function of the desire to make Kant's aesthetics fruitful for an understanding of the arts.[8] But as I have already said, the arts play only a minor role in Kant's reflections in the Third Critique. Once it is acknowledged that judgments of taste (whether on the beautiful or the sublime) primarily concern natural objects or phenomena, and that Kant's aesthetics consequently involves aspects of an objective and cognizable realm, such prioritization no longer makes any sense.[9] In light of the epistemological questions that I understand Kant to be pursuing in his aesthetics, the two parts form a whole—however complex—which does not permit a choice between the beautiful and the sublime. This leads me to mention that in my interpretation of the "Analytic of the Beautiful," I make extensive use of the First Introduction to the *Critique of Judgment*, which Kant left unpublished. As Giorgio Tonelli has persuasively argued, the First Introduction was written after the completion of the "Analytic of the Beautiful," the "Deduction of Pure Aesthetical Judgments," and the "Dialectic of the Aesthetical Judgment."[10] Unlike the Second (published) Introduction, the First Introduction enters deeply into the epistemological tenets of Kant's critique of the judgment of taste and its connections with the preceding Critiques, in particular the *Critique of Pure Reason*. The First Introduction is thus in some sense closer to his initial intentions for discussing the problem of taste, and remains a major source for any interpretation that seeks to understand Kant's aesthetics from the perspective of the epistemological innovations of his earlier work. Among other things, the unpublished introduction provides a great number of invaluable clues to the notion of mere form and is thus a significant resource for expanding upon the para-epistemic function of this notion. It also lends significant support to the argument that the pleasure caused by the perception—or rather judgment—of beautiful form has to do with the fundamental structure of cognition, and more precisely, with the minimal conditions of cognizability.

The approach that I have chosen will inevitably incur the charge that I have modeled the structure of aesthetic judgment exclusively upon the cognitive realm. Undoubtedly, the para-epistemic achievement of the reflective judgment of taste is made to stand out at the very beginning of this study. Yet the discussion of this essential aspect of reflective judgment not only focuses from the outset upon the relation between nature and reason but also highlights those structural features of the reflective aesthetic judgment of the mere form of an object that reveal the "presence" of reason (and, hence, of a maximum). I turn explicitly to the aesthetic and the moral only later, in Chapter 4's discussion of the structural ways in which the judgment of taste combines these two domains, specifically in the exposition of the double presentation involved in aesthetic judgments. But since this analysis must necessarily target pure judgments of taste, rather than empirical judgments in which the aesthetic and the moral dimensions mingle easily, and must furthermore heed the founding distinctions that characterize the transcendental inquiry, it yields only a structural resemblance (rather than identity) of judgments of taste to moral judgments.

Since the whole of the "Analytic of the Beautiful" is based on the notion of form, as is, indirectly, the "Analytic of the Sublime," Kant's aesthetic is certainly an aesthetics of form. By definition, the pure judgment of taste is a formal judgment, in that it concerns not the matter of the representation of an object but solely the object's form. Form is the unmistakable "space" of this aesthetics. But is it formalist in the sense understood by the formalist theories of modern and postmodern aesthetics? If "formalist" suggests the severance of the concern with form from all questions of cognition, then Kant's aesthetics cannot be labeled that way. Indeed, the notion of form in the transcendental idealism characteristic of the First Critique concerns the mind's capacity to gather the manifold of intuition: that is, the matter of what is given, which is manifold by definition. The "mere form" central to Kantian aesthetics is no exception to this; on the contrary, its distinguishing trait or accomplishment consists in its unifying a manifold of intuitions, or of laws, for which there is no determined concept, so as to secure what Kant repeatedly refers to as "cognition in general."

I would hold that reading the reflective judgment of taste in light of the epistemological advances of the First Critique (and against the background of Kant's practical philosophy) is the only way to do justice to the *Critique of Judgment* and to make sense of its reputedly strange architectonic. Indeed, in this Critique the subject matter is divided along the lines of the various domains of certain empirical objects—objects that cannot be accounted for from a cognitive perspective, and whose intelligibility, in the absence of concepts of the understanding, requires the intervention of the reflective judgment. Significantly, the order in which these divisions are made reflects the increasing role that reason plays in this employment of the faculty of reflection. There is a further consequence of interpreting the Third Critique as a development of Kant's transcendental approach to the question of the formation of objects of experience: it allows for a more balanced account of Kant's claim that the last Critique bridges the chasm between the two heterogeneous domains of the theoretical and the practical, and thus resists the lure of either romanticism or speculative idealism. Kant's critical investigation of the power of judgment brings to light transcendental conditions of possibility that are shared by cognitive and moral judgments—the play of the faculties and the formal purposiveness of representations—and such conditions permit a transition or passage between the two realms (rather than their unification). But this is not to say that the objects or domains that lead to the discovery of these conditions therefore gain some special privilege. In particular, the discovery of the transcendental passageway between nature and freedom does not imply a valorization of the arts. While the same transcendental principles guide reflection on uncharted aspects of nature and on certain artifacts and natural organized forms, these empirical objects are not therefore more fundamental. Nor are the merely reflective judgments called upon by these domains of objects—that is, aesthetic and teleological reflective judgments—in any way more fundamental than determining judgments. At most, the transcendental a prioris that guide these judgments are more fundamental; but, as I shall argue hereafter, the peculiar nature of these judgments means that the transcendentals in question can never be isolated with the same purity that characterizes those of determining judgments.

While Kant's theory of knowledge thus serves as the unavoidable background for the following study, I have kept explicit references to the First Critique to a minimum. However, in addition to emphasizing the First Introduction in my analysis of Kant's aesthetics, I have geared my commentary and close reading of its major sections to exhibit systematically the extent to which Kant's transcendental analysis of knowledge is presupposed in his elaborations on judgments of taste. I have chosen this approach not simply because it is more economical but also because it alone is capable of bringing forth the full complexity of what is being asserted, and the presuppositions on which these assertions are made. In my attempt to clarify Kant's theory of form and reflective judgment of form, I have also sought to avoid, whenever possible, a critical debate with the various and often contradictory interpretations that these and the related issues have received in Kant scholarship. Rather than challenging Kant's commentators, I have endeavored to think *with* Kant. As a result of the reading that I offer, many of the so-called inconsistencies and puzzles that commentators have enjoyed pointing out in this undoubtedly very difficult text of the Third Critique will appear, I hope, less problematic. Notwithstanding some indisputable discrepancies that are linked to the factual composition of the text, what emerges from the "uncritical" reading that I propose is a highly consistent set of strong arguments. Only by focusing on these arguments do the ambitiousness and the scope of the Third Critique come into view. It is with such arguments that philosophers ought to be concerned above all, and against such arguments that they should measure their criticism. Only thus will philosophers do justice to the Kantian enterprise.

I have entitled this book *The Idea of Form* even though, rigorously speaking, form is not an idea in the Kantian sense. According to the *Critique of Pure Reason*, form (along with its correlate, matter) is a concept of reflection (*Reflexionsbegriff*), and concerns the relations between concepts in a state of mind. Form and matter denote the difference between determination and the determinable in general; thus they underlie all other types of reflection and are intimately tied up with all employment of the understanding.[11] My title, *The Idea of Form*, might therefore seem to make only a customary use of the term "idea," in the sense of the thought, conception, or notion of form. But I have chosen the title for a very particular reason: my analysis of the "mere form" that is judged by aesthetic reflective judgments elicits the crucial role played by reason in the formation and judgment of form. Such intervention of reason in the realm of form is a prevailing issue in this study. While this does not make form an idea per se, it shows how instrumental the power of the ideas is to any representation of form. By entitling this book *The Idea of Form* I wish to make it plain from the outset that this is a study of how reflective aesthetic judgment structurally combines the dimensions of the cognitive and the moral.

A few words on the organization of the book may be warranted here. The analysis of how aesthetic judgment interlinks basic traits of cognition and morality culminates in Chapter 4. This chapter, in which the constitution of beautiful form is shown to require a double intervention of presentation (*Darstellung*)—schematic and symbolic presentation—is both a concluding chapter and the center of the book. Indeed, the subsequent discussion of what Kant qualifies as an appendix to his analysis of the beautiful—the part on the sublime—draws upon the conclusions reached in Chapter 4. The same holds of Chapters 6 and 7, which are devoted to explaining how Kant accounts for the beautiful of the arts in an aesthetics whose para-epistemic concerns lead to a privileging of natural over artificial beauty.

Finally, I should note that some of the chapters of this book appeared previously and have been substantially revised. However, the piece on hypotyposis, with which I began my work on Kant's *Critique of Judgment* some ten years ago, and which concludes the present study, I have left largely intact, despite a few formulations concerning the status of the transcendental in Kant's last critical work that I would no longer make in this way today. I have chosen to preserve this essay as it was published, and wish to express my appreciation for the warm reception it has enjoyed. I hope it will not prove excessively dissonant with the stance I take in the main body of this work.

1

One Principle More

Among the abilities of the mind that form the Kantian faculties (*Vermögen*), the power of judgment (*Urteilskraft*) is a faculty of a very peculiar kind. In the First Introduction to the *Critique of Judgment*, Kant writes that the power of judgment "is of such a special kind that it produces for itself no knowledge whatsoever, neither theoretical nor practical . . . but merely constitutes the union [*Verband*] of the two other higher cognitive powers, the understanding and the reason."[1] Its "function is simply to join [*nur zum Verknüpfen dient*] the two" higher powers, and thus judgment is "in no wise [an] independent cognitive capacity" but one whose role is merely to "mediate between the two other faculties."[2] From the very start, then, it would seem that, however important its function may be, the power of judgment is marked by a certain self-effacement, a subservience and a lack of independence. Now, insofar as the faculty is one of determining judgment—which holds "the capacity for *subsumption of the particular under the universal*"—no delineation could be more obvious: "it is merely a power of subsuming under concepts given from elsewhere."[3] But what about judgment in its reflective mode? Indeed, it is this latter kind of judgment that the critical investigation of the power of judgment takes up in the Third Critique. Characteristically, Kant qualifies reflective judgment in telling terms as "merely" reflective judgment. Unlike determining judgment, this judgment has seemingly no cognitive contribution to make, and Kant's qualification would appear to deprive it of any autonomy whatsoever.

A glance at how Kant distinguishes the two kinds of judgment would seem only to confirm reflective judgment's secondary status. In the First Introduction to the Third Critique, we read: "The judgment can be regarded either as a mere capacity for *reflecting* on a given representation according to a certain principle, to produce a possible concept, or as a capacity for *making determinate* a basic concept by means of a given empirical representation. In the first case it is the *reflective*, in the second the *determining* judgment."[4] The better-known definition of determining and reflective judgment, found in the Second (and final) Introduction, is more formulaic and considerably simplified; it is the version to which Kant resorts in the main body of the Third Critique and echoes in the *Logic* (1800). It runs as follows:

> Judgment in general is the faculty of thinking the particular as contained under the universal. If the universal (the rule, the principle, the law) be given, the judgment which subsumes the particular under it (even if, as transcendental judgment, it furnishes, *a priori*, the conditions in conformity with which subsumption under that universal is alone possible) is *determinant*. But if only the particular be given for which the universal has to be found, the judgment is merely *reflective*.[5]

Compared to determining (or determinant) judgment, which receives its law from the concepts that are given to it elsewhere and which accordingly subsumes the particular, the power of judgment called *merely* reflective has nothing definite to offer to the cognitive faculties, and thus appears to be an even less autonomous judgment. It is nothing more than a reflecting power, and seems to be doubly deprived of autonomy, in that it is not an independent cognitive capacity and even lacks the power of determining judgments to yield knowledge under the guidance of the understanding. Such "merely reflective" judgments, which include aesthetic and teleological judgments, would thus border on the insignificant. In consequence of such a reading, teleological judgment has more often than not received short shrift or been regarded as complete nonsense, and aesthetic judgment has been viewed by many of Kant's commentators as a contemplative, self-sufficient, or aestheticist approach to a domain characterized as disinterested, disengaged, nonserious, inconsequential, and merely playful—that is, the domain of art.[6]

Unlike theoretical and practical reason, the power of judgment is not an independent cognitive power. As we have seen, its sole function consists rather in linking these independent powers. The special task incumbent upon reflective judgment is thoroughly distinct from determining judgment, in that it is not involved in cognition or in practical matters. But is it possible that, paradoxically, this task might require reflective judgment to manifest an autonomy not foreseeable on the basis of reflection's determining and cognitive achievements? In other words, could it be that the power of judgment is capable of joining the two other powers only on condition that it can muster a freedom of its own? Before looking into precisely what reflective judgment amounts to and achieves, or inquiring into the "merely" reflective quality of reflective judgment, let me first establish, as succinctly as possible, what Kant understands by determining judgments. Such a clarification is warranted because these judgments must be either cognitive or moral: in other words, they must be judgments that either contribute to our knowledge of the world and its objects or determine action according to the moral law. In either case, determining judgments are distinguished by an unmistakable priority and significance. In what follows, I will focus on determining judgment in the cognitive sense. Although these judgments perform the valuable function of making the world known to us, we must still investigate what they tell us about it. This amounts to asking what theoretical cognition in fact amounts to for Kant. According to the lapidary definition in the Third Critique, in determining judgments, empirical representations (or particulars) are subsumed under the general concepts of nature, that is, the categories of the understanding. Consequently, such understanding is "only" categorial, that is, concerns exclusively the constituting conformity of the laws of objectivity in general with the objects of experience. Indeed, the categories are only the necessary conditions of experience and, as a result, are constitutive only of objects of experience in general. In other words, determining cognition amounts to "nothing more" than the cognition of nature in general. It follows that in determining judgments, and in the cognition they bring about, much remains undetermined. This is evident throughout the Third Critique even though, in the section of the *Critique of Pure Reason* entitled "Analytics of the Principles," Kant sought to bridge the gap between the conditions of experience in general and cognition of objects in experience by inquiring into the conditions of the possibility of objects such as those encountered in empirical experience.[7] In the Second Introduction to the Third Critique, Kant writes:

We find in the grounds of the possibility of an experience in the very first place something necessary, viz. the universal laws without which nature in general (as an object of sense) cannot be thought; and these rest upon the categories, applied to the formal conditions of all intuition possible for us, so far as it is also given *a priori*. Now under these laws the judgment is determinant, for it has nothing to do but to subsume under given laws.... But now the objects of empirical cognition are determined in many other ways than by that formal time condition, or, at least as far as we can judge *a priori*, are determinable. Hence specifically different natures can be causes in an infinite variety of ways, as well as in virtue of what they have in common as belonging to nature in general; and each of these modes must (in accordance with the concept of a cause in general) have its rule, which is a law and therefore brings necessity with it, although we do not at all comprehend this necessity, in virtue of the constitution and the limitations of our cognitive faculties. (19)

In the transcendental doctrine of the faculty of determining judgment, Kant has shown what kind of use (*Gebrauch*, *Anwendung*) must be made of the conditions of experience in general in order for the cognition of empirical objects to be possible. Nevertheless, in the case of certain objects of experience or empirical representations, determining—that is to say, cognitive—judgments are at a loss. They cannot muster a determined concept under which to subsume the things in question. In other words, cognition as understood by Kant comes to a halt before certain particulars, and before the manifold of particulars (i.e., empirical laws, or heterogeneous forms of nature). From the perspective of the transcendental laws of the understanding that make experience and cognition of nature in general possible, such particulars and their laws are contingent. Yet, as Kant stresses, if the contingent or particular does not have its own rules and lacks lawful unity, then the thoroughgoing connection of the whole of experience, a connection required a priori by our reason, is not possible. Now, determining—that is to say, cognitive—judgment is reduced to accounting for empirical representations, in the name of the transcendental concepts constitutive of nature in general. But it is not competent to deal with the particulars given in intuition, and thus reflective judgment, whether aesthetic or teleological, is needed. The task of such judgment consists in nothing less than "discovering" concepts and rules that the particular obeys. In short, the task of reflective judgment, as distinct from the task of determining judgment, is to render intelligible what is particular and contingent by showing it to have a unity that is thinkable by us, although it does not rest on the objective rules that are, of course, the prerogative of determining judgment. Considering the nature of what triggers it (to say nothing of the principle that serves as its guideline), the merely reflective judgment is thus anything but idle or empty play. Further, as should already be evident, the task that it faces is no small or insignificant one, and hence Kant's characterization of reflective judgment as "merely" reflective must in no way intimate his belittling of it.

In its more formulaic version, Kant's definition of both kinds of judgment states that determining judgment subsumes the particular under given universals, whereas reflective judgment seeks a universal for a given particular. Accordingly, the reader could be led to assume that one is just the symmetrical inversion of the other. From what we have seen so far, such an assumption would be quite misleading, since the judgments perform thoroughly distinct tasks. But something else needs to be set straight at this juncture: namely, that the opposition between the two forms of the power of judgment is predicated not on the distinction between determination and reflection but on the distinction between judgment in its determining mode and judgment in its *merely* reflective mode. Indeed, determining judgments are reflective as well, in the sense that they implicate reflection. If Kant does not give particular prominence to the operation of reflection in determining judgments, it is simply because reflection here follows the laws of the understanding.[8] The following passage about determining judgments from the First Introduction will certainly help to sustain this point:

In regard to the universal concepts of nature, under which a concept pertaining to experience but without particular empirical specification is initially possible, reflection already has its guide in the concept of nature in general, i.e., in the understanding, and the judgment requires no special principles of reflection, but *schematizes* these concepts a priori and applies these schemata, without which no experiential judgment would be possible, to each empirical synthesis. In this case judgment, in its reflection, is also determining, and the transcendental schematism of judgment provides it with a rule under which given empirical intuitions are to be subsumed.[9]

With unmistakable clarity, Kant thus establishes the presence of reflection in the determining, that is, theoretical or cognitive, judgment. Needless to say, the presence of reflection within determining judgments does not make them reflective judgments. By definition, determining judgments are never "merely" reflective. In *Critique of Pure Reason*, Kant explained: "*Reflection* (*reflexio*) does not concern itself with objects themselves with a view to deriving concepts from them directly, but is that state of mind in which we first set ourselves to discover the subjective conditions under which [alone] we are able to arrive at concepts."[10] Consequently, when Kant holds that to reflect, or to deliberate (*überlegen*), "is to compare and combine given representations either with other representations or with one's cognitive powers, with respect to a concept which is thereby made possible,"[11] the first type of comparison refers to the kind of reflection required in determining judgments (and which, indeed, is reflection in its logical mode), whereas the second type of comparison describes reflection in aesthetic reflective judgments. In all instances, judgments include a reflection upon the possible objective relation of the concepts in question, but in determining judgments concerning a manifold of representations, these concepts are a priori given to reflection. Reflection thus effaces itself before the pilot that the concept of nature in general represents. However, as Olivier Chédin has argued, it is most likely as an "analogy to the 'reflection' worked out in the First Critique that Kant develops the notion of an aesthetical reflective judgment"; even so, the analogy is only partial, because the reflection that characterizes aesthetic reflective judgment is endowed with features, and manifests an independence, not to be found in its theoretical employment.[12] Unlike determining judgments, in which reflection submits to the given concepts of nature, reflective judgments, properly speaking, are judgments in which reflection is no longer involved in operations of determination. What sets them apart from determining judgments is not that they are reflective but that they are, as Kant repeatedly emphasizes, *merely* reflective judgments.[13]

In order to elicit the exact nature and specific task of reflective judgments—"also called the critical faculty [*Beurteilungsvermögen*] (*facultas dijudicandi*)"[14]—it is thus necessary to explore the *merely* reflective quality of these judgments. Only under this condition does their difference from determining judgments (which also rely on reflection) come to light. The adverb "merely" (*bloss*) is not to be taken in a depreciatory sense. Just as "the *poet* merely promises an entertaining play with ideas, and yet it has the same effect upon the understanding as if he had only intended to carry on its business" (165), so the merely reflective judgment may seem a simple or even idle play with reflection but is in fact involved in a serious game of cognition in the broad sense. Rather than diminishing the status of this kind of judgment, the qualification "merely" serves to delimit a mode of reflecting comparison with respect to possible concepts, in the face of representations for which the understanding has no determined concepts to offer. Kant's commentators have attributed little importance to this restrictive "merely"; nor have they registered the extensive use that Kant makes of it and other restrictive adverbs such as *lediglich, nur,* and *allein* throughout the *Critique of Judgment* (though his use of "merely" in the context of teleological judgment is more rare).[15] When I bring these restrictive qualifiers into relief in the discussion below, my purpose will not be to draw up a complete inventory of occurrences of these terms in Kant's texts (if a complete inventory would even be feasible; the Third Critique is so replete with such terms as to produce curious and even amusing textual effects here and there). Rather, since the extensive presence of these restrictive terms cannot be accidental,[16] it seems crucial to figure out what reasoning imposes this device and governs its various uses, and even more important to assess whether the device tells us something specifically about reflective judgment itself. Does *merely* merely serve to indicate that reflective judgment is never determining? Were this the case, Kant could certainly have proceeded more economically. Rather, I believe that his abundant use of these restrictive terms betrays the difficulty of the task faced by Kant in this last critical work—the difficulty of isolating, with the required purity, the realm to be delimited. It could thus well be that rather than occurring incidentally in Kant's text, *merely* is used for systematic reasons, and that its status is that of a philosophical concept comparable, say, to that of the pure.

The discourse of the Third Critique has a transcendental thrust, in that it explores what precisely constitutes pure judgments of taste; Kant must, of course, proceed to confine certain phenomena within their bounds on the basis of clear-cut distinctions. It is a discourse intent on establishing the *purity* of reflective judgments, that is, their freedom from all sensible and moral elements. Kant pursues this quest in his analyses of free beauty —the kind of beauty that is central to the Third Critique's undertaking— specifically in his transcendental inquiry into the a priori principles; and while such principles are only regulatory, for teleological judgments, they constitute aesthetic judgments. It follows from this concern with the a priori principles that the Third Critique is also a quest into a pure, absolutely certain knowledge, that is, knowledge unencumbered by a direct appeal to experience, uncontaminated by any foreign admixtures, and able to guide such judgments when they are pure.[17] Yet this is precisely why the repeated recourse to restrictives is so surprising; for while such terms as *lediglich*, *nur*, *allein*, and *bloss* may be employed to confine meaning within limits and to narrow it down, they also seem to betray a patent vagueness, ambiguity, and hesitation. "Pure" and "mere" are not equivalent, interchangeable designations. What characterizes purity is that even though it stipulates separation and isolation, it is ultimately self-sufficient and consequently is definable from itself.[18] By contrast, what is said to be "merely" something is only negatively delimited; it is what it is only in distinction from, and with respect to, something else. It is defined only by way of derivation, and this secondarity explains a certain ambiguity or lack of precision that the qualification "mere" or "merely" carries with it. So, we may ask, what is the rationale for resorting to the "mere" in a quest for purity? How does the "mere" find its way into a discourse that aims at clearly severing the pure from any possible admixture? And if such a recourse to the "mere" is inevitable in the critical treatment of the reflective judgment, what does this reveal about the transcendental investigation in question? Could it signal something concerning the status and sweep of the discursive inquiry into reflective judgment? In other words, is the vagueness and ambiguity of the restrictive qualifier intrinsically part of the purity that is sought?

Of all the restrictives to which Kant resorts in the Third Critique, *bloss* is the one that stands out, and therefore it is with this term that I shall take issue. To begin with, I wish to emphasize that the ambiguity and vagueness that I have associated with the adverb "merely" have not escaped the notice of some philosophers, although in different contexts and without reference to the Third Critique. From a speculative point of view, the vagueness and ambiguity of something described as "merely" are due to the abstraction of this qualifier's conferred meaning. In terms of existence, what is qualified as "merely" something is only one side of what it is supposed to be in its essential nature and according to its concept. "Mereness" is thus only an initial determination of an object or a state, and calls for supersession by a fuller determination. Rather than being a positive index of a thing or a mental operation, as it seems to be in Kant, mereness is what by definition needs to be overcome. Hegel notes that what is characterized as merely something—"the abstract meaning of *mere* content"—"is destined in itself to be actually expressed [*zur Ausführung zu kommen*] and thereby made concrete."[19] Husserl treats "mere" even more harshly. While arguing that objective scientificity and its idea of truth have their ultimate root in what is commonly described as the "'merely subjective-relative' intuition of prescientific world-life," Husserl recalls that "'merely' has, as an old inheritance, the disdainful coloring of the doxa." "Mere" has no epistemic distinction; rather, it belongs to the inferior cognitive realm of opinion, and borders on error and falsity. For Husserl, the "stamp 'merely subjective and relative'" permits objective truth to discredit the whole dimension of the prescientific lifeworld and reveals a traditional association of the "mere" with nonphilosophical, nonscientific, everyday thought.[20] "Mere" is thus stigmatized as a modality of nondiscursive, nonrigorous, or even sloppy thinking. Such a verdict leaves us with no choice but to further investigate this term, in order to catch a glimpse of the reasons that have forced Kant, in his search for what constitutes the purity of aesthetic and teleological judgments, to make extensive use of such a controversial modifier.[21]

To begin our investigation, let us consider the range of meanings within the German word. But first I must note that the following etymological and lexicological inquiry into the term *bloss* is not intended to ground its meaning in some unshakable etymon but rather to focus our attention on the various semantic fields of the term that may be in play when Kant uses it. Needless to say, the first source for such an investigation is Adelung's German dictionary from 1793. *Bloss*, Adelung notes, means "to be deprived, or to have been robbed of one's cover, and is said, especially of such things that usually are covered." In other words, it is an adjective (or adverb) that marks a privation, in contrast to a prior and customary state of possession, protection, or endowment. *Bloss* designates a state that is exceptional, out of the ordinary. What is said to be *bloss* is distinct from, and even opposed to, the fullness that ordinarily characterizes something. According to this dictionary, *bloss* is an adjective that "only rarely allows for a comparative or superlative because it usually designates a deprivation that is so complete that it is no longer capable of any further degree of intensification." In its proper sense, the word refers to being naked, and is said of an unsheathed weapon such as a sword, but especially of a human body not being covered by clothes.[22] Figurally, *bloss* denotes above all the deprivation of a protective cover (such as the one used in fencing), so that a part of one's body is exposed and vulnerable to one's adversary. More generally, it refers to betraying a weakness or a secret. Finally, Adelung remarks that the term signifies "to be deprived of all other qualities, or predicates, to be alone, nothing but." In all cases, *bloss* designates a clear-cut demarcation: what is qualified as *bloss* is reduced, via a thorough deprivation of everything that it usually possesses, to a state of total nakedness and vulnerability, or to just what remains when it has been stripped of all former qualities. But while such divestment betrays a weakness or a secret, it also exposes something; in other words, it makes something plain for all to see. Reflecting on the term's possible etymological roots, Adelung notes that while it has been suggested that *bloss* derives from *lösen* ("to separate," "to detach"—a derivation to which I shall return), more probably it derives from the "old *las, laus*, appearance, and the verb *lassen*, or *laten*, to see and to appear . . . *bloss* then means properly to shine forth. A naked (a blank) sword whose deadly uncovered blade strikes the eye."[23] Thus the attribute designated by the adverb *bloss* starkly exhibits a quality that usually remains covered up, a secret quality, as it were, that occasionally becomes exposed for all to see, and whose meaning derives entirely from the opposing qualities that normally serve to cover it up, even though it is nothing more nor less than what it is, radically divested of all its former covers.

In their entry on *bloss* in the *Deutsches Wörterbuch* (1854)—where Kant, significantly enough, is the source for several of the examples—Jacob and Wilhelm Grimm make a number of observations about the term that may allow for a more nuanced account of its semantic field. After recalling some of the meanings we have already encountered in Adelung, they note that the term also serves to speak of the bareness of a landscape or a tree. Further, apart from meaning "simple," "plain," or "sheer," *bloss* suggests blankness, vacuity, or emptiness. The Grimms mention that, since "the representation of *nudus* touches upon that of *solus*," *bloss* can also signify "only," "sole." Occasionally (as we have seen with Adelung), the word also takes on the meaning of "open," "manifest," "for all to see."[24] In the Grimms' account, as in Adelung's, *bloss* is not equivalent to "pure," unlike the English "mere," which derives from the Latin *merus*, "pure," "unmixed." Indeed, if in the sense of "simple" and "naked," but also of "only" or "solely," *bloss* can suggest a sense of "pure," it is a purity that carries or is easily contaminated by the meanings of "empty," "bare," "sparse," or "puny."[25] At most, the simplicity, nakedness, and soleness that the word conveys delimit the bounds—the archaic English word "mere" signifies "boundary" or "landmark"—within which purity could be located. All by itself, "mere" outlines only the confines of a purity that does not define itself from itself but can be apprehended only in a negative fashion; in other words, only by way of what has been cut off by the *bloss*. Thus whenever the mereness of something is asserted, systematic attention must be paid to what precisely has been excluded. Our earlier investigation has already forced us to compare the merely reflective nature of judgment with the determining judgment and its characteristic logical reflection. But the very fact that the intelligibility of mereness depends on what has been stripped away, and that the specificity of the "merely" reflective nature of reflection can be made out only in contrast to determining judgment (rather than in its own terms) and can shine forth in all its nakedness only when the latter has reached its limits, betrays something about the nature and status of that specificity. Particularly, the purity sought in merely reflective judgments—and this means the a priori transcendental structures that constitute them—will in one way or another bear the mark of this essential dependence.

We have already revisited Kant's claim that in cognition the power of judgment stands "under laws of another faculty (the understanding)" and "proceeds only *schematically*."²⁶ He writes in the Third Critique: "The determinant judgment only subsumes under universal transcendental laws given by the understanding; the law is marked out for it, *a priori*, and it has therefore no need to seek a law for itself in order to be able to subordinate the particular in nature to the universal" (15–16). In determining judgment, which subsumes the particular under given concepts, the power of judgment is relieved, as it were, of the burden of searching for a law; as Kant writes, "it has no autonomy" (232). By contrast, in merely reflective judgment—which merely reflects on the particular in the absence of determining concepts and thus initially seemed to be even less of an entity than was the determining judgment—the power of judgment incurs the burden of searching for laws for the particular, a task that requires autonomy of some kind. Indeed, such autonomy is congruent with the reflection that characterizes merely reflective judgments. In the "Critique of the Teleological Judgment," where Kant returns to the distinction between determining and reflective judgment, he writes: "the *reflective* judgment must subsume under a law which is not yet given, and is therefore in fact only a principle of reflection upon objects, for which we are objectively quite in want of a law or of a concept of an object that would be adequate as a principle for the cases that occur" (232). This is not yet the moment for a detailed inquiry into the kinds of particulars that judgment may encounter and for which no law is given under which to subsume them; nevertheless, let me recall that, as with the divide between aesthetic and teleological judgments, such an encounter occurs when the mind is faced with one of two things: either a manifold of intuition, concerning single things and the multiple laws of nature for which no unifying concept is available, or the organized forms of nature that cannot be accounted for on the basis of mechanical causality alone. What judgment is left with in these cases is to reflect on the particulars in question, in view of a possible concept under which to subsume them. Now, Kant writes that since "no use of the cognitive faculties can be permitted without principles, the reflective judgment must in such cases serve as a principle for itself. This, because it is not objective and can supply no ground of cognition of the object adequate for design, must serve as a mere subjective principle for the purposive employment of our cognitive faculties, i.e. for reflecting upon a class of objects" (232). The merely reflective judgment is thus distinct from the determining judgment in that the former has a principle of its own. In its employment it follows a rule that is specifically its own, rather than one imposed on it by another faculty (the understanding). Moreover, reflective judgment gives this rule to itself. Now, what can it mean to say that, in the absence of objective concepts, the reflective judgment serves as a principle for itself? When it finds no determined concepts under which to subsume the particular, reflective judgment, if it is not to remain idle, needs a principle for its reflection upon the particular. Effectively abandoned by the understanding, it has no choice but to give a principle to itself. But in this case, as Kant remarks, it serves itself as a principle for itself; thus reflective judgment literally gives itself to itself. More precisely, as the power that constitutes the union between the understanding and reason—nature and freedom—reflective judgment gives unity and unification to itself, as the principle of its reflection. In giving itself to itself as its own principle—and as we will see, this principle is the (inner) formal purposiveness of the forms and products of nature, their adequacy to reason—merely reflective judgment becomes capable of approaching the particular in view of its possible comprehensibility. But this process of rendering unconceptualizable particulars intelligible becomes possible only when some degree of autonomy is demonstrated by the reflective judgment. Furthermore, by taking on the task of giving to itself its own (subjective) principle, the seemingly vain activity of mere reflection meets reason's qualifying demand for a thoroughgoing unity of experience.

However autonomous reflective judgment may be, we must recall that its autonomy exists only in distinction from the reflection that takes place in the understanding. In mere reflection upon particulars without objective concepts, the exercise of autonomy remains a function of the judgment's divestment of something that it ordinarily achieves. When judgment is merely reflective, it engages in an act that "is not based on the concept of object" and thus is, Kant writes, an act that it exercises for itself (*die sie für sich selbst . . . ausübt*).[27] In mere reflection, the power of judgment not only acts in view of itself but also acts all by itself, alone and independently. It is free from the constraints of the understanding. "Mere" indicates that in the act of mere reflection the power of judgment acts for its own benefit; but it further suggests that when it is merely reflective, the power of judgment takes place in a certain isolation (*Absonderung*) and in a state of severance or separation from the other faculties. Even though, as Adelung has noted, it is unlikely that *bloss* derives from *lösen, belösen*, "to separate," nevertheless in mere reflection the power of judgment is disengaged from those faculties that ordinarily help it or indeed impose themselves on it. It finds itself operating without the intervention of the understanding in its determining mode. When judgment is merely reflective and is "taken by itself [*für sich allein genommen*]," it represents "a separate cognitive power [*eine abgesonderte Erkenntniskraft*] . . . concerned with how just two faculties—imagination and understanding—are related in a representation prior to [the emergence of] any concept," Kant remarks.²⁸ In the mode of mere reflection, the power of judgment as a cognitive power is used in isolation: that is, a "separate use [*abgesonderter Gebrauch*]" is made of it. "Mere" in merely reflective judgments thus indicates an autonomy in the power of judgment, because in the experience of particulars for which no concepts are available, this power is disengaged from its usual ties to the determining mode of the other faculties.

Of course such a "mere" use of a cognitive faculty is not the exclusive prerogative of the power of judgment. We might recall, for instance, that intuitions can be blind and concepts empty. However, unlike other instances of the isolated performance of the powers, the insulated activity of "mere" judgment is not without effects. It does not spin in a void; indeed, in the aesthetic reflective judgment upon particulars, such mere use induces affects—the feeling pleasure or displeasure—and hence constitutes this judgment as synthetic. Although no cognition occurs in such judgments, they predicate a priori the pleasure or displeasure brought by certain particulars. This link of reflective judgments to affects is, as Kant notes in the preface to the Third Critique, "precisely the puzzle in the principle of judgment, which renders a special section for this faculty necessary in the *Critique*" (5). Such judgments, therefore, are not empty, idle, or vain. Kant explains:

In the faculty of judgment understanding and imagination are regarded as mutually related, and this can be considered (as happened in the transcendental schematism of the judgment) primarily as objective and cognitive; but this same relationship of two cognitive faculties can also be regarded purely subjectively, with respect to how one helps or hinders the other in a given representation and thereby affects one's mental state, hence as a relation which is sensible (a situation not encountered in the separate use of any other cognitive faculty).²⁹

Consequently, mere reflection is "devoid of concepts [*ohne allen Begriff*]."³⁰ It takes place in isolation—sundered from the other faculties, insofar as they are involved in cognition—by way of acts that it performs for its own sake. This does not mean, however, that in the reflective judgment the power of judgment reveals itself to be an absolutely independent (and perhaps more originary) power in its own right. Its qualification as a "merely" reflective judgment is precisely what prohibits this conclusion. In the first place, the power of judgment is nothing in itself; it is always only the union of other powers. If it is said to be a separate power when it is merely reflective, this is because, in this rather extraordinary employment, it links the imagination and the understanding (or the imagination and reason) in a relation that is merely subjective and that contrasts what ordinarily obtains in objective judgments.

I have already remarked that the isolated use of the power of reflection is not an inconsequential operation, in that this mere use affects the senses of the reflecting subject. In merely reflective judgments, beauty or sublimity is attributed to certain things, and such "predication" is accompanied by pleasure. But the absence of determined concepts also enables the power of reflection to bring forth a subjective predisposition without which no determining cognition would get under way; this is the free play of the faculties, which will be discussed in some detail in the following chapter. Rather than diminishing or even denigrating reflection, the qualification "mere" names the ability of this power of judgment to shed light on an affective dimension of cognition in a broad sense. More precisely, and in Lyotardian terms, it illuminates what thinking feels when it thinks,[31] over against, and in distinction from, the overpowering role of the understanding (and morality) in the ordinary employment of the faculties. To designate this purely subjective—and hence seemingly relative—use of the power of judgment, Kant has recourse to a modifier that has long been castigated as vague and imprecise. But this "mere" is in truth anything but relative. The isolation of the power of judgment may never be absolute, and may be visible as such only from the position of the understanding; nevertheless, Kant's use of "mere" reveals that, in its occasional isolation, the power of judgment is itself capable of isolating, and thus making manifest, a necessary subjective component of all cognitive mental life. The restrictive "mere" attached to reflection is not simply an unfortunate stopgap. It also attests positively to the condition of isolation under which the affective component in judgmental life has a unique opportunity to manifest itself and to have, as it were, a life of its own. The "mere" testifies to the exceptional, exemplary, and always singular occasion on which this subjective component is beheld, seemingly in all its nakedness. Above all, it testifies to the way in which the isolation that contextualizes these insights affects the status itself of what thus specifically comes into view, as well as that of its transcendental thrust.

At this point, I wish to return to Kant's characterization of the task incumbent on the merely reflective judgment. Kant has concisely elaborated it as the task of finding the proper universal for a sole given particular. He also characterizes such finding of universals for given particulars as judgment's obligation "to ascend [*aufzusteigen*] from the particular in nature to the universal" (16), or to more general laws.[32] This definition of the task is as prone to misunderstandings as is the equally summary definition of what sets determining and reflective judgments apart. Only patient attention to what Kant actually asserts in the Third Critique about reflective judgment—whether aesthetic or teleological—can overcome the danger of misinterpreting his formulaic definitions.

Let us recall that determining reflection does not have a principle of its own. In subsuming particulars under concepts of nature, reflection yields to the laws of the understanding. Only in taste, in aesthetic reflective judgment, does the power of judgment show itself to be a faculty that really has its own distinctive and a priori principle. It alone "contains a principle which the judgment places quite *a priori* at the basis of its reflection upon nature," and therefore, as Kant observes, "in a critique of judgment the part containing the aesthetical judgment is essential" (30). By contrast, the part on the teleological reflective judgment could be "appended to the theoretical part of philosophy" (6). Aesthetic judgment precedes all conceptual understanding of the object and hence has its determining basis in the power of judgment alone, free from any admixture of the other cognitive faculties. Teleological judgment, on the other hand, is based on "the concept of a natural end, [which] even if it is used in judging only as the principle of the reflective and not of the determining judgment, still cannot occur save through the union of reason with empirical concepts."[33] According to Kant, it follows from this that "the teleological judgment is not a special faculty, but only the reflective judgment in general, so far as it proceeds, as it always does in theoretical cognition, according to concepts" (31), though in teleological judgment these concepts do not serve to determine objects. Notwithstanding the fact that teleological judgment is only reflective judgment in general, and not a special faculty with its own a priori principle as is aesthetic judgment, it may allow us a better understanding of what occurs in merely reflective judgment. However, this choice is largely a matter of convenience and is not meant to privilege teleological judgment over aesthetic judgment, or to overlook the difference between the two kinds of reflective judgments.

Teleological judgments impose themselves when the mind is confronted with products of nature that manifest what Kant terms "*internal natural perfection*" (222)—products that cannot be accounted for on the basis of mechanical laws. These are nature's organized forms, for which no explication (*Erklärung*) is possible, and they include especially, but not exclusively, its life forms or organisms. From the perspective of the understanding (which knows only mechanical causality), the forms of such objects of nature are contingent, since it cannot come up with any necessary concepts for these natural phenomena. However, merely reflective judgment does not replace understanding regarding these unexplained products of nature, or provide an explanation for them that would extend the limits of what can legitimately be known. The task and the achievement of teleological judgment (and indeed, of reflective judgment in general) are not cognitive; they do not make up for the failure of the understanding but are of another order, as Kant emphasizes. The "different kind [*andere Art*] of investigation" that characterizes teleological reflection and serves "to supplement the inadequacy of [the investigation according to mechanical laws] even for empirical research into all particular laws of nature" (230) consists in bringing the unexplained products of nature "under principles of observation and inquiry" (206). In other words, this kind of investigation focuses on rendering the cognitively unaccountable empirical forms of nature susceptible to observation and investigation—perhaps even to experience—in the first place. But before we evaluate the scope and implications of the task to which teleological reflective judgment is committed, a point should be made: reflective judgment (whether teleological or aesthetic) needs a guideline (*Leitfaden*) in its attempt to structure (or form) the unexplained phenomena of nature in such a way that they become observable and susceptible to further investigation.

While defining the task of reflective judgment, Kant describes such manifold empirical laws of nature as "the labyrinth of the multiplicity of possible special [*besonderer*] laws."[34] Reflection is faced with the duty "to bring the particular laws under higher although still empirical principles, taking into account their differences under the same universal laws of nature as well."[35] But in this search, no universal concept is available, and reflection needs an Ariadne's thread in order to avoid "groping about [*Herumtappen*]" blindly in its attempt to discover a more general law.[36] The reference to Greek mythology is evident—the figure of a *Leitfaden*, Adelung notes, derives from the Theseus myth—and is certainly not accidental. Since mere reflection is conceivable only in contrast to determining reflection, the search for intelligibility that characterizes it inevitably resembles prerational modes of thinking. As it gropes about without the light of concepts of the understanding, mere reflection requires a guideline to make the labyrinth of the laws and forms of nature traversable and hence minimally intelligible.[37] But this requirement does not mean that mere reflection belongs to the realm of the mythopoetic. Indeed, its need for a guideline is basically no different from that of determining reflection. "Our *reflection* . . . requires a principle fully as much as determination, in which the concept underlying the object prescribes the rule to judgment and thus takes the place of the principle. . . . [Without such a] principle, all reflection would be carried on at random and blindly, and as a result with no sound expectation of its agreement with nature."[38] Now, in the case of reflective judgment, the principle is "a special principle of its own," devoted to the search for laws (13). It is a principle for reflective judgment alone, strictly insofar as it acts alone and for its own sake. It is, therefore, a singular principle; and indeed the principle cannot be "derived *a priori* from concepts, for these belong to the understanding" (5). As we have already seen, "judgment produces no concepts of objects for itself alone";[39] "judgment [in its determining mode] is only concerned with their application" (5). Reflection "must, therefore, furnish of itself a concept, through which, properly speaking, no thing is cognized, but which only serves as a rule, though not an objective one, to which it can adapt its judgment" (5). "Such a transcendental principle . . . the reflective judgment can only give as a law from and to itself. It cannot derive it from outside" (16). Mere reflection, unlike determining reflection, is entrusted with a certain spontaneity; it gives itself the rule for how to proceed in the absence of determined concepts for particulars. In the First Introduction, Kant writes, "the judgment itself posits a priori . . . the principle of its reflection . . . only in order to facilitate its reflection in accordance with its own subjective laws and needs while also in harmony with laws of nature in general."[40] Thus in its reflective mode, judgment is capable of a certain autonomy; but while it owes this distinction to its isolation, reflection is not simply a solo act. It takes place in accordance with the lawfulness of the understanding in general. We should further bear in mind that the power of judgment has been characterized as one of mediation. The principle that it gives to itself, in order merely to reflect on a particular for which there is no determined concept, therefore also concerns its ability to mediate. Let me emphasize that whatever acts reflective judgment performs, they all link the two higher powers and faculties of the mind; and the principle that it gives to itself is a principle that makes this mediation minimally possible. I will continue to elaborate on the peculiar nature of this transcendental principle, but first I will return to the question of teleological judgment.

In order to make the organized forms of nature available to possible observation and investigation, teleological judgment follows a guideline, which is the rational concept of a thing as a natural purpose (*Naturzweck*). Of this regulative principle Kant remarks: "The concept of combinations and forms of nature in accordance with purposes is then at least *one principle more* for bringing its phenomena under rules where the laws of simply mechanical causality do not suffice" (206). The concept of a natural purpose is a principle that the teleological reflective judgment receives from reason, and consequently it is not an a priori principle for judging. Though it is unlike the one used in aesthetic reflective judgments, what Kant establishes about this concept will help to throw a sharper light on the task and general achievement of mere reflection. The additional principle of natural purpose, or an inner natural purposiveness, serves as a guide that enables the mind to reflect on, meditate on, or think about (*nachzudenken*) the unexplained phenomena of nature (222).[41] Such phenomena are, of course, already given, and thus mere reflection consists in "a second-stage formation"—to use Cassirer's apt formulation—in which the preformed and apprehended phenomena are given a new meaning by way of a supplementary objectification.[42] To put it differently, in a teleological reflective judgment what is at stake is the very possibility of a meaningful approach to things that, for essential reasons (owing to the finite nature of our faculties of cognition), cannot be accounted for cognitively.[43] In this second-stage formation of natural products in teleological judgment, the mere possibility and meaningfulness of these entities becomes secured; and Kant holds that this formation proceeds from the "positing of the representation of a thing in respect of our concept and, in general, in respect of the faculty of thought" (250). When we perceive things as manifesting an inner organization, or purposiveness, we (already) conceive of them as *products* of nature (and hence as obeying a nonmechanical causality)—Kant writes that "the very thought of them as organized beings is impossible without combining therewith the thought of their designed production" (246). Thus it is the "one principle more" that makes it possible to identify a thing that the understanding sees as contingent, as barely a thing at all, and it does so by accounting for the very possibility of that thing's internal structure—and hence its unity as a thing—

on the basis of a notion of design. The additional principle simply secures the meaningfulness of the unexplained phenomena, by bestowing this unity upon them, and it thereby permits their subsequent observation and investigation. Reflection projects a surplus, or second-order, intelligibility upon these products of nature, above and beyond their categorial intelligibility, and as a result these products cease to be puzzling. This intelligibility—which may remind us of Claude Lévi-Strauss's dictum that it is better to have any order rather than no order at all—is an intelligibility "not in reference to the knowledge of nature or of its original ground, but rather to our own practical faculty of reason," Kant remarks (222). Now while the teleological judgment secures a minimal intelligibility of the unexplained phenomena of nature, this in no way makes them cognitively understandable. Kant leaves no doubt whatsoever that it would be sheer presumption to seek to introduce a "particular ground of causality" with this one principle more. Rather, it "only adds for the use of the reason a different [*andere*] kind of investigation from that according to mechanical laws, in order to supplement the inadequacy of the latter even for empirical research into all particular laws of nature." The idea of a natural purpose, Kant emphasizes, signifies only "a kind of causality of nature after the analogy of our own in the technical use of reason, in order to have before us the rule according to which certain products of nature must be investigated" (230).

In a teleological reflective judgment, the task of reflection is, unquestionably, solely one of securing a second-order intelligibility for phenomena of nature—phenomena that the understanding not only cannot explain but cannot even bring into view as such. Armed with the additional principle, reflection serves to establish the "contingent unity of particular laws" (233). If the one principle more elicits such intelligibility from organized forms of nature, the result is to render them susceptible to observation and investigation. But in what do such inquiries consist? Whenever the power of judgment must reflect upon objects (or their manifolds) that manifest internal organization, but for which we lack concepts, the additional principle provides the unique condition under which it is possible "merely to cognize [*bloss kennen zu lernen*, merely to get to know] nature according to its empirical laws" (232–33). For reasons that should by now be clear, such mere getting to know—when "we merely judge" (238) manifolds or organized forms of nature guided by the principle of a natural purpose (as opposed to a purpose of nature)—is not to be confused with a cognition.[44] It consolidates a simple awareness of the concrete inner stringency and unity of something that, from the standpoint of the understanding, is utterly contingent. Reflecting on, observing, and investigating organized natural forms, which the principle of a natural purpose brings forth in teleological reflective judgments, consist in nothing more (but also nothing less) than securing a thoroughly unified experience of the phenomenon's conformity to (an empirical) law, irrespective of what this law might be. And to the extent that merely reflective teleological judgment remains pure of any assumption of the real or material purposiveness of nature, this is all that such judgment accomplishes.[45]

In the absence of concepts of the understanding for phenomena of nature such as organized forms, teleological judgment is guided by the principle of a natural purpose, a principle furnished by reason in its demand for a thoroughly unified experience. Teleological judgment is thus capable of subsuming the organized forms of nature under a concept that merely guarantees a unity of meaning and hence an identity to these natural phenomena. The judgment that declares these phenomena to be natural purposes bestows on them an intelligibility and identity that they were denied by cognition. At this juncture, we may ask what this discussion of the task and achievement of teleological judgment tells us about the nature of the other—aesthetic—reflective judgment? In point of fact, what happens in aesthetic reflective judgment is not essentially different from what we have seen to take place in teleological judgment. Aesthetic judgment literally gives to itself the principle of a purposiveness of nature; in this latter case, however, it serves as an a priori principle. Since the chapters that follow are mainly concerned with aesthetic reflective judgment, I will limit myself here to a few brief remarks. Aesthetic judgment is guided by the concept of a purposiveness of nature that this judgment gives to itself a priori; thus aesthetic judgment, too, confers meaning where the understanding is incapable of doing so. Such conferral of meaning takes place precisely in the declaration that something is beautiful. The judgment that something is beautiful—whether it be nature as a whole or an individual empirical thing of nature or of art—merely recognizes formal intelligibility in its object. In the absence of determinate concepts for the manifold of natural laws, or for the intuitive manifold of something not yet recognized as a determined thing, the judgment of beauty makes it possible to experience these manifolds as having the form either of a system or of a thing. This is all a judgment of taste accomplishes as long as it is a pure judgment, not admixed with charm or concepts.

Since the principle that reflective judgment gives to itself cannot be one of a priori concepts or of objective categories, it must be a subjective principle. Kant contends that with this principle, which guides only reflection, the faculty of judgment "gives a law only to itself, and not to nature" (17). The power of judgment gives itself this principle a priori in order to be able to reflect on nature even where nature does not yield to concepts. Now this principle, "which serves as a principle for our investigation,"[46] is used for isolated employment of the power of judgment; thus the title "subjective" may not exhaustively describe its particularity, especially if "subjective" is taken to be the simple counterpart of "objective." The qualification of this principle as "subjective" tends to establish it as the mere reverse, or symmetric pendant, of those principles that hold true for objects of nature. But careful scrutiny of Kant's texts shows that the qualification "subjective" is, first and foremost, rooted in the biased viewpoint of the understanding and is not simply the opposite of the understanding's concern with objectivity. The characterization of the regulative ideas in teleological judgments as subjective (in spite of their universality) in chapter 76 of the Third Critique takes effect against the ultimate measure of the understanding. Kant writes here that it is the understanding that "limits the validity of these ideas to the subject.... That is, the understanding limits their validity to the condition that, according to the nature of our (human) cognitive faculties or, generally, according to the concept which *we ourselves* can *make* of the faculty of a finite intelligent being, nothing else can or must be thought, though this is not to assert that the ground of such a judgment lies in the object" (249). The understanding that is required to establish the objective validity of objects calls such regulative ideas subjective (and hence leaves its mark on them); thus it justifies the use of these ideas as necessary for conceiving of objects for which it cannot itself furnish any determined concepts. The qualification "subjective" marks the understanding's reappropriation of what happens when it is at a loss, and reason becomes animated, but the objects still have to be accounted for.

The "subjective" principle is thus a principle for mere reflection, that is, for an isolated use by the power of reflection—though, as Kant repeatedly reminds us, it is not without relation to the understanding as the faculty of concepts in general. The title "subjective," therefore, tends to conceal the fact that it can be only a "mere" principle. Indeed, whether a priori or not, the principle that belongs solely and expressly to the mere reflection of the faculty of judgment is a principle unlike any other: according to Kant, it is "a sheer [*blosse*] assumption on the part of the judgment for its own use in ascending continuously from particular empirical laws to more general, though still empirical ones."[47] The principle of mere reflection consists in a mere presupposition, or "mere idea," Kant adds.[48] Like the constitutive a priori of empirical cognition, the principle of natural purposiveness for merely reflective judgments is a transcendental one. But this principle, as a mere principle or mere idea, is even more elementary than the other transcendental structures; it is a mere transcendental, and its purity as a transcendental principle is, as it were, cut back. Of course, Kant repeatedly declares that there are good reasons for postulating such a principle. It is more than reasonable, he claims, to make the mere assumption in question. But the fact remains that there is no way of ever objectively confirming what the principle states, and therefore, however necessary it may prove to be, it must forever remain a mere assumption. The transcendental principle for reflective judgment in general (i.e., whether aesthetic or teleological) is the assumption that nature (i.e., nature as a whole, its single natural forms, and those products termed "organized forms") is purposive for our cognitive faculties. Kant writes: "This lawfulness, in itself contingent so far as all concepts of the understanding are concerned, which judgment (merely for its own advantage) presupposes of nature and postulates in it, is a formal purposiveness of nature, which we in fact *assume* in it but which is the basis neither for a theoretical knowledge of nature nor for a practical principle of freedom."[49] Mere reflective judgment thus approaches undetermined particulars in such a way as to "only *judge* [them] as if [*bloss nur so beurteilt werden, als ob*] their possibility rested on art."[50] Thanks to this special principle, all merely reflective judgment, whether aesthetic or teleological, is technical.[51] Its procedure is analogous to art, not in the narrow sense of the beautiful arts but in the broader sense of art as craft. "The reflective judgment . . . works with given appearances so as to bring them under empirical concepts of determinate natural things not schematically, but *technically*, not just mechanically, like a tool controlled by the understanding and the senses, but *artificially*, according to the universal but at the same time undefined principle of a purposive, systematic ordering of nature."[52] While this passage elaborates on the mere reflection on a manifold of forms of nature, with a view to establishing their systematicity, what Kant says here about reflective judgment applies to all its uses. Because of the mere assumption of a formal purposiveness of nature—that is to say, a purposiveness exclusively for our cognitive faculties—all reflective judgments are technical. Given the distinctions made in the above passage from Kant, this implies that no schematization is involved in them; or more precisely, no cognitive schematization takes place in reflective judgments. As we shall see in Chapter 4 of this study, schematization in reflective judgments is, indeed, intimately tied up with a symbolic hypotyposis.

The power of judgment becomes merely reflective when it is confronted with particulars for which no determined concept of the understanding is available. But what precisely are these particulars? As I have already pointed out, there are basically two different genres of such particulars: namely, the respective "objects" of aesthetic and teleological judgment. In each case, the genre divides into two species of particulars: for teleological judgment the species are, on the one hand, organized products of nature and, on the other, nature as a whole; for aesthetic judgment they are, on the one hand, single "objects" of nature or art and, on the other, the manifold forms of nature (or the particular empirical laws). Teleological judgments are primarily judgments that become inevitable when the mind confronts single organized products of nature. These especially include life forms whose factual possibility—that is to say, their nature as internally organized forms—cannot be accounted for on the sole basis of physical-mechanical necessity. But since the existence of natural purposes in nature raises associated questions about nature in its entirety, teleological judgment also concerns (though in a much more problematic way) the question of nature as a whole connected together by means of final causes. Aesthetic reflective judgments also regard two species of objects—Kant notes that formal purposiveness is "attributed to the thing *and* to nature itself."[53] However, in the objects of aesthetic reflective judgment, no empirical evidence of any inner or outer organization is observable, as it is in the products of nature regarded by teleological judgment.[54] To judge an undetermined empirical thing as beautiful is merely to state that it can be intuited (in its appearing) as having the phenomenal form of something determinable in principle; that is, something with open determinability. In other words, aesthetic reflective judgment is concerned first and foremost with establishing the purposiveness of what it beholds, its inner organization or form, so as to secure the very possibility of intuitive representation. This is the case for both species of particulars encountered by aesthetic reflective judgment—not only the single "objects" of nature or art but also the manifold forms of nature (or the particular empirical laws), which, as Kant says, "are so many modifications of the universal transcendental natural concepts left undetermined by the laws given, *a priori*, by the pure understanding—because these only concern the possibility of a nature in general (as an object of sense)" (16).

The a priori principle of a formal purposiveness of nature, which guides the mere reflection on these two sets of particulars in judgments of taste, is a principle that permits reflection to bring the phenomena into view as if they obeyed a unifying law. In other words, it is with the help of this principle that mere reflection subjectively secures the unity of experience on occasions when the concepts of the understanding are unavailable or insufficient. Kant holds: "This transcendental concept of a purposiveness of nature is neither a natural concept nor a concept of freedom, because it ascribes nothing to the object (of nature), but only represents the peculiar way in which we must proceed in reflection upon the objects of nature in reference to a thoroughly connected experience, and is consequently a subjective principle (maxim) of the judgment" (20). The objects of nature in question here are the manifold empirical laws and certain empirical intuitions of single "things"; thus the thoroughly connected experience, made possible by the principle of the purposiveness of nature, is not one of nature in general but only (or already) of nature as an empirical manifold of laws and forms. As Kant writes, in aesthetic judgments reflective judgment submits nature to a maxim that aims at nothing less than "the possibility of experience, and consequently of the cognition of nature—not indeed nature in general, but nature as determined through a variety of particular laws" (18). Compared to nature in general, which is cognizable and over which the understanding has sole jurisdiction, the nature for which the power of judgment is responsible—nature in its empirical manifold, and the empirical intuitional manifold of certain single things—is, as it were, a second-order nature.[55] The power of judgment prescribes a law to this second-order nature, in order to reflect upon and ensure a coherent experience of it; this is "the *law of the specification of nature* in respect of its empirical laws" (22). From the vantage point of the understanding, the laws that must exist for the natural manifold and the empirical intuition of certain things can only be higher empirical laws, which means contingent laws. "Yet, if they are to be called laws (as the concept of a nature requires), they must be regarded as necessary in virtue of a principle of the unity of the manifold, though it be unknown to us," Kant claims (16). It is to the end of forming this second-order nature that the reflective judgment offers the principle of formal purposiveness. This principle of mere (aesthetic) reflection is "a principle *a priori* of the possibility of nature, but only in a subjective aspect" (22). It allows reflection to consider "particular empirical laws [and, I add, the intuitional manifold of certain things], in respect of what is in them left undetermined by these universal laws, . . . in accordance with such a unity as they would have if an understanding (although not our understanding) had furnished them to our cognitive faculties, so as to make possible a system of experience according to particular laws of nature" (16). In sum, whether faced with the manifold of empirical laws or forms, or with an empirical intuitional manifold of a singular thing, the principle guiding aesthetic reflective judgment instructs the power of judgment to reflect upon the empirical data as if they contained a unity of law in the combination of its manifold—a unity without which this manifold could not lend itself to a possible experience in the first place. The understanding does not have the power to prescribe such a law to the empirical manifold. Hence, in order for a coherent experience to be possible, it is incumbent on the power of judgment to presume that nature (in its contingency) is in harmony with our cognitive powers.

In its merely aesthetic reflective mode, the power of judgment gives itself the principle of purposiveness as a mere idea, in order to reflect upon the empirical manifold. For the moment, suffice it to say that reflection remains mere reflection if it is limited to establishing that the empirical manifold of nature, or of the intuition of certain single things, can be subsumed under higher empirical laws. Reflection remains merely reflective if it is restricted to the recognition that nature has the unity of a system and that certain things of nature or art have form. But as soon as it is guided by the principle of a transcendental purposiveness of nature, and begins to flesh out the discovery that there is a general law of particular experiences, mere reflection is no longer aesthetic but becomes logical. When the principle in question turns into a principle designed to further explore nature, the inquiry becomes a search for specific laws. As far as the manifold of the empirical laws and the forms of nature as a whole are concerned, such investigation serves to give substance to the aesthetic experience of nature as a system. From that moment on, however, reflective judgment is no longer simply aesthetic, and hence is no longer (purely) a merely reflective judgment. It is a cognitive judgment, and while it is distinct from teleological judgment, they are similar to the extent that both belong "only to the reflective and not to the determining judgment."[56] The aesthetic judgment of reflection—that is, the merely reflective judgment upon the empirical manifold of nature and the intuitional manifold of single things, which gives itself the mere principle of a purposiveness of nature—is limited to merely securing the possibility of a (thoroughly coherent) experience of these aggregates. As Kant remarks, if nature is necessarily harmonious not only "in regard to the agreement of its transcendental laws with our *understanding*, but also in respect to the agreement of its empirical laws with the *judgment* and the power of the latter to exhibit [*Vermögen der Darstellung*] an empirical apprehension of nature's forms by means of the imagination," this is "simply for the furtherance of experience."[57] However, the experience made possible by the subjective principle of the purposiveness of nature—the "one principle more"—is what, following Kant, I would like to call "mere experience [*blosse Erfahrung*]" (although he uses the expression only once, and possibly just in passing).[58] It is not more profound than empirical experience, even though it actualizes the conditions of experience in general, but it is an experience of nature when the understanding fails to muster the concepts required by empirical experience as such. At its most elementary, and especially in its aesthetic mode, merely reflective judgment is really about the possibility of mere experience: on this side not only of determination but also of logical reflection in all its forms, whether concerning the system or the purpose of nature. This possibility of securing the mere form of experience is what the focus on the mereness of mere reflection will have brought into view. If such a judgment, which secures the mere possibility of an experience of uncognizable manifolds, is called aesthetic, it is because such experience is subjectively pleasurable—pleasurable, that is, in that it ensures the agreement between nature and reason.

By way of a conclusion, I would like to return to the question concerning the status of this mere experience, and hence of mere reflection. Just as merely reflective judgment is no more profound than is determining judgment, so mere experience is no deeper than empirical experience. Although it is perhaps less common than experience in the cognitive and moral sense, mere experience is undoubtedly no less real and concrete, and the Third Critique is evidence of this fact. Indeed, both the occasion on which merely reflective judgment becomes necessary and what actually happens in such judgment are exceptional in several ways. Merely reflective judgment secures mere experience only where the understanding has exhausted its resources, or where something that has been determined still appears in need of further determination. On such occasions, an isolated use of reflection takes place, a use that is free from the understanding's usual leverage over reflection. Furthermore, the mere experience thereby gained is an experience that, as such, differs significantly from what is usually meant by experience in a theoretical or practical sense. Indeed, the mere experience of the intelligibility of nature as a whole or of its individual forms in the absence of concepts actualizes a condition without which no experience in a determined sense could take place but that never becomes thematic in ordinary cognitive experience. From a transcendental perspective, merely reflective judgment is thus of particular interest. The mere experience that is secured by the reflective judgment is brought about with the help of the "one principle more," the transcendental a priori of natural purposiveness. Kant refers to this principle as a transcendental structure, even though it is only a "mere idea" and arguably lacks the purity of the constitutive principles of theoretical cognition and moral action. Mere reflection gives this principle to itself in order to orient itself when it faces uncharted phenomena of nature. The principle of natural purposiveness guides the faculties of the mind in forming an arrangement that benefits cognition in general; this subjective arrangement of the powers of representation is what Kant calls "the free play of the faculties." The arrangement consists in a relation of the powers of cognition that is so basic that it must be presupposed by any kind of experience. But given Kant's precise sense of "transcendental," can this condition that must obtain in all kinds of judgments be called a transcendental condition, strictly speaking? Is it not rather proto-transcendental because the play of the faculties is presupposed by all determined operations of the mind? In any event, does the principle that is required by any and every cognition, and that comes to light only in merely reflective judgment, manifest itself on this occasion as a transcendental in the full sense of the word? In the following chapter on the play of the faculties, I will discuss this condition of all determined reflection in greater detail; consequently, here I shall simply remark that while the conditions of experience in general are actualized in mere experience, they are never actualized as such. As conditions of possible experience, Kantian transcendentals, including the "one principle more," are never the direct object of an experience. Mere experience is not a more profound experience, because it is never an experience of a universal structure. Rather, in mere experience, a principle that underlies all determined experience and all its principles becomes the sole principle responsible for securing an experience to begin with. But if (formal or objective) purposiveness serves as the a priori guideline for judgments about natural objects that establish these objects' conformity to reason, then what makes these judgments possible—the principle of a formal purposiveness of nature—coincides with what they judge—the purposiveness of single natural objects. As a result, the necessary condition of merely reflective judgment is imbued with ineradicable contingency. Indeed, the conditions that constitute mere experience are always realized only in singular ways—in the singular judgments upon contingent empirical manifolds to which reflection responds guided by the mere idea of a purposiveness of nature. But furthermore, in a merely reflective judgment, the purposive arrangement of the faculties for any possible cognition—the "one principle more" of natural purposiveness and the play of the faculties—does not enable determinate judgments or cognitions but instead secures only mere experience and cognition in general. It is a para-epistemic experience that is realized exclusively in occasional and singular judgments of mere reflection. One way to formulate its paradoxical nature would be to say that the universal conditions of any experience give rise to experiences in their own right—experiences that are different from cognitive experiences but on par with them; in these experiences nothing but these conditions themselves are effectuated, and always in singular ways. As a transcendental principle, the "one principle more" is therefore always only in the position of serving as an example of itself.

The autonomy of the power of judgment is hard won from its merely reflecting activities. However significant its accomplishments are, and however important the glimpses that it procures into general conditions of experience, it is an activity of the mind that lacks the ordinary support of the understanding, and that—as we have seen from the outset—is in no way an independent cognitive power. Forced to give itself its own principle, it achieves an independence that is fragile because it is denuded of the categorial guidance that thinking usually enjoys in theoretical reasoning. It represents a mode of thought that is deprived of all protection. Thus exposed, it is, of course, also vulnerable to becoming idle or vacuous, that is, becoming "mere reflection" in a depreciatory sense.

The Third Critique's inquiry into mere reflection brings to light a dimension of thinking that admittedly is neither theoretical nor practical. Capitalizing on a fundamental requisite for all determined cognition, mere reflection ensures experience where neither theoretical nor practical reason can prevail. Mere reflection is engaged in what I called a para-epistemic operation. But this is also an operation in which thinking is no longer of the order of either the empirical or the pure. Undoubtedly, the analysis of the different types of mere reflection triggered by certain empirical givens reveals a principle that is of interest to the transcendental philosopher. However, as the qualification "mere" indicates, this kind of reflection comes into view never purely but only in relation, and in opposition, to the understanding. Mere reflection is inevitably bent upon the cognitive faculty, and to such a degree that in spite of its autonomy, it never attains the security of being firmly within boundaries of its own. As a result, the transcendental search for a principle is also put into play in the analysis of this kind of thinking. Mere reflection would thus also seem to blur the traditional divide characteristic of philosophical thinking—the one between the empirical and the transcendental. Permeated by "mereness"—a qualification that by now needs to be recognized as a philosophical, more precisely, epistemological, concept similar to the pure, though distinct from it in that it inscribes an ineradicable relation to the empirical—mere reflection appears to perform a mode of thinking that gives more food for thought than any concept could hope to exhaust. What is actualized in such thinking concerns a condition without which no experience is possible; nevertheless, because it manifests itself only singularly, it is impossible to definitely classify and situate what thus comes into view. Kant finds himself in want of conceptual tools to describe the precise structural reasons for the constant and intrinsic instability of this reflective thought; it is, as he explains in the preface to the *Critique of Judgment*, "a problem so involved by nature" that he feels compelled to excuse himself "for some hardly avoidable obscurity in its solution" (6).[59] But if, finally, the mereness proper to merely reflective judgment signifies this judgment's unique philosophical nature, its peculiarity is owing not to a lack of rigor on Kant's part but rather to the philosophical nature of the problem that it brings into view, and that refuses, as it were, the identity of the concept.

2

Transcendentality, in Play

In *Critique of Pure Reason*, Kant held a critical treatment of the beautiful conducted under rational principles to be fruitless. In *Critique of Judgment*, however, he demonstrates not only that such a treatment is possible but that aesthetic judgment itself is grounded on a priori principles. This reversal need not be taken to signify a discontinuity between these two Critiques. Indeed, as Andreas Heinrich Trebels has convincingly shown, the *Critique of Pure Reason* can be seen "as having laid the philosophical foundation for the problematic of the aesthetic, namely of what grounds and makes possible the aesthetical judgment."[1] Although certain concepts instrumental to the analytic and deduction of aesthetic judgments are significantly recast and expanded in the Third Critique, these modifications not only draw on possibilities implicit in their first critical treatment but take place within the perspective of goals implicitly outlined in the First Critique and thus congruent with its concerns. Still, the *Critique of Judgment* is not simply the realization of the possibilities for the understanding of the realms of the beautiful, the sublime, or the natural order latent in the First Critique. Kant does claim that the Third Critique ends his whole critical undertaking since the critique of the faculty of judgment permits the connection of the legislation of understanding with that of reason,[2] and this claim can undoubtedly still be read as a response to exigencies present in the earlier work. But the fact that judgments of taste, for instance, would become crucial in the attempt to bridge the outstanding gap between the theoretical and the practical comes more as a surprise. Having first been denied the possibility of rational treatment, the beautiful and the sublime (as well the objective purposiveness of nature) are, indeed, raised in the last Critique to positions of importance that could not have been anticipated from the first.

The notions of play and imagination, for instance, which appeared in a rudimentary way in the First Critique, are considerably refined and developed in the Third Critique when Kant attributes a reflective function to them, thus bringing them more centrally into the argument as a whole. In the *Critique of Pure Reason*, these notions—found in Kant's references to a "play of the faculties" and, in particular, the "play of imagination" and the "play of understanding"—signify an activity that has no objective validity; play stands in opposition to cognition, and its product is *Erdichtung* (fiction or invention). The reemergence of these notions in the last Critique certainly underscores a fundamental continuity in Kant's work. What is unpredictable from the perspective of the First Critique, however, is the idea that in play the faculties in question could enter into relation with one another. The truly new problematic that arises with the Third Critique, to quote Trebels, is that of the "singular relation of understanding and imagination [respectively, of reason and imagination], both of which are in free play, but which must also be seen as relating to one another."[3] The innovative introduction of this question of the relation of faculties in play in the last Critique is, of course, intimately linked to Kant's attempt to account in a rationalist or, more precisely, transcendental fashion for something like judgments of taste. Such treatment requires, indeed, that judgments of taste be not only synthetic but a priori, in other words, judgments that can claim universal assent. To demonstrate the a priori nature of judgments concerning the beautiful and the sublime, Kant had no other choice than to open up the possibility of relation, and its various modalities, between the powers of cognition in play, that is, freed from their regular involvement in theoretical cognition or practical reasoning. Kant acknowledges as much when he writes that the universality of judgments of taste can be grounded on "nothing else than the state of mind, which is to be met with in the relation of our representative powers to each other" (52). Consequently, any evaluation of Kant's continuation of his transcendental philosophy in the third and last Critique, of what it means to have brought that philosophy to an end, and of the singular role that judgments of taste play in such a conclusion, must be based on an elucidation of how the faculties relate in free play. However, in this chapter I shall limit the discussion to the relations of the mental powers in the judgment of the beautiful. In Chapter 5 I will take up the question of the play of the faculties in the context of the sublime.

The determining ground of a judgment of taste concerning the beauty or nonbeauty of a representation rests not on a priori proof according to definite rules but on the subject's feeling of pleasure or pain, something entirely subjective, Kant holds. A judgment of taste thus signifies nothing in the object, but rather predicates the way the subject is affected by a representation, more precisely the way the subject feels itself (*sich selbst fühlt*) when faced with this representation. Still, the determining ground of such a judgment is not simply any subjective feeling of pleasure or pain but only a feeling of pleasure or pain insofar as it names the subject's feeling of life (*Lebensgefühl*) (37–38). Although this reference to the feeling of life in Kant's discussion of judgments of taste has received little notice, the idea of life, as Rudolf A. Makkreel has demonstrated, provides "an overall perspective for understanding the reflective functions of the imagination" and even plays "a transcendental role in Kant's aesthetics."[4] For the purpose of my argument I must go over much of the same material Makkreel has covered in chapter 5 of *Imagination and Interpretation in Kant*, but I shall linger in greater detail on the relation of the feeling of life to the question of agreement and accord in the play of the faculties. Now, if judgments of taste are not cognitive judgments, it is because reference to the subject implies exclusion of any "cognition whatever, not even . . . that by which the subject *cognizes* itself" (40). The feeling of life predicated in judgments of taste is a noncognitive awareness of being alive. The pleasure predicated of representations in judgments of taste is the pleasure of coming to life, as it were. Yet what sort of life is this? Obviously, the subject must already be alive in some way for it to experience such a coming to life. This life thus cannot refer to biological life but rather refers to the life of the mind (*Gemüt*); this life is therefore intimately tied to its own, albeit noncognitive, self-awareness. This question of life, to whose simplicity (*lediglich*) (40)—or, rather, complex simplicity, as we shall see—all representations must be referred in judgments of taste, shall remain the frame within which I intend to discuss the faculties' relations to each other in play.[5]

Kant provides a preliminary answer to the question concerning the life of the mind when he says that in the subject's feeling of life to which representations are referred in a judgment of taste inheres the singular power of distinction and of judgment that compares (*gegen . . . hält*) "the given representation in the subject with the whole faculty of representations, of which the mind is conscious in the feeling of its state" (38). In short, then, the feeling of life is a mental awareness of the full range of its representational faculties, more precisely, of its powers of representation as a whole.

Toward the end of the "General Remark upon the Exposition of the Aesthetical Reflective Judgment," Kant, after having referred to Burke's psychological observations as affording rich material for empirical anthropology, remarks that it is "not to be denied that all representations in us, whether, objectively viewed, they are merely sensible or are quite intellectual, may yet subjectively be united to gratification or grief, however imperceptible either may be, because they all affect the feeling of life, and none of them, so far as it is a modification of the subject, can be indifferent" (119). His affirmative gesture toward Epicurus—who contended that ultimately all feelings of pleasure or pain, whether originating in imagination or the understanding, are corporeal—shows Kant to conceive of life as an intimate mix of the mental and the corporeal. He writes: "life without a feeling of bodily organs would be merely a consciousness of existence, without any feeling of well-being or the reverse, i.e. of the furthering or the checking of the vital powers." Although "the mind [*Gemüt*] is by itself alone life (the principle of life)," life is felt. This feeling of life arises from the way in which representations affect the body, or organs. Moreover, not only is life made to feel itself through the pleasure or pain caused by the mind's representations, but the mind's life can even be furthered or hindered by these feelings. In the "Remark" concluding the "Deduction of Pure Aesthetical Judgments," Kant returns, during of a discussion of laughter, to the issue of "the influence of the representation upon the body and the reflex effect of this upon the mind" (177). In light of his statements about the general influence of representations on the subject's feeling of life in his account of Burke's physiological approach to questions of taste, the analysis of laughter is crucial insofar as Kant here assesses the effect of the "mere play of representations" and of the play of thoughts (*Spiel von Gedanken*) on the body (177–78). According to Kant, in laughter the organs of the body are put into an oscillation (*Schwingung*) "which promotes the restoration of equilibrium" (177). The mind, too, is "put into a state of oscillation [*Schwankung*]. This . . . occasion[s] a mental movement, and an inner bodily movement harmonizing therewith, which continues involuntarily" (179). Although these discussions concerning the invigorating effects of representations might still be couched in anthropological terms, they are a first indication of how one is to conceive of the animation of the mind in what Kant calls the "free swing [*Schwung*] of the mental powers" (156). It is in his definition of spirit (*Geist*) that a principle of the animation of the mind by the faculties in play is spelled out: "*Spirit*, in an aesthetical sense, is the name given to the animating principle of the mind. But that by means of which this principle animates the soul, the material which it applies to that [purpose], is what puts the mental powers purposively into swing, i.e., into such a play as maintains itself and strengthens the mental powers in their exercise [*welches sich von selbst erhält und selbst die Kräfte dazu stärkt*]" (157).

But let me set aside for a moment the question concerning the feeling of life in order to establish what happens in judgments of the beautiful. Although in such judgments it is imagination, and not understanding, that refers a representation to the subject's feeling of pleasure or pain, such referral also includes the intervention of the understanding. An aesthetic judgment is after all a judgment and as such is not made without the participation of the faculty of concepts. Kant writes that the latter faculty belongs to aesthetic judgment "not as a faculty by which an object is cognized, but as the faculty which determines the judgment and its representation (without any concept) in accordance with its relation to the subject and the subject's internal feeling" (65). The intervention of the understanding, therefore, cannot mean that the judgment is "*based* on concepts . . . [or has] concepts as its *purpose*" (44). It means rather that "the satisfaction in the beautiful must depend on the reflection upon an object, leading to any concept (however indefinite)" (41). Imagination, the faculty required to gather together the manifold of intuition, is likewise free in judgments of taste. Although in cognitive judgments the imagination is subservient to understanding, in judgments of taste "understanding is at the service of imagination" (79). As a result, imagination enjoys "*free conformity to law*." It is "productive and spontaneous (as the author of arbitrary forms of possible intuition)" (77). Both cognitive powers, as they participate in an aesthetic reflective judgment, are thus "in free play, because no definite concept limits them to a definite rule of cognition" (52). Further, not only are they in free play individually, but they also relate to and "agree with each other [*unter einander . . . zusammen stimmen*], as is requisite for *cognition in general*" (52). The peculiar feature of a judgment of taste consists in this: in such a judgment, "conformity to law without a law, and a subjective agreement [*Übereinstimmung*] of the imagination and understanding—without such an objective agreement as there is when the representation is referred to a definite [*bestimmten*] concept of an object—can subsist along with the free conformity to law of the understanding" (78). Kant also characterizes this relation of the faculties in free play as a mutual agreement (*wechselseitige Zusammenstimmung*) of the faculties with the conditions of universality. As is obvious from chapter 15, *Zusammenstimmung* refers to a manifold's collection (*Zusammensetzung des Mannigfaltigen*) (66) so as to achieve a unity of concept—an undetermined unity, of course—in a judgment of taste (63–64). Further, this mutual agreement of the powers of cognition in free play is also referred to as a relation in which the imagination finds itself in *Einstimmung* with the power of the concepts (82). *Einstimmung*, apart from meaning "agreement," "joining in," "consent," "unanimity," also suggests a being put into the right mood for something (and, as we will see in a moment, the monophonicity of one voice). Indeed, the state of the mental faculties in free play is a state of mind, a *Stimmung* of the cognitive faculties (75). In aesthetic judgment about the beautiful, imagination and understanding not only are in agreement and gathered into a unity but also are put into a mood suitable for cognition in general. In this context, Kant speaks of their relation as "that proportion of them which is suitable for a representation (by which an object is given to us) in order that a cognition may be made out of it." In the cognitive process, the proportion in which the attuned faculties find themselves is always "a different proportion according to the variety of the objects which are given." In the judgment of taste, by contrast, "this internal relation, by which one mental faculty is excited by another, shall be generally the most beneficial for both faculties in respect of cognition (of given objects)" (75–76). The relation, then, between the faculties in an aesthetic judgment about the beautiful consists only in the single and singular proportion needed for cognition in general. This minimal relational attunement of the faculties in free play is "the subjective condition" without which "cognition as an effect could not arise" (75). The proportionate accord of the faculties in play thus consists in a precognitive function that is unthematized in *Critique of Pure Reason* but clearly required by determinate knowledge as such. Indeed, this requirement could easily have been formulated on the premises of the First Critique alone. Seen as *the* distinguishing trait of judgments of taste, the condition for cognition in general discovered and elaborated in *Critique of Judgment* fully accords with everything set forth in the First Critique, and access to it through the aesthetic could thus be understood merely to serve as a convenient example for the exposition of a principle whose ultimate importance lies in the theoretical realm. Unlike most critics of Kant's theory of the aesthetic form, who tend to limit the role played by the accord of the faculties to the production of determinate knowledge, Makkreel has argued that "cognition in general" extends beyond this purely precognitive function and "includes the reflective concern with the systematization of knowledge."[6] As should be evident from the preceding chapter, I agree with this assessment of the purposive disposition of the faculties in cognition in general, an assessment that "points beyond the production of empirical knowledge to its possible integration."[7] Undoubtedly, as the First Introduction evidences, beauty is predicated not only of the aesthetically pleasing form of certain natural objects but also of nature as a whole when it displays systematicity. But Makkreel's interpretation of "cognition in general" as the condition for the systematization of nature reads the play of the faculties primarily from the perspective of what Kant, in the First Critique, had established about the role of universal concepts (i.e., concepts of reason), namely, that they unify the manifold of the understanding. Thus the originality of the notion of "cognition in general" does not come sufficiently into view. However, for my purposes I will not take up Makkreel's interpretation of "cognition in general" but will limit myself to a discussion of the play of the faculties as a necessary requirement of objective knowledge.

In search of an aspect of the free play of the faculties in judgments on the beautiful that would not simply be derivative from the First Critique, I return to my analysis of the play between the imagination and the understanding to make two remarks. First, the attunement of these faculties into a coherent whole is not of an intellectual nature. Second, this attunement, rather than becoming conscious intellectually, manifests itself as an enlivening sensation. The indeterminate (*unbestimmte*) yet harmonious activity (*einhellige Tätigkeit*) in which imagination and understanding engage in the contemplation of a beautiful object is a function of the animation (*Belebung*) of these faculties, Kant contends (53–54). They become vivified, endowed with life, by being yoked together "into that proportionate accord which we require for all cognition," and which consequently has to be regarded "as holding for everyone who is determined [*bestimmt*] to judge by means of understanding and sense in combination (i.e. for every man)" (54). How then are we to conceive of this animation of the mental powers, which results in a mood favorable to cognition in general? At this point, let me recall Kant's occasional references in the First Critique to a "putting into play [*ins Spiel setzen*]" of the faculties, and in particular to the "play of imagination" and the "play of the understanding." As Trebels has shown, "play" seems here to indicate the ability of a mental power to operate in isolation from the other powers. Cognition, according to the First Critique, requires the collaboration of imagination and understanding. But in play a faculty freely engages in its own activity, in isolation from any other. As Trebels holds, "such play does not exclude the possibility of real cognition, on the contrary, it lays the foundation for it." Speaking of the play of understanding, he notes: "This play must be understood as the fundamental condition of all cognition. It only turns into reality when empirical data as givens are added to it."[8] A mental power's isolated activity predisposes it for the task it is to achieve in conjunction with another power in that this free activity endows the faculty in question with spontaneity.[9] But whereas in the *Critique of Pure Reason*, the free play of the faculties seems to animate them only for the specific task of cognition and of bringing about objective truth, in the *Critique of Judgment*, that free play amounts to a relation between faculties, that is, between faculties in isolation, a relation that, as play, must remain isolated as well, as we shall see, from the intellectual relation that obtains in the objective schematism of the power of judgment. The animation of the faculties that occurs in a judgment of taste follows from their being linked to begin with, a linkage that predisposes them for a common task. But this linkage does not override their isolation. The powers of imagination and understanding that become attuned in a judgment of taste are still free. Indeed, it is only insofar as they are involved in a free activity that they enter the agreement that is the subjective condition for cognition in general.

With this I circle back to Kant's description of the relation between the faculties in play in a judgment of the beautiful as one of mutual animation. In the "free and indefinite purposive entertainment [*unbestimmt-zweckmäßige Unterhaltung*] of the mental powers with what we call the beautiful" (79), "only the purposive form in the determination [*Bestimmung*] of the representative powers which are occupying themselves therewith" is brought to our notice, Kant writes (64–65). This harmonious attunement or "accordance [*Stimmung*]" of the powers of representation "can only be determined [*bestimmt*] by feeling (not according to concepts)," he adds (76). The agreement of the powers with each other, the proportionate relation beneficial for cognition in general that they achieve, is of the order of feeling, of sensation, more precisely, of a state of mind or a mood. If the subject, or rather, the mental powers that as a whole make up the subject, is the ground of determination of an aesthetic judgment, then this whole is constituted by the powers' cohering in mood (*Stimmung*). On the side of the subject there is thus a mood in which the powers of the mind are attuned to one another, in which they cohere in mood, or as a mood, to achieve unity among themselves. This attunement, while beneficial for cognition in general, remains separated from the configuration of the powers of the mind in their objective or logical employment. However, as mental dispositions, moods have a quality, and thus the question arises as to what sort of mood it is in which the cognitive powers are made to agree with one another. Yet what mood other than that of pleasure can this be? It is none other than the pleasurable "feeling of a furtherance of life" that the beautiful directly brings with it (83). When Kant ascertains that in the case of the beautiful, pleasure "must be bound up [*unmittelbar mit . . . verbunden*] with the mere act of judging, prior to all concepts" (131), it should be clear that it is judging itself, that is, the purposeful relating of the faculties for cognition in general, that is pleasurable.[10] But pleasure is also said to be the feeling in which "we are conscious of a mutual subjective harmony of the cognitive powers with one another" (53). Pleasure is predicated of the representation through which the beautiful object is given. Yet the pleasure in question is only the pleasure predicated (immediately) of a state of mind that itself is pleasurable insofar as it is a mood in which the cognitive faculties are in harmony with one another. The pleasure to be predicated follows the pleasure felt. In chapter 9 of *Critique of Judgment*, Kant expresses the view that "the merely subjective (aesthetical) judging of the object, or of the representation by which it is given, precedes the pleasure in the same and is the ground of this pleasure in the harmony of the cognitive faculties" (52–53). Indeed, for aesthetic judgments to be synthetic (and a priori) judgments, the pleasure predicated of the pleasurable state of mind must be distinct from it. Whereas the pleasure felt, the pleasure in which the harmony of the mental powers consists, is a subjective and empirical pleasure, the pleasure that follows the judgment properly speaking is that of the universal communicability of the state of mind in question. The pleasure by which the pleasurable subjective condition for judging becomes determined is that of the universal communicability of that very pleasure. Since most commentators on the Third Critique have understood "aesthetical" to refer only to the subjective determining ground of judgments of taste, and not to the pleasure that precedes it as the condition for judging to begin with, I emphasize the following points. First, in the case of the beautiful, the pleasure is linked up immediately with the judgment. Second, the faculties' purposeful play itself has the quality of a mood. Their harmonious agreement is neither intellectual nor logical. It occurs as a state of mind through the faculties' mutual animation. Third, since "the pleasure itself [*das Gefühl selbst*]" that coincides with "the consciousness of the mere formal purposiveness in the play of the subject's cognitive powers" (57) is such a pleasure only "because it contains a determining ground of the activity of the subject in respect of the excitement [*Belebung*] of its cognitive powers, and therefore an inner causality (which is purposive) in respect of cognition in general" (58), this pleasure serves to perpetuate the accord and hence keep the pleasure of the mutually self-animating faculties alive. Kant writes that this pleasure "involves causality, viz. of *maintaining* without further design the state of the representation itself and the occupation of the cognitive powers. We *linger* over the contemplation of the beautiful because this contemplation strengthens and reproduces itself" (58). Pleasure, then, is not only the immediate effect of the powers' playful agreement—hence not straightforwardly distinct from its cause—it is instrumental in the conservation of that agreement for its own sake. It not only keeps the play in place for its own sake but also contributes to the animation of the faculties that have entered an enlivening relation in view of their self-maintenance. Kant speaks of taste as a "tone of mind which is self-maintaining [*Gemütsstimmung, die sich selbst erhält*]" (67). Pleasure is thus not merely an effect—an aesthetic manifestation of awareness—it is intimately tied up with taste as a state of mind in which powers freely become attuned to one another in pleasure, or rather as pleasure itself.[11]

Now, this proportionate accord of the order of a subjective attunement, a state of mind or mood in which pleasure plays a determining role, is "the subjective relation [of imagination and understanding], suitable for cognition in general," hence valid for everyone, and universally communicable, "just as if it were a definite [*bestimmte*] cognition, resting always on that relation as its subjective condition" (52). This accord is the ground of satisfaction in pure aesthetic judgments and the basis of the judging subject's belief that he speaks "with a universal voice [*allgemeine Stimme*]" and that he can consequently claim the assent of everyone. "In the judgment of taste nothing is postulated but such a *universal voice*, in respect of the satisfaction without the intervention of concepts, and thus the *possibility* of an aesthetical judgment that can, at the same time, be regarded as valid for everyone" (50). Since the universality of this voice rests on a disposition for cognition that all human beings must be able to share, it is distinct from the empirical certitude "based on any collecting of the suffrages of others [*Stimmensammlung*]" (122) or on "a hundred voices . . . [however] highly praising" they may be (125). Because the agreement (*Übereinstimmung, Zusammenstim-*

mung) of the imagination and the understanding in a judgment of taste achieves a minimal consistency and relation among the faculties—a consistency that, owing to the faculties involved, is a general condition for any cognition—the subject can assume a minimal cohering, correctness, balance, attunement, on the one hand, and on the other, a mood that is common to everyone. *Stimme*, then, is not merely the relating of the faculties that allows for cognition but also a lived accord, one that includes a strong feeling of life. This is the first sense of the postulated *allgemeine Stimme*.[12] But in judging something to be beautiful, the subject in question also claims to speak in a voice that is universal since it voices a cohesion that is nothing but the mood for cognition in general. Still, "the judgment of taste itself does not *postulate* the agreement [*Einstimmung*] of everyone (for that can only be done by a logically universal judgment because it can adduce reasons); it only *imputes* this agreement to everyone, as a case of the rule in respect of which it expects, not confirmation by concepts, but assent by others. This universal voice is, therefore, only an idea" (50–51). In judging something beautiful, the subject only "promises himself the agreement [*Beistimmung*] of everyone" (51). This is the second sense of the postulated universal voice. But the universal voice as mere idea articulates also a demand of reason, that of the end, destination, or vocation (*Bestimmung*, now in a teleological sense) of our mental powers. As idea, the universal voice is "the subjective principle, viz. the indefinite [*unbestimmte*] idea of the supersensible in us," that is, of "the point of union for all our *a priori* faculties" (186–87). The universal voice is thus, third, to be understood as the subject's destination to "make ... [his] reason harmonious with itself" (187). In short, then, by pointing to cohering, agreement, union as an end, *Stimme* articulates the subjective condition not only for cognition through determining judgments (*bestimmende Urteile*) but for assent (*Beistimmung, Einstimmung*) in common sense between subjects that share the power of cognition, and, finally, for a supersensible destination or vocation of the faculties involved in cognition. It is only a subjective condition: a voice that the subject claims for himself on the one hand and, on the other, a voice lived, more felt than heard, that speaks to him in the *Stimmung* of the subject's powers of representation for cognition in general. *Stimme* names here the complex and intelligible structure of the feeling of pleasure involved in judgments of taste. Seen as the structure of that one feeling that is universally communicable, *Stimme* gathers all the different senses of *stimmen, bestimmen, übereinstimmen, einstimmen, zusammenstimmen*, as well as the sense of "voice," "dictate," "vote." Only insofar as it possesses the outlined complexity is the feeling of pleasure this "deep-lying general ground of agreement [*Einhelligkeit*] in judging [common to all human beings] of the forms under which objects are given" (68). If *Stimme* realizes the conditions for cognition in general, the feeling of agreement in question is made up (*zusammengesetzt*) of the minimal structural features from which the possibility of determined (*bestimmt*) knowledge can be derived, as can the possibility of achieving unity in the manifold of cognition by bringing concepts of reason to bear on it (*Bestimmung* in a teleological sense). According to Kant, the analysis of the judgment of taste has laid bare "a property of our cognitive faculty which without this analysis would remain unknown." It is a property, he adds, "noteworthy, not indeed for the logician, but for the transcendental philosopher" (48). Undoubtedly, the analysis of aesthetic judgment has yielded insight into an aesthetic condition, a condition of subjective universality, without which cognition properly speaking would not be possible. Without the proportionate relation of imagination and understanding characteristic of judgments about the beautiful, these faculties could not proceed to a determining, or cognitive, judgment. As Kant's claim would seem to suggest, this discovery of a nonpsychological and hence necessary condition is, indeed, a transcendental discovery in that the minimal purposeful relation of the faculties in question concerns the way in which we know objects. Gilles Deleuze in particular stresses this possibilizing role of the free play of the faculties when he writes, "a faculty would never take on a legislative and determining role were not all the faculties together in the first place capable of this free subjective harmony."[13] Further on, he states:

Reflective judgment manifests and liberates a depth which remained hidden in . . . [determining judgment]. But . . . [the determining judgment] was also judgment only by virtue of this living depth. . . . The point is that any determinate accord of the faculties under a determining and legislative faculty presupposes the existence and the possibility of a free indeterminate accord. It is in this free accord that judgment is not only original (this was already so in the case of determining judgment), but manifests the principle of its originality.[14]

A note of caution might be appropriate at this point. To claim, as Kant does, that the play of the faculties is a necessary condition mandated by all empirical cognition of course does not imply that all cognitive judgments are based on prior aesthetic judgments. It implies even less that all objects that are known are also beautiful. Cognitive and aesthetic judgments, qua judgments, rest on the same universal conditions. But in the case of determining judgments an objective use is made of these conditions, without giving rise to aesthetic judgments properly speaking. Yet even though a judgment of cognition excludes as such a judgment about the purposeful play of the faculties involved since in cognition these faculties are from the start under the yoke of a determining concept, it is perhaps possible to assume that everything that can be cognized could also, in an entirely distinct act, be judged to be beautiful. But to be able to judge everything this way, one would have to make only a subjective use of the condition for cognition in general, and this use would require one to abstract from everything one already knows of the object. In the following, this subjective use will be elaborated further.[15]

I recall that the universally communicable state of mind that is the determining ground of aesthetic judgment, and which Kant exhibits through his analysis of judgments of taste concerning the beautiful, is said to be a discovery noteworthy for the transcendental philosopher. Considering what transcendentals are, namely, universal a priori conditions of possibility of cognition, the question that imposes itself as a result of the Third Critique's analytic of the beautiful is that of the relation of the universally communicable play of the faculties of cognition to the transcendentals exhibited in *Critique of Pure Reason*. Is the harmonious attunement of the faculties in a reflective judgment on the beautiful a transcendental in the same right as what has been discussed under this title in the First Critique? Can the aesthetic a priori be construed as just a final transcendental condition without which the analysis of experience would not be complete? Or should one understand it rather as a transcendental anterior to the transcendental conditions of possibility of knowledge? As a transcendental of the transcendental, a proto-transcendental, or quasi-transcendental? Undoubtedly, the harmonious agreement of the faculties in a representation of a beautiful object, on which rests the universal communicability of a judgment of taste, articulates a connection of mental powers that must also obtain if judgments are to be determining. But this indispensable condition of possibility is not present in determining judgments in the same way that it is in aesthetic reflective judgments. Overshadowed by the objective relation of the faculties in theoretical cognition, the free play of the faculties, by contrast, is front rank in the judgment of the beautiful. Although it is by nature a possibilizing transcendental, and perhaps even a proto-transcendental for theoretical cognition, the playful agreement of the faculties in the case of the beautiful seems to secure only cognition in general. Or rather, the free interplay of the faculties, having no determined cognitive end and enacted purely as such, is what Kant terms cognition in general. It takes place, as it were, for its own sake, enabling nothing else but itself. In aesthetic judgments, the pure power of judgment "is itself, subjectively, both object and law," Kant writes (130). To sharpen this difference between the enabling role of the a priori principle of the purposeful play of the faculties in judgments of taste and in determining judgments, let me once more go over the specifics of the play that constitutes a judgment of taste. I shall do so by focusing on the corresponding developments in the "Deduction of Pure Aesthetical Judgments."

Having noted that judgments of taste are similar to determining judgments even though the former do not subsume representations under any concept, Kant returns to the distinction between the two types of judgment. In chapter 35, he characterizes the basis of judgment of taste as that of "the subjective formal condition of a judgment in general" (129). He writes:

> The subjective condition of all judgments is the faculty of judgment itself [*das Vermögen zu urteilen selbst, oder die Urteilskraft*]. This, when used with reference to a representation by which an object is given, requires the accordance [*Zusammenstimmung*] of two representative powers, viz. imagination (for the intuition and comprehension of the manifold) and understanding (for the concept as a representation of the unity of this comprehension). Now because no concept of the object lies here at the basis of the judgment, it can only consist in the subsumption of the imagination itself (in the case of a representation by which an object is given), under the conditions that the understanding requires to pass from intuition to concepts. That is, because the freedom of the imagination consists in the fact that it schematizes without any concept, the judgment of taste must rest on a mere sensation of the reciprocal activity [*der sich wechselseitig belebenden*] of the imagination in its *freedom* and the understanding with its *conformity to law*. It must therefore rest on a feeling, which makes us judge the object by the purposiveness of the representation (by which an object is given) in respect of the furtherance of the cognitive faculty in its free play. Taste, then, as subjective judgment, contains a principle of subsumption, not of intuitions under concepts, but of the *faculty* of intuitions or presentations (i.e. the imagination) under the *faculty* of the concepts (i.e. the understanding), so far as the former *in its freedom* harmonizes with the latter *in its conformity to law*. (129)

The play of the faculties, that is, the harmonious agreement of imagination and understanding construed up to this point as the subjective condition of cognition in general, is now reformulated in such a way as to become the subjective condition of judgment. By describing the play as an attunement and subsumption of the mental powers themselves, rather than as a relating by the imagination of a representation to an undetermined concept of the understanding, "play" turns out to be a power itself, the power of judgment. In the reciprocal animation of the two faculties in play, this power to judge manifests itself as such as the "internal feeling of a purposive state of the mind" (138). The power of judgment said to be the principle of taste is nothing but this feeling of "fitness" of the cognitive powers to legislate, a feeling that arises at the moment those powers become animated by entering freely into the purposive relation in question. The "merely sensible relation between the imagination and the understanding mutually harmonizing in the representation of the form of an object" (133), their felt relation, the feeling of their being alive, is the feeling of life as the power to judge itself. In Kant's view, this feeling of purposiveness, or the faculty of judging itself, is the "link in the chain of the human faculties *a priori*, on which all legislation must depend" (140). Harmonious agreement of the faculties, or the power of judging itself, then, is an a priori transcendental condition of experience in the theoretical sense. No cognition whatsoever is possible without this subjective, merely felt, arrangement of the faculties in purposeful play beneficial for cognition in general in the precognitive sense.

Yet this purposive arrangement of the mental powers is also the basis of judgments of taste in the case of the beautiful, and secures their universal communicability. Unlike cognitive judgments, however, this most fundamental condition of empirical cognition in aesthetic judgments about the beautiful does not proceed to generate knowledge. Speaking of the beautiful in its distinction from the sublime, Kant remarks that it requires "the representation of a certain *quality* of the object, that can be made intelligible and reduced by concepts," only to add that "it is not so reduced in an aesthetical judgment" (107). The specificity of aesthetic judgments consists precisely in this: in them, what functions as a fundamental transcendental principle for determining judgments does not become involved in such an operation of conceptual reduction. Although a judgment concerning the quality of an object can be reduced to concepts and thus be made intelligible, this does not mean that this possibility must or will eventually be realized. As long as the judgment remains aesthetically reflective, the indispensable transcendental possibility of cognition in general does not turn into the possibility of an actual act of determined cognition. The aesthetic reflective judgment is based on a possibility intrinsic to all cognitive judgments, but in such a judgment this possibility is divested of its enabling power. Although aesthetic judgments can be transformed (*verwan-*

delt) into logical judgments, and "a logical judgment [can be] based on an aesthetical one" (50), such transformation, and grounding, takes place to the detriment of the aesthetic judgments' specificity. An aesthetic judgment is at all times distinct from a logical judgment and makes room for a logical one only through an entirely different act of the mind. Even though the two types of judgments share the same a priori principle, all this principle does in the case of judgments of taste is to assert itself and to secure the possibility of judging in the first place. In logical judgments, by contrast, this principle is at the service of a "solution satisfying a problem" (79). In these judgments, the principle in question is thus a transcendental condition of possibility in the strict sense.

To do justice to judgments of taste, it is thus imperative to reflect on and further conceptualize their self-sufficiency. What keeps a judgment of taste from becoming a logical judgment must itself be thematized. In other words, we must consider the "without" of "without interest," "without concept," "without objective universality," "without purpose," "without a law," and so on, which constitutes the oneness or uniqueness (*Einigkeit* or *Einzigkeit*) (64) of aesthetic judgments. Only by "separating off [*Absonderung*]" (51) all objective realization and remaining "independent" (53) does a judgment of taste acquire specificity to begin with. Needless to say, in determining judgments the play of the faculties is also beneficial to the task of cognition, but it is never nothing but such benefit. It is not, in Kant's language, free. Since judgments of taste share with logical judgments the same transcendental and universal condition, it is thus a question as to how to conceive of such a condition on its own, distinct from its objective employment. In short, it is a question concerning a transcendental condition that refrains from its enabling role, and that seeks to maintain itself as such in isolation from its theoretical destination.

At this point, I wish to call up again several of the aspects of the judgment of taste previously discussed. First, the mental powers in play are powers that are active in isolation, and it is in this capacity that they are linked in the power to judge itself. Since this power is likewise in play, it impedes the making of any definite judgment. Kant notes, indeed, that "the aesthetical purposiveness is the conformity to law of the judgment [*Urteilskraft*] in its *freedom*" (361). Second, the play of the faculties is a play that by itself maintains and strengthens itself. The feeling of life in the reflective judgment is that of the life of the faculties themselves. Strangely enough, I add in passing, the question of life emerges with full force at the precise moment at which Kant investigates an activity of the mind that, however fundamental in a transcendental sense, remains withdrawn from everything that it could effectively condition, or make possible. Isolated from the serious business of cognition and morality, life discovers here the possibility of its own autonomy.

It would thus seem that the price of integrating the beautiful into transcendental philosophy amounts not merely to opening up a reflective, that is, subjective realm of conditions for theoretical and practical reason, but further to allowing this realm, and what constitutes it, to operate and strengthen itself in isolation. If anything, the acknowledgment of such a viable isolation is the truly new thought that emerges with the last Critique. It is a viable isolation because, as we have seen, it accomplishes a significant epistemic, or rather para-epistemic, task. How does the thought of such isolation square with Kant's general assumption of a unity of consciousness as well as with the holistic thrust of the Third Critique? Does such isolation still refer back to the unity in question, or does it represent a necessary possibility at the margins of unity—the possibility of the life of the unity of consciousness, of a life of life itself? I leave these questions in abeyance (they will find an answer with the role that reason plays in aesthetic reflective judgment). But, since the possibility of such isolation concerns nothing less than a priori principles, I briefly return, in conclusion, to the question of transcendentality.

"A transcendental principle is one by means of which is represented, *a priori*, the universal condition under which alone things can be in general objects of our cognition," Kant writes in *Critique of Judgment* (17). In the introduction to *Critique of Pure Reason*, Kant entitled "*transcendental* all knowledge which is occupied not so much with objects as with the mode of our knowledge of objects in so far as this mode is to be possible *a priori*."[16] The pure forms of space and time, as well as the synthetic knowledge a priori of the categories, are transcendental in this sense. Now, whereas the pure intuitions of space and time are the conditions under which objects are given to us as objects, the pure concepts analyzed in the transcendental logic are a priori cognitive concepts capable of being applied to objects in general. A transcendental logic is, indeed, a science that "concerns itself with the laws of understanding and of reason in so far as they relate *a priori* to objects."[17] It is thus a logic of concepts that always, and without exception, relates to objects in a priori fashion. Transcendental conditions of possibility for knowing objects are conditions that, before all empirical knowledge, necessarily refer to such objects. The transcendental, in the Kantian sense, is thus intrinsically a knowledge of objects. The transcendental conditions make sense only as constitutive of objects, or as legislating about their cognition. In addition, Kant remarks that although "in a transcendental logic we isolate the understanding . . . separating out for our knowledge that part of thought which has its origin solely in the understanding . . . the employment of this pure knowledge depends upon the condition that objects to which it can be applied be given to us in intuition."[18] From the perspective of the First Critique, all isolation per se of transcendental conditions would thus be rigorously excluded. But, as we have seen, the lively free play of the faculties, without which cognition in the empirical sense is not possible, is played out entirely for itself in aesthetic judgments on the beautiful without giving rise to any determined knowledge whatsoever. This play is undoubtedly a transcendental condition, and yet in judgments of taste it hovers on its own. If to be in play means to be active in isolation, then the transcendental function itself is here in play as well. It is free from its determined enabling condition, and would seem therefore to exist, strictly speaking, no longer in the quality of a transcendental principle. However, by putting itself into play, and hence also putting itself at stake, the transcendental has, on its own terms, included in transcendental philosophy a domain first held to be exclusively subject to merely empirical rules—the domain of beautiful form.

3

On Mere Form

According to Kant, beauty resides in the form of an object; a feeling of sublimity, however, can arise when the spectator is confronted with a formless object. Of course not just any formless object inspires such feeling, but only one in which boundlessness is represented. From this, there is no mistaking that Kant's aesthetics is an aesthetics of form. But is it therefore a formalist aesthetics, that is, an aesthetics that makes form absolute? What is form, anyway? Kant's notorious inconsistency regarding the use of key terms is an obstacle as well to clarifying what he understands by form. Or, rather, the way form is understood in his writings is context bound, and this to such a degree that one must distinguish several concepts of "form." In *Critique of Pure Reason*, space and time are the constitutive a priori pure forms of objects of experience. Distinct from them is the beautiful form of objects dealt with in the Third Critique. Since the notion of form is broached in the part of the Third Critique entitled "Critique of the Aesthetical Judgment," and since it is commonly believed that aesthetics must primarily be about art, it is also often taken for granted that "form" in the Third Critique must suggest an ascendancy over content, or matter, and that an aesthetics of form is thus necessarily formalist. But such reasoning misses out on the very peculiar notion of form that we find here.

As the object of pure judgments of taste, form excludes charm (*Reiz*); in other words, "the matter of representations, viz. simply sensations."[1] As Kant holds, charms are aliens (*Fremdlinge*) that "disturb the beautiful form" (61). A pure aesthetic judgment, one solely about the form of an object, leaves all objective determination, whether theoretical or practical, aside as well. Aesthetic judgment does not take into consideration what a thing properly is. But even though all matter—sensible, theoretical, and moral—is thus ignored in pure judgments of taste, does this make them formalist, that is to say, judgments about one facet of things to the detriment of another? Do these exclusions imply, in particular, that the object of an aesthetic judgment concerns the (inner or outer) formal composition of the object? In other words, is the concept of form in Kant's aesthetics necessarily a formalist concept of form? Undoubtedly, some of the examples found in the Third Critique seem to suggest that the beauty of form consists in its outer shape, figure, or outline; in the tasteful arrangement of parts in the whole of a figure, or in the mere play of such figures in space or time. One could think, for instance, of the beautiful forms of the canoes and clothes of the Caribs or the Iroquois (139) or the "flowers [the notorious tulips and roses], free delineations, outlines intertwined with one another without design and called foliage" (41), but also of "the house we see, the coat that person wears, the concert we hear, the poem submitted to our judgment" (47). A formalist concept presupposes a contrast between form and matter. Indeed, without this distinction the absolutization of form makes no sense; without it the problem that formalism cannot account for the formation of form could not arise. Now, on some occasions, Kant seems to endorse this Aristotelian distinction between form and matter. Take, for example, the following passage: "Genius can only furnish rich *material* [*Stoff*] for products of beautiful art; its execution and its *form* require talent cultivated in the schools, in order to make such a use of this material as will stand examination by the judgment" (153). Further, when Kant holds that "beauty in nature can be rightly described as an analogon of art because it is ascribed to objects only in reference to reflection upon their *external* aspect, and consequently only on account of the form of their external surface" (221–22), form seems to relate to the outer shape, the organization of the surface of a thing, as distinct from its matter. Undoubtedly, judgments of taste make judgments about form in this sense. But it would be misleading to conclude from this that for Kant aesthetic judgments primarily concern the external figure of things, and that "form" in the Third Critique refers exclusively to how a material is shaped. It is certainly not insignificant that the distinction between form and matter surfaces for the first time in the chapters on genius, in which Kant—after having elaborated in depth on pure aesthetic judgment, which primarily concerns natural beauty—turns to the production of artworks and to the kind of aesthetic judgments that occur when an artwork (as distinct from a natural thing) is judged to be beautiful. As is evident from the discussion of the arts in general and the beautiful arts in particular, form, in this context, designates to some extent the being-formed of a material (matter in the case of the arts in general, aesthetic ideas in the case of the arts of genius) according to rules (in the case of literary works, rules of prosody or versification, for example)—in short, form here is what Kant terms at one point "the form of the schools" (150). Does Kant evoke this concept of form with respect to man-made art and to judgments about already known art objects in order to tell us retrospectively how the form of beautiful objects discussed in the "Analytic of the Beautiful" is to be taken? Without yet broaching the question of what precisely occurs in the production (and reception) of a *beautiful* work—this will be postponed until Chapter 7—one thing can be made clear at this point: if indeed an artwork is only the (perfect) realization of a concept according to the rules and the forms of the schools, it is not different from any artifact. Is the concept of beauty predicated of form in this sense—which construes the beautiful object as an object whose law of composition is form and in which construction, formation, and composition prevail—truly capable of accounting for what is judged beautiful on the grounds of the object's form alone? If beauty is merely a function of the polished realization of an end, beauty is based on perfection, and hence, as Kant emphasizes in chapter 15, on a judgment that is no longer aesthetic. Consequently, it is rather unlikely that what Kant calls "the mere form" of beautiful things, and which is the sole object of pure judgments of taste, could be understood from a concept of form that implies perfection.

But if the form of beautiful objects does not refer to their outer surfaces, what about the "inner form" of objects—a concept that was to become important, especially in romantic aesthetics? Is such inner form what aesthetic judgment is about? First, it must be remarked that this concept of "inner form" becomes an issue for Kant only with respect to teleological judgments, which, though reflective, are not aesthetic judgments. Precisely because certain objects found in nature display an internal organization that no concept of the understanding can explain, reflective judgment must turn teleological. It is true that qua products of genius, works of art, when judged as such and not merely as beautiful things, also reveal an inner organization, whose possibility must be taken into account in such judgments. Kant writes:

If the object is given as a product of art and as such is to be declared beautiful, then, because art always supposes a purpose in the cause (and its causality), there must be at bottom in the first instance a concept of what the thing is to be. And as the agreement of the manifold in a thing with its inner destination, its purpose, constitutes the perfection of the thing, it follows that in judging of artificial beauty the perfection of the thing must be taken into account. (154)

The inner purposiveness of a thing of art, the inner form that it reveals to the extent that it is a product, thus concerns the way in which the manifold of the thing coheres in view of realizing the concept that precedes it as its cause. However, the very presence of such a concept of the thing in a judgment of taste precludes its being a pure aesthetic judgment. What is found beautiful in a pure judgment of taste, an artwork's mere form—its appearing to be structured without a purpose—cannot be of the order of such inner agreement of the parts of the thing since such cohering is not possible without reference to a purpose.

It needs to be pointed out that many of Kant's commentators who have favored an aestheticist and formalist interpretation of form have relied on chapter 14 of the *Critique of Judgment*, entitled "Elucidation by Means of Examples."[2] Indeed, Kant gives here his most explicit definition of form, in the context of a discussion of Euler's undulatory account of color.[3] After expressing his disagreement with Euler on this subject,[4] Kant admits that were color and tone to be explained by an undulatory theory, they could no longer "be reckoned as mere sensations, but as the formal determination of the unity of a manifold of sensations, and thus as beauties" (60). This formula is refined when, in order to distinguish the form of an object from an object's quantitative and qualitative perfection, Kant writes in chapter 15 that the "formal [element] in the representation of a thing, i.e. the agreement of the manifold with a unity (it being undetermined what this might be), gives to cognition no objective purposiveness whatever" (63). In the context of chapter 14—where Kant refers to "isochronous vibrations [*gleichzeitig aufeinander folgende Schläge*]," the "regular play of impressions (and the form of the combination of different representations)," and the uniformity [*Gleichförmigkeit*] of the simple mode of sensation—the definition of form as the unity of a manifold bears a likeness to a formalist definition of form. Without overlooking for a moment that form, as it is used in the Third Critique, has something to do with the unity of a manifold, I wish to ask whether this formal way of defining form in chapter 14 is truly the gist of what Kant wishes to establish about the form of a beautiful object.

Since so many commentators have relied on the chapter "Elucidation by Means of Examples" to define what Kant supposedly means by form, I begin with the most obvious question: what is the overall status of this chapter within the "Analytic of the Beautiful"? To answer this, let us first recall the distinction made in the "Deduction of Pure Aesthetical Judgments" between the critique of taste as an art and the critique of taste as a science. When we inquire critically into the rules determining the accordance or discordance of imagination and understanding in a representation of a beautiful object—a representation that elicits a judgment of taste—we can proceed in two different ways, Kant argues. We can either show these rules by way of examples (in which case the critique of taste is an *art*) or derive the possibility of judgments of taste from the nature of the faculties of imagination and understanding (in which case it is a *science*). Accordingly, in the chapter "Elucidation by Means of Examples" in order to illustrate what form implies in a transcendental, or scientific, critique of taste—which is the only critique of concern in the *Critique of Judgment*—Kant implicitly compares the procedures of this critique to those of the critique of taste as "an *art* . . . [which] shows this by examples" (128). Indeed, the true addressee of the "Elucidation" is not the transcendental philosopher but the cultivated reader or art critic, who, by contrast with a reader "whose taste is yet weak and unexercised," knows that "in painting, sculpture, and in all the formative arts . . . the *delineation [Zeichnung]* is the essential thing; and [that] here it is not what gratifies in sensation but what pleases by means of its form that is fundamental for taste" (61). There is a distinction to be made between, on the one hand, form, in the sense of harmonious composition, or regular and uniform construction, and on the other hand, color, for instance. On this difference rests the critique of taste as an art; and Kant thus avails himself of it as an example familiar to the art critic, in order to sensitize his cultivated reader to a more fundamental distinction on which rests the critique of taste as a science. The distinction instrumental to the transcendental approach must thus be one in which pure form, free of all charms as well in order for it to be judged beautiful, differs from the art critic's formalist conception of it as residing in the object's delineation. In light of Kant's argumentative strategy in "Elucidation," that is to say, his referring to what the art critic understands by form to illustrate what form means in a transcendental perspective, it seems unjustified to make the formalist definition of form Kant deploys here into a prime means of explanation for the notion of form in a transcendental perspective. Furthermore, Kant's commentators seem not to have noticed that, while a transcendental critique concerns the conditions of possibility of a judgment upon the beautiful in general (including natural beauty and the beauty of art), the formalist concept of form is evoked with respect to man-made artworks alone: more precisely, already recognized products of beautiful art, from which this formalist concept of form is subsequently abstracted by the art critic.

A further reason for hesitating to take the formalist definition of form at face value is provided by Kant's statements about regularity and symmetry in the "General Remark on the First Section of the Analytic." "Geometrically regular figures, such as a circle, a square, a cube, etc., are commonly adduced by critics of taste as the simplest and most indisputable examples of beauty"; yet they are not beautiful in the sense that term takes in the *Critique of Judgment*, Kant holds. He states that geometrically regular figures are "mere presentations of a definite concept which prescribes the rule for the figure (according to which alone it is possible)," while he "regards purposiveness apart from a concept as requisite for beauty" (78). In a "judgment of taste, which when pure combines satisfaction or dissatisfaction—without any reference to its use or to a purpose—with the mere *consideration* of the object," regularity and symmetry are of no concern. Neither one is a characteristic of the beautiful form; rather, they are both of the order of cognition and the unity of the manifold that it achieves.[5] Undoubtedly, "every violation of symmetry . . . displeases," but it does so "because it contradicts the purpose of a thing" and not because it would be adverse to the standards of taste (79). In sum, then, if beauty is linked to an agreement of a manifold with a unity, such agreement is not to be understood in terms of regularity, symmetry, and uniformity. The opposite, as it were, would seem to be true. Kant associates regularity with constraint and identifies it as something by means of which the understanding "puts itself in accordance with the order [*in die Stimmung zur Ordnung*] that it always needs" (80); in the remaining parts of the "General Remark," he goes on to advocate the "separation from every constraint of rule" requisite for taste to "display its greatest perfection in the enterprises of the imagination." He even goes so far as to endorse a measure of the grotesque, albeit "under the condition, however, that the understanding is to suffer no shock thereby" (79).[6] But even though regularity and symmetry are not elemental characteristics of the beautiful form, form is not therefore of the order of the irregular and the asymmetric. Rather, as is shown in chapter 22 by Kant's criticism of one W. Marsden, who thought a pepper garden with its parallel rows to be more beautiful than the Sumatran jungle, the mere form of an object judged beautiful combines with a certain prodigality and even luxuriance. Neither regularity and symmetry nor their opposites constitute the beautiful form; instead a certain richness of the form itself, its indeterminateness, or dynamis (of possibilities), constitutes that beauty. Rather than being opposed to content, form, in this sense, gestures toward what is otherwise than form and content—an exuberance of indeterminateness prior to any fixing of objective meaning and its constraining formal characteristics.

Although Kant amply clarifies that pure judgments of taste—which occur only if no determined concept is available for the object under consideration, so that the object is unknown—concern exclusively "free beauty," commentators have scarcely noticed that such beauty is encountered especially in the wild. The form that is thus judged beautiful is form in the wild —form that, for a lack of concepts, never achieves the fixed shape of a delineation or outline and is still free of inner or outer regularity and symmetry. Let me therefore return to Kant's discussion of Marsden. Kant writes:

> Marsden, in his description of Sumatra, makes the remark that the free beauties of nature surround the spectator everywhere and thus lose their attraction for him. On the other hand, a pepper garden, where the stakes on which this plant twines itself form parallel rows, had much attractiveness for him if he met with it in the middle of a forest. And he hence infers that wild beauty, apparently irregular, only pleases as a variation from the regular beauty of which one has seen enough. But he need only have made the experiment of spending one day in a pepper garden to have been convinced that, if the understanding has put itself in accordance with the order that it always needs by means of regularity, the object will not entertain for long—nay, rather it will impose a burdensome constraint upon the imagination. On the other hand, nature, which there is prodigal in its variety even to luxuriance, that is subjected to no constraint to artificial rules, can supply constant food for taste. (80)

As Kant emphasizes against Marsden, only the free beauty of nature—wild beauty—because of its prodigality, variety, and luxuriance, offers the imagination a way to entertain itself for the longest time, that is, without coming to rest in a definite act of the understanding. The parallel rows of stakes on which the pepper plants grow subject the entwined tendrils to an order that, according to Kant, is not the form considered by a judgment of taste; rather it is what gives rise to determining judgments. The form judged by pure aesthetic reflective judgments is thus obviously that of the freely entwined tendrils and the wild growth of the jungle. That artificial objects require such intertwining as well if they are to be judged beautiful therefore comes as no surprise. I mention only the "free delineations, outlines intertwined with one another [*ineinander geschlungene Züge*] without design and called foliage" (41), and "the delineations *à la grecque*, foliage for borders or wall papers, [which] mean nothing in themselves" and are said to be free beauties (66). It is also worth noting in this context that many of the artifacts that Kant judges to be beautiful are those of peoples that in Kant's time were considered wild savages—the Caribs and the Iroquois, for example (139). If a palace, as distinct from "a regular, purposive building," can by mere observation be judged beautiful, this is precisely because it lacks a definite purpose and hence is in a colloquial sense "wild" (38). But "the beautiful figure of a wild flower" (141) encountered in nature, that is, the figure of a flower whose species one does not know, is perhaps the paradigm of beautiful form. Kant writes:

> Flowers are free natural beauties. Hardly anyone but a botanist knows what sort of a thing a flower ought to be; and even he, though recognizing in the flower the reproductive organ of the plant, pays no regard to this natural purpose if he is passing judgment on the flower by taste. There is, then, at the basis of this judgment no perfection of any kind, no internal purposiveness, to which the collection of the manifold is referred. (65–66)

When judged beautiful, flowers are the objects of a mere observation in the absence of all determined concepts and are consequently by definition always wildflowers. One might object to this that the tulip, to which Kant refers twice, is hardly a wildflower. According to Kant, "a flower, e.g. a tulip, is regarded as beautiful, because in perceiving it we find a certain purposiveness which, in our judgment, is referred to no purpose at all" (73). However, as Kant insists, such a judgment occurs only with respect to "an individual given tulip," that is, in the absence of all consideration regarding the species to which it belongs (127). What is true of wildflowers is true, too, of the tulip: this flower, which had just been imported to Europe from Turkey, was, in Kant's time, a wildflower in all senses of the word.[7] In short, wild objects of nature are the privileged objects of judgment upon beautiful form (whereas "nature excites the ideas of the sublime in its chaos or in its *wildest* and *most irregular* disorder" [84; emphasis mine]). The notion of form at the core of the transcendental inquiry of judgments of taste is thus necessarily the notion of a form whose traits, rather than being forcibly gathered into a recognizable shape, remain intertwined in such a fashion as to defer all definiteness. Such form is still wildly rich in potential determinateness.[8]

But if an aestheticist and formalist concept of form does not come close to what Kant means by form in the *Critique of Judgment*, we must still ask whether the considerably more complex Heideggerian reading of Kantian form that Walter Biemel gives is capable of doing it justice. Form for Kant, Biemel writes, concerns the *how* of an object's appearing. It is what remains if an object is stripped of all its determinations—that is, determinations of *what* it is. According to Biemel, Kant's claim in "Elucidation by Means of Examples" that in all the formative arts "delineation is the essential thing" reveals an influence by Winckelmann, for whom delineation and contour are the essential moments of an artwork; thus Biemel further notes that delineation proceeds by means of delimiting lines. Lines, he continues, organize a manifold into a whole, outlining the limits within which an object in its own unity can come into appearance. By means of delineation, and of the emerging lines that delimit the object, the latter acquires a figure, a visible contour, a *Gestalt* within which it can come into appearance. Biemel writes: "With the form we experience nothing that concerns sensibility, or the intellect as the power of concepts. Form, as Kant understands it, is that which informs the object. It is what makes it possible for it to show itself by means of the determined articulation of the formal as such which, for the intuition, is space and time."[9]

First, let us remark that the starting point of Biemel's analysis of form is chapter 14, "Elucidation by Means of Examples," the same chapter from which the formalist interpretation of form draws its resources. The following passage from that chapter, a passage on which Biemel draws heavily, needs in particular to be mentioned here:

Every form of the objects of sense (both of external sense and also mediately of internal) is either *figure* [*Gestalt*] or *play*. In the latter case it is either play of figure (in space, viz. pantomime and dancing) or the mere play of sensations (in time). The *charm* of colors or of the pleasant tones of an instrument may be added, but the *delineation* in the first case and the composition in the second constitute the proper object of the pure judgment of taste. (61)

As the whole context of chapter 14 makes amply clear, especially the paragraph preceding the one from which the above quote is drawn, the objects of sense that Kant alludes to are primarily artifacts and works of (figurative and tonal) art. The forms of the objects of (internal or external) sense that are invoked here are the forms of objects that are not only already constituted but also determined as objects of art. Delineation as the formal distinguishing trait of figures, as distinct from their materiality, concerns first and foremost the perception of the forms of the figurative arts. Kant's allowance, in chapter 14, that charm could potentially enhance the beauty of something (that is to say, enhance its form) by making it "more exactly, definitely, and completely, intuitable" (61) is further evidence that he is referring here to existing objects that are fully determined as artworks. Although Kant makes only sparse use of the term "figure," it serves, undoubtedly, as a characterization of form. For example, in the First Introduction, he writes that the "formal technic" of nature "yields purposive figures, i.e., forms such that, in the act of representation, imagination and understanding are of themselves harmonious with the possibility of the concept."[10] But unless one understands the formal technic of nature to be analogous to art—to painting in particular, which Kant terms "the art of delineation" in order to rank it highest among the arts (175)—this example about the forms of natural objects for which no determined concept is available—that is, objects that exist but have not yet been construed as definite objects, and whose form thus is precisely what is in question—also makes one wonder whether "delineation" catches the formal traits that allow for the representation of an indeterminable natural object. Is it delineation that causes a figure to be purposive and hence to have form? The subjective qualification of the purposiveness of natural objects refers to the harmonious arrangement of the faculties beneficial for cognition in general. The figure or form of unknown objects—of phenomena whose objectivity is not yet specified—is not an objective property like the delineated shape, or outline, of a work of art. It is, so to speak, constituted in the act of judging the object purposive, and hence beautiful.[11]

Second, it must be remarked that Biemel's interpretation of delineation rests on Kant's contention, at one point, that form consists in delimitation. At the beginning of the first chapter of the "Analytic of the Sublime," in order to distinguish the sublime from the beautiful, Kant writes, "the beautiful in nature is connected with the form of the object, which consists in having [definite] boundaries [*die in der Begrenzung besteht*]" (82). But what does Kant mean by *Begrenzung*, that is, "delimitation"? Kant does refer to these boundaries as the limiting lines within which an object can show itself. As Louis Guillermit has argued in his genetically oriented account of the Third Critique, the notion of *Begrenzung* must be traced back to the technical conception of infinite judgments, that is to say, judgments made according to the third moment of quality in the table of the categories.[12] Such judgments, Kant explains in the *Logic* and the *Critique of Pure Reason*, are judgments that do not determine the concept under which an object is to be subsumed but merely indicate that the concept possibly to be applied to an object belongs to the sphere exterior to the one of a given concept. Such a sphere, Kant writes in the *Logic*, is "actually no sphere at all but only the *bordering of a sphere on the infinite*, or *limitation itself*." According to the *Logic*, such judgments are of no importance to a general logic.[13] But in the First Critique, Kant writes: "These judgments, though infinite in respect of their logical extension, are . . . , in respect of the content of their knowledge, limitative [*beschränkend*] only, and cannot therefore be passed over in a transcendental table of all moments of thought in judgments, since the function of the understanding thereby expressed may perhaps be of importance in the field of its pure *a priori knowledge*."[14] Kant's analysis of judgments of taste according to a transcendental perspective gives these infinite judgments their due. Thus if the reduction of the beautiful of nature to form—a form that consists in having boundaries—is the clear consequence of an (infinite) judgment in which the judgmental function of quality dominates, then such limitation of the form of the object means that, while it fits under no given concept, it is not for that reason just anything. What the infinite judgment establishes is that the object is limited to (merely) having form, in other words, of possessing the qualities required for a possible concept to be applied to it! This understanding of limitation does not warrant an interpretation as Heideggerian as the one proposed by Biemel. Finally, Biemel's interpretation of form as the boundary within which things come into their appearing conflates the sensible form of a given object judged to be beautiful with the formal constitution of objects in general—that is, of phenomena, or *Erscheinungen*. Considering the shift in the meaning of the notion of aesthetics between the First and Third Critiques, one cannot simply transpose the problematic of the pure forms of intuition to the analysis of aesthetic reflective judgments. Undoubtedly, in the writings preceding the *Critique of Judgment*, and in particular in the *Reflexionen*, Kant identifies the form of the beautiful with the form of the phenomenon.[15] But Claudio La Rocca has convincingly demonstrated that Kant abandons this conception in the Third Critique. Indeed, he must have abandoned it, because, as La Rocca notes, "on the basis of such an identification of form and appearance (phenomenon) it is impossible to explain why the objective reason of a judgment of taste cannot be reduced to an empirical predication, to an objective discourse."[16] The analysis of form that I shall put forward below in this chapter not only musters further evidence for the necessary distinction between the form of the phenomenon and that of a given beautiful object but also outlines what precisely form in the aesthetic sense describes. Here I limit myself to the following observation: the reflective judgment concerns objects given in experience—that is, already constituted phenomena, as well as "the connection of phenomena which is given in [natural products] according to empirical laws" (17)—and judges "the form of [these empirical] things (of nature as well as of art)" (28). It follows from this that the form of these empirical things—rather than consisting in the a priori laws of sensibility, that is, the laws of a possible experience in general—involves the connection of empirically intuited features of a thing, and is thus itself an "empirical unity" whose lawfulness is "in itself contingent, so far as all concepts of the understanding are concerned."[17] Because form in the aesthetic reflective sense relates to empirically given things, it is not the *one* form of phenomenality in general, but always necessarily manifold. This notion of form concerning individual empirical things must be understood in conjunction with Kant's statements about *"experience as a system according to empirical laws,"* which statements bear upon nature as a whole. In both cases, it is a question of an empirically experienceable formal unity of a phenomenally constituted thing, or manifold of things.[18] In the *Critique of Judgment* Kant gives no extensive exposition either of the reasons for distinguishing the formal constitution of objects in general from the beautiful form or of what the exact distinguishing traits are. Nonetheless, the necessity of separating the two is clearly established, in particular when, toward the end of the "Critique of the Aesthetical Judgment," Kant distinguishes between "the *ideality* of the objects of sense as phenomena . . . [as] the only way of explaining the possibility of their forms being susceptible of *a priori* determination," and "the *idealism* of purposiveness, in judging the beautiful in nature and art . . . [as] the only hypothesis under which critique can explain the possibility of a judgment of taste which demands *a priori* validity for everyone" (196). However, Kant's relative silence about what sets the form of the beautiful object apart from the form of the phenomenon obliges his commentators to answer this question, by carefully scrutinizing Kant's assertions about beautiful form in the Third Critique. Any elucidation of the notion of form in the *Critique of Judgment* must observe, first and foremost, that the beautiful form of an object is not the phenomenal form of the object, which concerns only the possibility of the object, but the *empirical* unitary law for the intuitive manifold of certain existing objects, which from the point of view of our understanding is contingent.[19]

Some of the more astute commentators upon form in the Third Critique have clearly seen that the form called beautiful is not that of the object in general—the cognizable phenomenon or appearance—but is rather the form of a given, that is to say, an empirical object.[20] Few of these commentators, however, wondered why, according to Kant, a judgment of taste concerns only the "mere form" of such an object (64), or "the mere representation of the object" (39).[21] But does Kant's emphasis on the restrictive "mere" to qualify the form of beautiful things not deserve special consideration here as well? Kant's extensive use throughout the "Critique of the Aesthetical Judgment" of the restrictive adjective "mere" to qualify what is judged beautiful makes it plain that a very specific kind of form is at stake in aesthetic judgments upon certain empirical objects. Hence, "mere form" must be distinguished from form generally. Undoubtedly, "mere form" is pure, unmixed form, considered absolutely, that is to say, exclusive of its materiality and its possible conceptual determinations. But apart from standing free of all admixture of charms and concepts, what else does "mere form" suggest? More precisely, what is a mere form of an empirical object in its mere representation? The answer is not self-evident. Kant exacerbates the difficulty by saying that such mere form comes into view only in a very particular kind of sighting: in what Kant terms the "mere observation [*blosse Betrachtung*]" of a thing, or an object (38).[22] What does such mere sighting consist in, and what does it reveal about the mere form of the object that it sees?

Kant's repeated insistence that a judgment of taste concerns only the mere "representation by which an object is *given* to us" (56) leaves no doubt that what is judged is an object that is already given. But as this statement also shows, the judgment concerns only two things: the "representation through which the object *is given*" (51) and the question whether "this mere representation of the object is accompanied in me with satisfaction" (39). An aesthetic reflective judgment, Kant remarks in the First Introduction, is one "about a particular object [*über einen gegebenen Gegenstand*]."[23] In other words, aesthetic judgments about objects (or the representations thereof) presuppose the formal constitution of those objects as phenomena, or *Erscheinungen*. Rather than judging "the *form* of appearance," or "that which so determines the manifold of appearance that it allows of being ordered," the aesthetic judgment concerns something other than "the pure form of sensibility" since in given objects it considers merely the form.[24] So again, what is this "mere form" of the object (64), or of its representation, that is at issue in a judgment of taste? What has it to do with "the representation through which the object *is given*"? Although I have already discussed the nature of reflective judgments, I need to take up this issue one more time to further clarify not only the general nature of reflective judgments, of which the judgment of taste is a specimen, but also, and especially, the occasion on which such judgments are deemed necessary. Kant writes:

> A merely *reflective* judgment about a particular object *can be aesthetic* . . . if even before it contemplates comparing the object with others, the judgment, with no concept antecedent to the given intuition, unites the imagination (which merely apprehends the object) with the understanding (which produces a general concept [*in Darstellung eines Begriffs überhaupt*]), and perceives a relation between the two cognitive faculties which forms the subjective and merely sensitive condition of the objective employment of the faculty of judgment—namely, the harmony of those two faculties with one another.[25]

An aesthetic reflective judgment precedes any comparison by means of which the understanding secures a determinate concept for the intuition of a given object. To put it differently, a reflective aesthetic judgment takes place in the absence of any concept that would unify (*zur Einheit bringen*) the collected manifold (*Zusammensetzung des Mannigfaltigen*) of a given intuition (75). One could thus say that the judgment deals with "the object itself" (55) before all logical determination, before all representation through which the object is thought. Since the object is given in an intuition, it has, of course, been apprehended (*aufgefasst*) by the imagination. As Kant defines it in the First Introduction, apprehension—the taking in of "the manifold of intuition"—is the first act of the cognitive faculty in search of an empirical concept.[26] But no determinate empirical concept is available to produce a cognition of the thing in question. In other words, the intuited manifold has not yet been subjected to collection, which itself presupposes an act of spontaneity. It follows from this that the possibility of an aesthetic reflective judgment arises when the imagination has apprehended the manifold of a given object in the absence of a determinate concept, that is, a concept for which the manifold, having first been collected (*zusammengesetzt, zusammengefasst*) by the imagination, could become the presentation (*Darstellung*). Before further exploring the passage quoted above, we must refine our understanding of the very condition of aesthetic reflective judgment—the apprehension by the imagination of a manifold of intuition in the absence of any determinate concept.

I recall: reflective judgments, according to the Third Critique, divide into aesthetic and teleological judgments. Both kinds of judgments presuppose a purposiveness of nature for our powers of cognition, and therefore the reflective power of judgment as such is also to be called technical. The difference between the aesthetic and the teleological powers in question is that in aesthetic reflective judgments, which occur in the absence of determined concepts, the presumed purposiveness of nature is judged to be subjectively purposive, or formal, whereas in teleological reflective judgments, which require given concepts, nature is deemed objectively purposive. Now, Kant's emphasis on this division in the *Critique of Judgment* makes it easy to overlook another distinction that pertains to the reflective judgment in its subjective, hence aesthetic, mode. Indeed, Kant draws this distinction only in the introductions, particularly in the First Introduction. This division within aesthetic judgments—a division that, as a footnote in the First Introduction suggests, is patterned after the Aristotelian distinctions between genre and specific difference, that is, also between matter and form[27]—concerns the subjective purposiveness of either nature as a whole or individual objects. Both judgments are aesthetic: not only those that find the form of given single objects subjectively purposive (which judgments are commonly regarded as the sole theme of Kantian aesthetics) but also those that judge nature as a whole to have the form of a system. For none of these judgments are concepts available, and, therefore, the judgment that finds nature to have the form of a system, hence to yield to a unified experience, is not a teleological judgment. Both judgments on the whole of nature and those on its single objects have their ground of determination in the feeling of pleasure or displeasure.

As is manifest from the introductions to the Third Critique, there are two distinct occasions on which the mind faces empirical manifolds for which the understanding lacks determined concepts.[28] One occasion is when we confront the "*infinite multiplicity of empirical laws*" and the "*great . . . heterogeneity of natural forms*"[29] to which experience in the theoretical sense gives rise; the other is when we face the intuited manifold of certain single objects of nature or of art. Whereas the manifold of intuition of individual things, along with the judgment of taste to which it gives rise, is thematized primarily in the "Analytic of the Beautiful," the manifold of empirical laws, as well as forms of nature that also call for aesthetic reflective judgments, is almost the exclusive subject of the introductions.[30] In the cases of both single objects and empirical laws, aesthetic reflective judgments are warranted.

In light of what we will see these reflective judgments to achieve, we should note here that in an aesthetic reflective judgment, objects of art are basically judged the same way as are objects of nature. Even though in my discussion of the arts of genius in Chapter 7 I will slightly modify this statement, for the moment it is important to stress that in judgments of mere taste no difference is made between objects of nature and of art (142). Kant writes in the First Introduction that "the judgment of artistic beauty will have to be regarded . . . as a mere derivative of those principles, which are the foundation of judgment concerning natural beauty."[31] This means that in a purely aesthetic judgment, a work of beautiful art should be looked at as one looks at natural beauty. One is reminded here of Kant's dictum in the Third Critique that works of art ought to have the look of objects of nature. Indeed, as soon as the work of art is judged as a product following from "the causality of human powers of representation that is called *art* (in the restricted [*eigentlichen*] sense of the word)"—that is to say, judged according to an *intentional* purposiveness—the judgment is no longer a merely reflective judgment but a "determining judgment (which underlies all human art works)."[32] If a purely reflective aesthetic judgment does not discriminate between objects of nature and objects of intentional artistic production, this is, as we shall see, precisely because of what, in such a judgment, is called "form."

But first let me return to the mechanics of the aesthetic reflective judgment. In the First Introduction, Kant lists the three acts of the faculty of cognition that must combine in order for empirical concepts to emerge. In addition to the apprehension (*apprehensio*) of the manifold, which we have already discussed, one must also distinguish "(2) the *synthesis*, i.e., the synthetic unity of consciousness of this manifold in the concept of an object (*apperceptio comprehensiva*); [and] (3) the *presentation* (*exhibitio*) in intuition of the object corresponding to this concept."[33] While apprehension requires the faculty of imagination, reason—in the sense of *Verstand* (understanding)—is needed for the synthesis, and the power of judgment for presentation. As we have seen, a reflective aesthetic judgment takes place in the absence of any determined concept that would comprehend the apprehended manifold of a "something." Whereas, in determining judgments, the concept of the understanding allows the imagination to collect the manifold of intuition and thus to turn the manifold into the presentation in intuition of the concept in question, in aesthetic reflective judgment, judgment and the imagination have no such concept at their disposal. But in a merely reflective judgment, the imagination, serving as the faculty of apprehension, can nonetheless call on the understanding—not to provide the imagination with a definite concept but instead to enter, as the faculty of concepts in general, into a "relationship in which [the faculties] must stand to one another in the judgment generally."[34] Where such a relationship succeeds, the apprehended manifold has become collected or comprehended in what Kant calls *comprehensio aesthetica* (90). However, since no concept is involved in such comprehension, the collected manifold is not a presentation in a determinate cognitive judgment. In the relationship of the faculties in question, the imagination in its actual apprehending of the manifold of a particular intuition has become the presentation of the understanding insofar as the latter is the faculty of concepts in general; and the ramification is that, since only a relationship beneficial for a determinate judgment has been secured, a reflective judgment remains merely subjective.

Yet, in order for the apprehension of the manifold of a "something" in the imagination to agree with the presentation of a concept of the understanding in general (regardless of which concept), the "something" to be reflectively judged must, it would seem, have specific characteristics. With a view to elaborating on the character (*Beschaffenheit*) of the objects that lend themselves to aesthetic reflective judgments, I return to the "*infinite multiplicity of empirical laws*" and the "*great . . . heterogeneity of natural forms*" that derive from the theoretical cognition of nature. Even though the mind has no concept unifying the particular laws and forms of nature, the empirical manifold gives rise to reflective judgments if this manifold of "the *aggregate* of particular experiences"[35] presents itself in such a manner as to reveal some order. More precisely, the aggregate in question must be of such a nature that reflection can proceed on the heuristic assumption that it is a lawful whole, that is, that the aggregate has the "form" of a system. What the empirical manifold of nature must thus allow the mind to assume of it

is a formal purposiveness [and not a 'teleology,' as Haden translates] of nature, which we in fact [*schlechterdings*] assume of it, but which is the basis neither for a theoretical knowledge of nature nor for a practical principle of freedom; nonetheless it gives a principle for judging nature and investigating it in search of the general laws of particular experiences, according to which we must posit them to bring out that systematic connection needful for coherent experience.[36]

This formal purposiveness does not postulate anything objectively about the *Beschaffenheit* of the things of nature or of nature in its entirety. No more does the formal purposiveness thus ascribed to nature establish anything about the possible existence of natural things. It "is a mere Idea, which serves as a principle for our investigation, and hence is only subjective," Kant writes.[37] In short, the formal purposiveness of nature is the a priori principle for judgments concerned with empirical manifolds of natural laws and forms, in the absence of any determinate concept.

To conclude my discussion of the aesthetic reflective judgment concerning natural manifolds, I wish to consider briefly the implications of the idea of a formal purposiveness of nature in its entirety. Kant spells them out when he writes that this principle of purposiveness consists in the assumption "that for all things in nature empirical concepts can be found; in other words, that one can always presuppose in the creations of nature a form which is possible under universal laws accessible to our knowledge."[38] For the particular laws in nature, and for nature's heterogeneous "empirical forms for which one has concepts already," reflection produces empirical concepts under the guidance of the principle in question, concepts that correspond to "*generically harmonious* forms [*generisch-übereinstimmende Formen*]." In other words, on the basis of an assumed formal purposiveness of nature, aesthetic reflective judgment is capable of showing that "nature has observed in its empirical laws . . . a similarity among forms [*Gleichförmigkeit*]";[39] that is to say, it has observed an always contingent, always empirical formality. This form of the empirical manifold of nature is quite different from the forms of intuition that Kant analyzes in the "Transcendental Aesthetics" of the First Critique; for it is felt to be pleasurable, since it allows the mind's powers of representation to experience nature as a systematic ordering, or as one nature. Succinctly, the idea of an inner formal purposiveness of nature permits aesthetic reflective judgment to detect a harmonious empirical form in what Kant terms "the labyrinth of the multiplicity of possible special laws."[40] Where reflective judgments are able to discover empirical forms that harmoniously tie together the natural manifold, such judgments are accompanied by "a very marked pleasure" (24). The aesthetic pleasure that comes with such discovery arises from "the comprehensibility [*Fasslichkeit*] of nature" (24), which is composed in its empirical manifold of particular laws and heterogeneous forms. When nature proves comprehensible because it yields to forms or systems of forms, it is found to be beautiful. Nature's formal purposiveness is the ground of a sense of pleasure, since such purposiveness "is harmonized with our design" (23).

As long as reflective judgment represents nature only as internally purposive, it remains subjective and aesthetic and does not predicate anything of nature itself. However, because aesthetic reflective judgments can be about the systematicity of nature, they are easily confused with teleological reflective judgments. To avoid this confusion, one needs to distinguish the formal purposiveness represented by aesthetic judgments, which is internal and merely subjective, from the purposiveness represented by teleological judgments, which, while also merely formal, is an objective purposiveness. In turn, the objective formal purposiveness represented by teleological judgments must be distinguished from the objective material or real purposiveness represented by determining judgments. Objective formal purposiveness, unlike subjective or aesthetic purposiveness, is not a principle whereby one finds nature's manifold to be a priori comprehensible; rather it is a principle concerning the *possibility* of certain objects within nature and, to a lesser degree, of nature as a whole. But objective formal purposiveness does not account for the *existence* of the objects of nature— it is merely formal even though it is logical. Objective material or real purposiveness, on the other hand, which is the matter of determining judgments, is about nature in its existence. Hence, of objective purposiveness, only the purposiveness that concerns nature's inner, or absolute, objective organization is the stuff of teleological judgments. Where reflection on the purposiveness of nature and its forms has become teleological, it is no longer satisfied with merely discovering nature's manifold to have the form of a system. Even though distinct from determining judgments concerning objective mater.ial or real purposiveness in nature, teleological reflection on the possibility within nature of certain of its forms is already cognitive in a certain sense. As a result of its indifference to the subjective purposiveness of the manifold, the reflection is no longer aesthetic.

Aesthetic reflective judgment involves not only the (empirical) forms of the manifold of natural laws and nature's heterogeneous forms but also the forms of certain individual objects, in the absence of determinate concepts of the understanding. The objects in question are primarily objects of nature, but can also be objects of art as long as they are not apprehended simply as the result of art. Before I analyze how, in the aesthetic reflective judgment of taste, the manifold of such objects becomes the presentation of a concept in general, and what "concept" means in this case, I will dwell momentarily on the particular kind of sighting in which certain objects are beheld that subsequently are judged beautiful.

A judgment of taste always takes "the form of a singular judgment about an object," Kant remarks in *Critique of Judgment* (127). This means that the judgment covers only the one object that is estimated according to its beauty. "I describe by a judgment of taste the rose that I see as beautiful" (50), but I make no claim about other roses, or roses in general (which would amount to an objective generally valid judgment). In judgments of taste, objects are thus encountered outside their possible discursive and conceptual contexts. They are envisaged in isolation: as it were, for themselves, in advance of any possible comparison. By contrast with the judgment of an object according to a concept, and hence in conformity with the way others have looked at it, a judgment of taste presupposes that one "submit[s] the object to . . . [one's] own eyes," Kant writes (50). He adds, in the "General Remark upon the Exposition of the Aesthetical Reflective Judgment," that since the object is being looked at in the very contingency of its appearance, the mode of its representation is one of "immediate intuition" (110). In the "mere observation [*blosse Betrachtung*]" (38) of a thing—and I note that when Kant speaks of the object of a judgment of taste, he calls it not only indiscriminately *Object*, or *Gegenstand*, but also *Ding*, or *Sache*, expressions referring generally to something that eludes precise determination—one looks at it "as poets do, merely by what strikes the eye [*nachdem, was der Augenschein zeigt*]" (111). What strikes the eye in the mere observation of a single thing is nothing less than "the mere form" of the object (50). Since what such a mere observation sights is "immediately referred to my feeling of pleasure and pain" (50), the judgment that occurs in these circumstances "only judges the forms (without any reference to a purpose) as they present themselves to the eye," Kant adds (168). Yet what is such form—the form of a single, empirical thing of nature or of art? Why does its perception cause such pleasure, and prompt the universal claim that this object is beautiful?

The search for a response to these questions requires us to look again at what happens in a judgment when it concerns the apprehended manifold of one single thing. Kant writes in the First Introduction:

if . . . the form of a given object is so produced [*so beschaffen ist*] in empirical intuition that the *apprehension* of its manifold in the imagination agrees with the presentation of a concept of the understanding (regardless of which concept), then in simple [*blossen*] reflection understanding and imagination mutually harmonize for the furtherance of their work and the object is perceived as purposive for the [power of] judgment alone. Hence the purposiveness as such is thought as merely subjective, since a definite concept of the object is neither needed nor produced by it, and the judgment made is not a cognitive one. Such a judgment is called an *aesthetic judgment of reflection*.[41]

Under the condition that the merely apprehended intuitive manifold of a single object lends itself to being collected into the presentation of a concept in general, a harmonious agreement of the imagination and the understanding takes place, and thereby represents the minimal condition for cognition in general. But such agreement depends "on the form of a given object . . . in empirical intuition." This is to say that if the form of an object is perceived to have the *form of form*, an aesthetic reflective judgment in which the object is seen as beautiful becomes possible. The object has the form of form if its form appears to be subjectively purposive. Kant renders this notion of form a bit more precise when he writes that what is judged to be purposive in this case—that is, as I discussed earlier, in the absence of any determinate concept of the empirical manifold of the intuition—is an "indeterminately purposive *natural form* . . . [*Naturformen*]."[42] Formal purposiveness of the object obtains when that object has a natural form, but one that is indeterminately purposive; in other words, one to which only a concept in general corresponds, and not any determinate concept. If such an object can be judged to be purposive, although no concept fits it, this is because this object displays form. Yet if it has form, it is no longer simply a "something"; rather, it has the form of a determinable thing, the form of an object of nature, and hence is eminently cognizable. To put it bluntly, what is found beautiful in the judgment upon the mere form of an object is that the thing judged conforms to the form of an empirical object or a thing (irrespective of what it is), rather than refusing itself to such a representation (and consequently, to representation as such). A judgment of taste savors not the phenomenal nature of what is judged but its susceptibility to empirical concepts. Because of its form, a beautiful object is, as it were, exquisitely cognizable. At this point, the full reason why a judgment upon the beautiful makes no distinction of essence between objects of nature and objects of intentional art comes into view. Indeed, what such a judgment is concerned with is exclusively whether the objects under consideration have an indeterminately purposive natural form; in other words, whether they have the form of an object of empirical experience at all. What causes the pleasure of such a judgment is merely that the powers of cognition achieve a representation of a natural form, hence of something that has the qualification of cognizability. No consideration of objective purposes enters the purely aesthetic judgment, be it one about a natural or an artificial object. As we will see in our discussion of the beautiful arts, it is even questionable whether one can still speak of beauty at all, or for that matter of pleasure, if an object of art is viewed exclusively on the basis of its intentional production.

Before circumscribing this concept of form any further, let me emphasize that its conception is entirely non-aestheticist or formalist. Form, in the case of a single object of experience for which no concept is available (at least for its immediate intuition) here names only the form of empirical "object" or "thing" as something that is in principle cognizable because it has this form. Dieter Henrich's contention that the *Critique of Judgment* must be understood within "the framework of . . . [the] new epistemology that Kant had worked out in the *Critique of Pure Reason*," a structure based on "the possibility of our knowledge of objects," shows here all of its pertinence.[43] Whether it regards natural beauty or the beauty of art (as long as the latter is not judged primarily as an intentional production), the judgment of taste focuses on the thing's form as the form of a thing. The judgment of taste is thus involved in what I have termed a para-epistemic act. Kant writes: "A natural beauty is a *beautiful thing*; artificial beauty is a *beautiful representation* of a thing" (154).[44] Kant could hardly be more precise as to how he wants "form" to be understood than he is when he subsequently remarks, "the beautiful representation of an object . . . is properly only the form of the presentation [*Darstellung*] of a concept" (155).[45]

The form of the object considered in a judgment of taste is the form of an empirically given object, or of an actual representation of such an object.[46] But since this form does not objectively predicate anything of the object, the undetermined empirical object, on the occasion of which the judgment is made, remains undetermined. Nevertheless, because it has form, the object has the figure of something eminently cognizable—it appears to have a natural form, the form required by cognitive experience. Certainly it is an empty object, but exquisitely determinable, as it were, and still inherently rich in potential determinations. It is marked by open determinability. Since the formal purposiveness of the object is merely subjective, it attributes nothing to the thing itself but instead asserts something about the state of the faculties of representation and cognition: namely, that the cognitive faculties relate harmoniously in the minimal relation necessary for there to be a possible cognition. From certain of Kant's statements in the Third Critique, it is evident that if judgments of taste admit of universal communicability and can make universality claims, it is because of this "accordance of the cognitive powers with a cognition generally and that proportion of them which is suitable for a representation (by which an object is given to us) in order that a cognition may be made out of it" (75). What the preceding developments have made clear, however, is that the universality of the "subjective condition of cognition" (75) cannot be understood solely on the basis of a minimal relating of those powers required for cognition in general; rather, the powers must stand in a relation corresponding to the one required for any representation by which an object is given at all. In other words, the basis upon which the universality of an aesthetic judgment rests is that of "mere form"—the form of the object, the form of what is eminently cognizable.

Since, after all, certain objects of nature and of art invite judgments of taste in which these things are called beautiful because of their form alone, one is easily tempted to understand form as an objective determination of the thing. This may, indeed, be the particular temptation of formalist aestheticism. But what, precisely, is the status of the beautiful thing of nature, or of art, in a (pure) judgment of taste—that is to say, in a judgment distinct from the determining judgment that proceeds on the assumption of a real ground of the purposiveness of the object and that makes objective claims? In the "Analytic of the Beautiful," Kant admits that on the basis of the object's form alone, "beauty [is] attributed to the object" (60). He remarks that one says "the *thing* is beautiful" (47); he even speaks, at one moment, of the "determination [*Bestimmung*] of an object as beautiful" (56). In a judgment of taste, one "compares [the object's] character [*Beschaffenheit*] with the feeling of pleasure and pain" (43–44). Yet there is no way of revoking Kant's claim that judgments of taste are only subjective and do not "extend to the object" (49). A judgment of taste, he holds, "brings to our notice no characteristic [*Beschaffenheit*] of the object, but only the purposive form in the determination of the representative powers which are occupying themselves therewith" (64–65). It would thus seem that the form is the form not of the object (*genitivus objectivus*) but only of the representational powers harmoniously preconditioning the emergence of cognition in general. In the First Introduction, Kant notes that the "relation [between the power of apprehension and the power of presentation], by its form alone, causes a sensation which is the determining ground of a judgment."[47] Rather than belonging to the object, the form would be the form only of the organization of the faculties involved in a judgment of taste, an organization that Kant calls "free play." But let there be no mistake: for its occurrence, such formal arrangement of the faculties needs (beautiful) objects. How are we to reconcile these seemingly contradictory propositions?

Let me begin to answer this by further emphasizing the duplicity of this concept of form. In the First Introduction, Kant distinguishes formal and real technics of nature, which are the respective grounds of aesthetic and teleological judgment. He writes, as we have already seen, that the "formal technic" of nature "yields purposive figures [*Gestalten*], i.e, forms such that, in the act of representation, imagination and understanding are of themselves harmonious with the possibility of a concept."[48] The formal technic of nature is manifest inasmuch as the intuited empirical manifold of nature's laws has the figure of a system; and the variegated aspects of a single thing, rather than presenting themselves as a formless chaos, show this manifold to have the formed coherence of the figure of an object. Now, in the passage cited, the representation of this form of the manifold is said to incite the imagination into the harmonious relation required for producing a possible concept. In other words, the form or figure of what in the intuition offers itself to the powers of representation, makes these powers take on the harmonious form of free play. The form of the object is thus clearly distinct from the form of the powers of representation. But consider the following point: "Judgment can a priori create and construct [*angeben und konstruieren*] purposive forms of intuition, for instance when it devises for the purpose of comprehension forms appropriately illustrative of a concept [*als sie sich zur Darstellung eines Begriffs schickt*]."[49] Kant shows here that judgment is in a position to detect purposive forms in the empirical manifold in intuition and to construe them as the presentation of a concept in general; I understand this passage to imply that the form of the given thing in representation is purposive only insofar as it lends itself to the presentation of an indeterminate concept. In itself such a form is, for all intents and purposes, nothing. Or, more precisely, only in representation does a given thing acquire form; independently, if such a thing would be possible, it has none. The thing acquires the status of form solely if it is made into a sensible presentation of a concept. However, if in truth only the harmony achieved by the powers of cognition is found pleasurable, it follows that in the process of agreeing to such a form, the empirical manifold of intuition (which sets off the free play) has been transformed from a formless chaos into an empirical order, or into something that has the figure of an empirical object. The latter remains the object of a judgment of taste that states, "This thing is beautiful," and its beauty stems from its being perceived as having the form of an empirical object, in that it is the sensible presentation of an indeterminate concept. But does a statement such as "This thing is beautiful" not also tell us something, in a certain way, about the object itself? As La Rocca has convincingly argued, from Kant's assertion that the feelings of pleasure and pain denote nothing in the object one cannot conclude that "the aesthetical experience does not manifest anything at all about the nature of the thing that constitutes its theme, and that this thing is nothing more than the indifferent occasion on which the experience in question arises."[50] Undoubtedly, what the object that is judged to be beautiful reveals is that it has form, the purposive form of an object. But how is one to understand such manifestation, if it cannot be "objective"?

In an effort to further circumscribe the difficulty in question, I wish to take up Kant's distinction, in the First Introduction, between inner and relative purposiveness. This distinction applies to both subjective and objective purposiveness; for what interest me, I need consider this distinction only as it bears on the former. Moreover, since relative subjective purposiveness defines "only the *possible* [not 'teleological,' as Haden translates] purposive *use* of certain sensuous intuitions," a use by means of which sublimity is attributed to objects of nature, I shall limit myself to the definition of inner subjective purposiveness on the basis of which "judgment attributes *beauty* to the objects of nature." But let me first cite Kant on the distinction itself:

All *purposiveness*, subjective or objective, can be divided into *inner* and *relative*; the first kind is based on the representation of the object as such, the second simply on its contingent *use*. Accordingly, the form of an object can in the first place be perceived as [internally] purposive for reflective judgment, i.e., in sheer intuition apart from concepts, and as a result subjective finality is attributed to the thing and to nature itself. In the second place, perception of the object may hold for reflection absolutely no purposiveness of its form as such, but the representation of it arousing a feeling of a purposiveness lying a priori in the subject (perhaps the suprasensuous determination of the subject's mental powers) can give rise to an aesthetic judgment.[51]

Inner subjective purposiveness allows the perception of the form of an object to take place free of all concepts of the understanding, in an act of "mere intuition." It is a form that can be intuited not only for itself (*für sich*), as an "object" in its own right, but also as purposive with regard to the reflective power of judgment, that is, as offering itself as the presentation of a concept in general and furthering in this manner the powers of cognition. As Kant remarks, when such a perception of an inner subjective purposiveness of the form of an object takes place, "subjective finality is attributed [*beigelegt*] to the thing and to nature itself." In other words, such perception gives rise to a kind of determination both of the thing and of nature. The thing is judged to have the form of a potentially cognizable object, and nature is viewed as having the form of a system that makes it inherently cognizable. The thing and nature have thus become endowed with intrinsically universal characteristics. But although these characteristics are nonprivate and universal, we must still pause to ask whether they are therefore objective. Aren't they rather pre-predicative features, on the sole basis of which objective attribution can possibly take place? Indeed, what is attributed to the thing and to nature in an aesthetic judgment is nothing but their subjective inner purposiveness for the power of judgment. Somewhat like phenomena or appearances, empirical manifolds of intuition (of a thing or of nature as a whole) are *in themselves* merely what the powers of cognition have projected into them. One is reminded here of Kant's claim in the First Critique that the conditions of possibility of objects are the conditions of possibility of experience in general. However paradoxical it may sound, the objects of nature and its manifold, to which beauty (that is to say, form) is attributed, have the objective characteristic of being subjectively purposive. Kant writes, indeed, that "a judgment of taste consists in calling a thing beautiful just because of that characteristic in respect of which it accommodates itself to our mode of apprehension" (123).

Kant himself seems to grapple expressly with this difficulty concerning the status of the form attributed to beautiful objects, in the very title of chapter 11 of the *Critique of Judgment*—"The Judgment of Taste Has Nothing at Its Basis but the Form of the Purposiveness of an Object (or of Its Mode of Representation)." Does Kant waver here on attributing form to the object or to the mode of its representation? The formula that he uses to speak of form in this chapter is indeed worth noting. Form is the harmonious "relation of the representative powers to one another, so far as they are determined by a representation," he writes (56). Since the ground of a judgment of taste can consist neither in sensible pleasantness nor in the representation of perfection, "therefore it can be nothing else than the subjective purposiveness in the representation by which an object is *given* to us, so far as we are conscious of it, which constitutes the satisfaction that we without a concept judge to be universally communicable; and, consequently, this is the determining ground of the judgment of taste" (56). Kant seems to insinuate here that the form of purposiveness of an object (which form belongs to the object) is "the mere form of the purposiveness in the representation by which an object is *given* to us" (56). To phrase it differently, form, as an attribute of the object, is the subjective purposiveness of the form of the faculties in the representation of this object. How is one to understand this equation? Chapter 34 of the *Critique of Judgment*, in which Kant returns one more time to his definition of the form of the beautiful object, may offer a clue to solving the puzzle. Kant refers here to "the reciprocal subjective purposiveness (of the powers of cognition), the form of which . . . in a given representation, constitutes the beauty of the object [*dass ihre Form in einer gegebenen Vorstellung die Schönheit des Gegenstandes derselben sei*]" (128). The beauty of the form of an object of a representation by which that object is given is, thus, the form of the powers of cognition in harmony. But the passage also allows us to solve the difficulty we have been trying to come to grips with, since it states two points with unmistakable clarity. First, it affirms that an object is beautiful only insofar as it has been represented—insofar as it is an object of representation, that is to say, an object in a representation by which an object is *given* in the first place. Second, it proposes that if the form of the object is identical with that of the harmonizing powers of cognition, this is because the form of the object (and hence its beauty) is the form of representation itself—a representation that gives a coherent object, rather than a formless aggregate of particular aspects. If, at one point, Kant can claim that "the satisfaction in beauty is such as presupposes no concept, but is immediately bound up with the representation through which the object is given (not through which it is thought)" (67), clearly he does so because he understands the mere form of the object to be the form of the representation itself by which an object is given. In chapter 35, Kant explains that the judgment of taste rests upon the feeling emerging from the reciprocal activity of the cognitive powers, "which makes us judge the object by the purposiveness of the representation (by which an object is given) in respect of the cognitive faculty in its free play" (129). It follows from this that an object has form if its representation is merely the *giving* of an object. It also follows that such form cannot be "a concept of the object" (133); in the designation of form nothing becomes predicated of the object, because it is "merely" the form of the object. If such form is the form of an object in a representation by which an object is given in the first place, it is necessarily also the form of the representative powers, if not of (objective) representation itself, in the arrangement that furthers cognition.

From all of this it should be evident that the "mere form" of reflective aesthetic judgments is not the objective form of an empirical manifold of intuition that occasions these judgments. "Mere form" is anterior to any possible objective attribution in that it secures the form of empirical objectivity for the intuited in the first place. "Mere form" concerns exclusively the possibility of being given in a representation, that is, of having the form of an object. Consequently, what is judged beautiful on the basis of its form alone is the form that permits the representation of something as an undetermined empirical object. Yet, since the form in question is already the form of cognizable objectivity, it is not something that strictly speaking can be attributed to objects; and this is true simply because prior to it, objects are not yet given. "Mere form," then, is the pre-objective and pre-predicative condition under which empirical manifolds of intuition can be gathered into figures of objectivity, in the absence of determined concepts. The eventual attribution of form to a formless manifold of nature, or of intuition, is pleasurable because by this feat of the mind, the possibility of objectification and predication is potentially secured.

Since I have been seeking to ward off the aestheticist and formalist temptation to construe the concept of form in pure aesthetic judgments as the form of already constituted objects, or of objects shaped according to formalist principles of composition, I may have inadvertently caused another misunderstanding of "mere form." Defined as the form of an object, and hence as a universal condition of cognition that is found to be universally satisfactory, what is judged to be beautiful in the representation by which an object is given to us seems to have all the qualities of an abstract generality of the understanding. But let us recall that in judgments of taste one judges single things—this rose that I have before my eyes, for example! Indeed, what is found beautiful in such a single thing is not that it has the form of an object in general but that this one thing has the single form of a cognizable thing. Only form as the single form of a single thing is judged to be subjectively purposive and hence beautiful. It is never apprehended in its generality. Such apprehension would presuppose comparison, and therefore would no longer be an aesthetic judgment. If the objects of aesthetic judgments are given empirical objects, then the judgment that secures their form in the absence of a concept secures it as the form of a particular object. What is deemed pleasurable in such a judgment is that this object is knowable not as a phenomenon, or as an appearance in general, but as an object that is potentially cognizable in its very singularity.

From everything we have seen, it follows that according to a judgment of taste, objects are beautiful only if they have the form of cognizable objects. In themselves—objectively, as it were—objects cannot be declared beautiful; it is not within the power of aesthetic judgments to make objective statements in this respect. One might argue that although this might be plausible in the case of objects of nature, it would certainly not apply to the beautiful objects of the arts. Taking as a premise what we have established with respect to "mere form"—that it is the form of the (single empirical) object—one could try to make the point that artworks, or some artworks, at least, are subjectively purposive representations made into material objects. Artworks could thus be understood as reflections on the necessary requisites for becoming an object; more precisely, as staging the minimal conditions that must be met for a material manifold to be recognizable as having the form of an object. Needless to say, understanding art in this way could serve to account for numerous trends in contemporary art, and prove that Kant's elaborations on art and its form are still significant for the understanding of art today. But it must also be remarked that unless the rule presiding over the production of artworks that concern the very possibility of being an object (whatever its determination may be) has been rendered indeterminate, judging man-made works of art to be the purposive staging of what it takes to be an object is not an aesthetic judgment. To judge art with an eye to the potential purpose of materially realizing the minimal conditions under which a manifold can have the form of an object is to shift to a different register than that of aesthetic judgment; namely, to determining judgment. If on this register one continues to refer to the form of the object, or to an object's formal beauty, these terms can no longer be taken as aesthetic terms. From a Kantian point of view, they have become objective determinations and no longer admit of the pleasure or displeasure specific to judgments of taste.

4

Presenting the Maximum

Kant's fundamental doctrine concerning the heterogeneity of intuition and concept grants a place of central importance to presentation (*Darstellung*) in cognitive judgments. All concepts under which a particular is to be subsumed must undergo a presentation—that is to say, an intuitable exhibition in the unitary shape of a sensible manifold—before cognitive judgment can proceed to the subsumption properly speaking. In the event that these concepts are a priori concepts, or categories, the presentation required by Kant's conception of cognition as a synthesis of intuition and concept is, as Kant has shown in the chapter on schematism in the First Critique, an a priori presentation. However, despite the central role of presentation in the *Critique of Pure Reason*, the term enjoys no special treatment there. Only in the discussion of pure mathematical concepts in "The Discipline of Pure Reason in Its Dogmatic Employment" does Kant finally get around to overtly defining presentation, here called "construction," as the (mathematical) procedure by which these pure concepts are a priori given a corresponding intuition.[1] In the *Critique of Judgment*, by contrast, presentation becomes so central an issue that a whole chapter is dedicated to illuminating the notion in question. In chapter 59, Kant goes so far as to refer to *Darstellung* under its Greek name "hypotyposis," or its Latin equivalent *exhibitio*, thereby granting the notion of presentation a philosophical and conceptual dignity that it did not enjoy before. One needs to ask, therefore, what it is in the Third Critique that warrants this more detailed discussion of presentation. Why, precisely, does the elaboration on the aesthetic reflective judgment and its object require that the issue of presentation be expressly and explicitly addressed? Since "presentation" is thematized only in the first part of this work, an overhasty explanation may be that the *Critique of Judgment* is about art, and hence about representation and its limits. But is this so? Undoubtedly, the analysis of aesthetic judgment takes up most of the Third Critique. However, aesthetic judgments concern above all the beautiful of nature, rather than that of art; and beautiful man-made art is considered only to the extent that it resembles products of nature. The sublime, on the other hand, is said to be primarily a state of mind, and not something attributable to objects—not even to those objects of nature with which the sublime is usually associated. Consequently, the distinction between an original and its representation cannot be central to the overall concerns of the Third Critique. The meaning of "aesthetic" in this work, moreover, bears little resemblance to what is known under that title in the history of aesthetics, both before and after Kant. As Kant uses the term it does not refer to artistic representation at all, but to that which concerns the senses in judgments, and is subjective. Finally, presentation is not the same as representation: neither in the common sense of a likeness or an image of a model nor in the Kantian sense of a *Vorstellung*, an activity of the mind that encounters no boundaries, since everything is susceptible of becoming an item in the mind. Even though ideas of reason cannot be presented, they are still representations of the mind!

Before investigating the reasons for the heightened visibility of presentation in the Third Critique, let me first recall in what presentation consists, and in particular, under which of the powers of the mind it falls. Presentation achieves prominence in a study of judgments about mere form, but is also central to judgments about what is absolutely great. One might therefore expect that the eminence of presentation results from the effort to account for the specific kind of judgments that make up the judgments of taste. However, even though Kant pays particular attention to the notion of presentation during the discussion of aesthetic judgments upon the beautiful and the sublime, this in no way amounts to privileging the sphere of the aesthetic with respect to *Darstellung*. Certainly, the notion of presentation is not very conspicuous in the discussion of the teleological judgment; but as Kant notes in the Second Introduction, presentation plays a decisive role in teleological judgments as well as in aesthetic ones. In aesthetic judgments, he writes, "we can regard *natural beauty* as the *presentation* of the concept of the formal (merely subjective) purposiveness," whereas in teleological judgments, we can regard "*natural purposes* as the presentation of the concept of a real (objective) purposiveness."[2] In any event, in this chapter I will continue my elucidation of mere form and of judgment thereupon, and my discussion of presentation will primarily rely on Kant's statements regarding this notion within the exposition of the judgment of taste (and in the two introductions as well). I wish to discuss presentation initially in the context of what seems to be an exclusive concern with the specifically formal characteristics of reflective aesthetic judgment, in the hope that this elucidation of presentation will help clarify the concept of mere form itself.[3] This approach will further bring to light a dimension of form that has received little attention in Kant scholarship: a minimal, yet essential, function of reason in the formation of form.

Presentation (*Darstellung*) is not representation (*Vorstellung*). Kant insists that "free beauties," such as "delineations *à la grecque*, foliage for borders or wall papers, mean nothing in themselves; they represent nothing— no object under a definite concept" (66). Beauty is not a representation, in the sense that it is not a depiction of a conceptually definite thing. But Kant's use of the notion of representation is much broader than such reference to a concept might suggest. For Christian Wolff, who was the first to introduce the notion of *Vorstellung* in German-language philosophy, *Vorstellungen* are often distinct from logical concepts, and designate the mental images of perceptions. However, Kant's own use of the term rests on another tradition, in which *Vorstellung* derives from the Latin *repraesentatio*. Following this tradition, *Vorstellung* functions for Kant as a generic term that includes both intuitions and concepts. Very generally speaking, he uses "representation" to refer to any mental item; and, in this sense of the word, the perception of a beautiful thing, for example, is a representation. But presentation must not be confused with this very broad meaning of representation. As a result of Kant's occasional terminological laxness, one may come across passages in which "representation" and "presentation" blend into each other. Nonetheless, "presentation" has a meaning—or rather a set of meanings—that are clearly distinguishable from "representation." During the eighteenth century, and prior to Kant, *Darstellung* (**presentation, or exhibition**) became a *terminus technicus* in the theory of art (especially the art of theater); thereafter, with Friedrich Gottlieb Klopstock, it became the central term of the theory of poetry.[4] There are, of course, a number of instances in Kant's work where his use of "presentation" points to this semantic stratum of the term. But another use of the term by Kant needs to be mentioned here. In the First Introduction, Kant argues that since applications of theoretical knowledge "obey no other principles than those under which, as sheer laws of nature, the understanding recognizes the possibility of the thing," these applications belong to theoretical knowledge and are not to be confused with practical knowledge. Kant here makes use of the verb *darstellen* to designate (the act of) the effective realization of a concept. He writes that the "proposition expressing the possibility of the thing as an effect of will . . . must borrow its basic principle from the theory of nature in order to produce the representation of an actual object [*um die Vorstellung eines Objekts in der Wirklichkeit darzustellen*]."[5] "Presentation" is thus clearly distinct from "representation." For the moment, I leave in abeyance the question of the dependence of representation on presentation, which this passage seems to suggest, and point only to Kant's use of presentation as production. I single out this particular meaning of *darstellen* as production—a meaning that conforms to its employment in chemistry throughout the eighteenth century—because it is related to the specific use that Kant makes of the term. This specific Kantian use of "presentation" corroborates a more general observation: that the term achieves its first philosophical, or more precisely, epistemological, status in Kant's critical philosophy.[6] Indeed, as we have seen already, Kant argues that no empirical cognition of a manifold of intuition is possible without the sensibly intuitable presentation of the concepts of the understanding.[7] Presentation concerns concepts, and consists in rendering them intuitable, in a process that is subservient to cognition. In Dieter Henrich's words, "To exhibit a concept means to associate with it in intuition a manifold of a distinctive unitary (temporal and/or spatial) shape."[8] Concepts must be able to take on a unitary presentation according to the pure forms of intuitions—space and time—if the fundamentally distinct orders of intuition and concept are to come together in the first place, and thereby make determined cognition possible.

Kant remarks in the Second Introduction:

> If the concept of an object is given, the business of the judgment in the use of the concept for cognition consists in *presentation* (*exhibitio*), i.e. in setting a corresponding intuition beside the concept. This may take place either through our own imagination, as in art [in the sense of *téchnē*] when we realize a preconceived concept of an object which is a purpose of ours, or through nature in its technique (as in organized bodies), when we supply to it our concept of its purpose in order to judge its products. (29)

In theoretical judgments in which the concept is given, and in judgments about organisms of nature to which we bring a concept of a natural purpose, presentation produces an intuition that conforms with the given concept. Distinct from these are the judgments about objects given in experience for which no concepts are available, and it is this latter kind of judgment that the Third Critique investigates. But what role can presentation play in judgments in which concepts are nonexistent, and in which the presentation cannot come up with corresponding intuitions for given concepts? Is it the very obscurity of the function of presentation in such judgments that leads to this function's being so conspicuous and pronounced in *Critique of Judgment*? Or could it be that, in judgments that are merely reflective rather than determining, a hitherto unthematized dimension of presentation in general comes to light: a dimension that will require special treatment? Reflective judgments of taste concern only mere form, and when there is a radical lack of form, they concern the absolutely great. I will limit myself here to the consideration of mere form, in anticipation of what remains to be established about the absolutely great. We have already seen that mere form secures a minimal objective intelligibility for objects of nature for which we have no determined concepts. The prominence that the problematic of presentation enjoys in the "Analytic of the Aesthetical Judgment" suggests that presentation must be involved in a significant way in reflective judgments. In other words, presentation must play a distinct role in the formation of mere form, and in judgments thereupon.

Presentation consists in making a concept intuitable. On the basis of the seemingly unequivocal declaration in the Third Critique that "the imagination is the faculty of presentation" (69), the task of providing a concept with a sensible shape is generally attributed to the imagination. However, Kant scholars have rarely taken notice of other statements on presentation in the Third Critique that complicate the attribution of presentation to the imagination. The following passage from the First Introduction, for instance, is one of several in which the task of presentation is ascribed to the understanding. Regarding the determining ground of aesthetic judgments of reflection, Kant writes here that this ground is the "feeling brought about by the harmonious interplay of the judgment's two cognitive faculties: imagination and understanding, when the former's power of apprehension and the latter's power of presentation are mutually assisting each other in the given representation."[9] Other passages from the Third Critique even seem to suggest an involvement of reason in the act of presentation. One instance of this occurs in the context of the analytic of the sublime; Kant writes that when reason is confronted with an unlimited series of numbers, it "desires comprehension in *one* intuition, and so the [joint] *presentation* of all these members of a progressively increasing series" (93). If presentation consists not only in rendering a concept intuitable but in rendering it sensible by way of *one* intuition—that is, in a unitary way—presentation is thereby also linked with the faculty of the ideas (of totality). In the same context, Kant holds that "by the principles of the schematism of the judgment (being so far, therefore, ranked under freedom), [the imagination] is the instrument of reason and its ideas" (109–10). Finally, the First Introduction also imputes the power of presentation to the power of judgment. Kant writes: "Nature is necessarily harmonious, not merely in regard to the agreement of its transcendental laws with our *understanding*, but also in respect to the agreement of its empirical laws with the *judgment* and the power of the latter to exhibit an empirical apprehension of nature's forms by means of the imagination."[10] With unmistakable clarity, Kant emphasizes that a judgment is necessary for "the *presentation* (*exhibitio*) in intuition of the object corresponding to [a] concept."[11] How is one to understand and contrast these different statements concerning the agency of presentation? Needless to say, presentation and what it accomplishes cannot be satisfactorily described until the confusion about which faculty is responsible for presentation has been dispelled.

The presentation that is generated by the imagination is the presentation of concepts of the understanding. The imagination renders these concepts intuitable in presentation in order to ensure their usability, for otherwise they would remain abstract or empty. Presentation thus takes place to the end of applying the concepts of the understanding within cognition, and hence can be said to be in the service (at least) of the understanding. Presentation of concepts occurs as an intuitive manifold that has a temporal and spatial unitary form. Furthermore, precisely this unity of the intuition presenting the concept also ties presentation (in a way that will be determined hereafter) to the faculty of the ideas. In all of this, however, we must not neglect the power of judgment, which Kant, particularly in the First Introduction of the Third Critique, puts in charge of presentation. What does the power of judgment consist in? Throughout Kant's writings, the faculty of imagination commands a variety of operations: the apprehension of the manifold of intuition and the synthesis of representations, for example. In this sense, the imagination provides the sensible representation for the presentation of a concept. But the presentation of a concept consists in adding to a concept an intuition that properly *corresponds* to this concept. Securing such conformity between intuition and concept, however, is not in the power of the imagination; for this reason it is misleading to equate the imagination with the power of presentation, and thus to ignore Kant's other references to the facultative origin of presentation. In point of fact, only the power of judgment is capable of ensuring that an intuition conforms to a concept. If the concept is a determined concept, only a determining judgment can ensure the correspondence between the concept and the intuition; if it is an undetermined concept, as is the case for aesthetic reflective judgments, it is the reflective power of judgment that secures the conformity.

In his essay "Urteilskraft und Darstellung," Javier Ibanez-Noé examines the different modes of presentation that Kant distinguishes: construction (or schematic presentation of a priori concepts); the example (that is, empirical presentation); symbolic presentation (or the presentation of an unpresentable concept); and the presentation of an undetermined concept (or of a concept in general). Ibanez-Noé goes on to argue that though the imagination indisputably provides the intuition in the presentation of a concept, the Third Critique's analysis of reflective judgments also reveals that the power of judgment is required to ensure that the presentative intuition corresponds to the concept. Indeed, since "the presentation of a concept whose relation to the particular of intuition is not determined a priori (that is to say, the presentation of all concepts with the exception of the schematized categories), presupposes an examination of this particular's appropriateness to the concept, that is to say, a *reflection*," any judgment concerning "the presentability of a (determined or undetermined) concept by means of a particular of an intuition" is intimately interwoven with the presentation by imagination. In other words, even though it is the "imagination [that] brings forth the *preconceptual* interconnection of the manifold" of intuition, to be affiliated with a concept, it is in fact the power of judgment that seeks "to relate the preconceptual unity of the manifold to the unity of apperception in the concept." Ibanez-Noé concludes: "The result of this act is called presentation. Imagination is therefore only a power of presentation by way of the power of judgment. For the presentation is not simply a presentation but one that is adequate to the concept." Since judgment alone is capable of evaluating an intuition's adequateness to a concept, the "imagination *as the faculty of presentation* (and not simply as apprehension), is at the service of the power of judgment."[12]

With a view to establishing the precise role of presentation in reflective aesthetic judgments, let me first take up Kant's remark in *Critique of Judgment* "that whatever we present [*darstellen*] in intuition according to the precept of the judgment (and thus represent aesthetically [*ästhetisch vorstellen*]) is always a phenomenon, and thus a quantum" (88). Although it occurs in the "Analytic of the Sublime," this statement concerns reflective judgment in general. In conjunction with this claim, Kant observes that a judgment about the mere size of something—a judgment that is, as we will see, merely reflective, although it concerns neither the beautiful nor the sublime—can apply to anything, including beauty. Beauty, for example, can be said to be great or small because what is judged to be beautiful is always a phenomenon: an object in space and time, something that has unity and hence size, and that in Kantian terminology is therefore a quantum. I underscore once again that reflective judgments, whether aesthetic or not, concern phenomena that are given in experience, have no determined concepts, and have an empirical form. In reflective judgments, phenomena of this kind are intuitively set forward, but not as presentations of objective concepts, as would be the case in determinate judgments, since objective concepts are precisely what are lacking. Instead, as the reference to aesthetic representation suggests, they are the presentation of a subjective susceptibility to concepts in general. Natural beauty comprises the phenomena of nature that, qua natural phenomena, already have the unity of phenomena but that also display an empirical form for which no concept is available. Such natural beauty can, according to Kant, be regarded as the presentation of "the concept of the formal (merely subjective) purposiveness" (30). In the presentation that operates in reflective judgment, the objects under consideration are the sensibly intuitable shapes that are added to the subjective power of what Kant calls concept in general, rather than to given concepts. Kant notes that anything presented in intuition, according to the precept of reflective judgment, is represented aesthetically. Thus not only is presentation distinct from representation, but it in fact seems to be an essential ingredient in the making of representations; in any event, aesthetic representations rest on a presentation in the sense we have just discussed. Consider the following passage: "the beautiful representation of an object . . . is properly only the form of the presentation of a concept, by means of which this latter is communicated universally" (155).[13] Rather than providing an intuition of an object that corresponds to a given (objective) concept, a beautiful representation is constituted by a presentation that has only the form of such a sensible illustration. It holds the object under consideration against the subjective power of concept in general, or of mere (indeterminate) cognition. The object presented in reflective judgments is one for which no determinate concept is available and by way of which concept in general, or the mere form of concept, becomes universally communicated. As we have seen, reflective judgments concern the mere form of objects, in the absence of objective concepts. Thus the kind of presentation that is constitutive of aesthetic representations is a presentation "reduced" to the mere form of the kind of presentation we experience in cognitive judgments. In such presentations the mere form of the object serves as the sensible intuition of "the concept of . . . formal (merely subjective) purposiveness"; that is, of concept in general, or mere concept. In short, the mere form of undetermined objects of nature—that is, empirical rather than transcendental—is the intuitable substrate of presentation in aesthetic reflective judgments upon the beautiful. What is presented by the mere form of a beautiful object is the mental power to cognize (in a very broad sense), despite the lack of concepts that inhibits cognition in a definite sense. Any further elaboration on presentation in judgments upon the beautiful requires us to deepen our understanding of the sensible appearance that triggers aesthetic presentation, and to speculate on what sort of concept is thus rendered intuitable.

Pure aesthetic reflective judgments upon the beautiful (to which I limit the following investigation) admittedly concern only "the mere representation [*blosse Vorstellung*] of the object" (39). The restrictive adjective "mere," while it does not belittle what it modifies, indicates that the object in mere representation is not the object of a cognition in a strict sense. A mere representation is thus distinct from a representation through which the object is thought (67). But what does a mere representation positively amount to? Kant also repeatedly speaks of mere representation as representation "through which the object *is given*" (51). In the *Critique of Pure Reason*, Kant argues that for concepts to have objective reality, the object must be given in one way or another; in the same passage he defines objective givenness as follows: "That an object be given (if this expression be taken, not as referring to some merely mediate process, but as signifying immediate presentation in intuition [*in der Anschauung darstellen*]), means simply that the representation through which the object is thought relates to actual or possible experience."[14] To "give" an object, that is, to present it in immediate intuition, is to relate it to a concept of the understanding of which that object then becomes the presentation. But in the pure judgment of taste, the representation of an object in intuition does not relate it to, and hence make it a presentation of, determinate or possible concepts. It follows that the object given in a mere representation is one in which determinate concepts can have no signification and meaning. Furthermore, there is a clear distinction between what it means for an object to be given in a mere representation and the linkage to determinate concepts effected in cognition. Finally, the function of presentation in mere presentation also must differ from its role in cognitive judgments.

Concerning the determining ground of a judgment of taste, Kant remarks that it

> can be nothing else than the subjective purposiveness in the representation of an object without any purpose (either objective or subjective), and thus it is the mere form of purposiveness in the representation by which an object is *given* to us, so far as we are conscious of it, which constitutes the satisfaction that we without a concept judge to be universally communicable; and, consequently, this is the determining ground of the judgment of taste. (56)

Hence, in the mere representation of an object, one is less concerned with the characteristics of the object itself than with the representation, and more precisely, with the form of the representation as the form of an object. Indeed, how could it be otherwise, given that it is in the absence of any purpose or concept? If in such a mere representation an object *is given*, this means only that what is given in such a representation is something that has the form of an object. In other words, in the mere representation of an object, "the mere form" (64) of the object is all that is given; and this form, because it is judged to be purposive, is found to be pleasurable. Now, if this form of the object is *given* in a mere representation, it follows that, qua immediate intuition, it must be linked to "something" of the order of cognition, of which it is the presentation. As we know from the Third Critique, in a judgment of taste the mere representation of the object is held not against general concepts but against concepts in general: that is to say, against the power of cognition in general. Indeed, if a mere representation is found to be pleasurable, it is "merely [because of] the purposiveness of the form" (59). What is given by this representation is beneficial for cognition as such; since no determinate concepts are available, this cognition remains indeterminate, but it is no less of the order of the cognitive. It thus becomes possible to elucidate the precise role of presentation in judgments of taste.

In the absence of all concepts for a given representation of an object, the mere form of the representation by which an object is given becomes its presentation—that is, the immediately intuitable figure of cognition in general. At the hands of the reflective aesthetic judgment, presentation makes it possible to link the representation of a manifold of intuition, for which there is no concept, to the powers of cognition in general. It opens this possibility by offering that representation as one that has the form of a (cognizable) object, and that is consequently purposive. If presentation gains a conspicuous role in the Third Critique, this is not because reflective aesthetic judgment is aesthetic in the sense that it would deal with the beautiful in art and artistic representation. After all, aesthetic judgment as understood by Kant includes, for example, judgments about nature's having the form of a system. Rather, presentation is important because aesthetic reflective judgments originate when one is faced with a manifold of intuition that precludes determinate concepts. On these occasions, the imagination, holding the power of presentation, faces a task unlike the one that it has in determinate judgments. Its responsibilities now include enabling reflection on this manifold of intuition in the first place. To secure this possibility, imagination comprehends the apprehended manifold of intuition in such a way that the latter displays the mere form of a still-undetermined object. Subsequently, this apprehended form can serve as a presentation for the purposive play of imagination and understanding required for cognition generally.[15] Even though in such situations no determinate cognition occurs, such presentation furthers the powers of cognition by animating them.

The chapter "Of the Ideal of Beauty" forms part of the discussion of the third judgmental function of the aesthetic judgment, namely relation. It is here that Kant introduces the crucial notion of purposiveness without purpose (on which all other aspects of the beautiful depend), and also elaborates in some detail upon the role of the imagination in aesthetic judgments concerning the mere form of an object. A careful commentary on certain sections of this chapter will help us to further explore how the imagination gathers the manifold of an object in a pure judgment of taste, in order that this manifold may then serve as a sensible illustration of the concept in general. In addition to shedding greater light on the nature of presentation itself, this analysis will also demonstrate the extent to which the question of presentation is in evidence in the expository part of the aesthetic judgment. Even though the question of presentation is explicitly addressed only in the penultimate chapter of the "Critique of the Aesthetical Judgment," it pervades both analytics, and in the "Analytic of the Beautiful," even has a structuring role in the exposition of the argument itself.

As Kant remarks at be beginning of the chapter "Of the Ideal of Beauty," there can be "no objective rule of taste," because judgments of taste are aesthetic judgments, and thus grounded in the feelings of the subject. Any rule would be based on a concept of the object that would serve to measure the quantitative and qualitative perfection of that object; for taste, this is impossible. Yet notwithstanding the absence of a universal objective rule of taste, the feeling that certain things are beautiful not only claims universality but is also universally communicated. Kant writes: "the agreement, as far as it is possible, of all times and peoples as regards this feeling in the representation of certain objects—this is the empirical criterion, although weak and hardly sufficing for probability, of the derivation of a taste, thus confirmed by examples, from the deep-lying general grounds of agreement in judging of the forms under which objects are given" (68). Since from time immemorial diverse peoples have more or less agreed on what is or is not beautiful, this shared taste is empirical evidence of a deeper (transcendental) ground of agreement in judging the forms by which objects are given. But these shared views by all peoples at all times are more than examples by which a universal communicability of the feeling of beauty is empirically confirmed; these examples of good taste, or at least some of them, have also served as models for taste. Kant notes: "Hence we consider some products of taste as *exemplary*. Not that taste can be acquired by imitating others, for it must be an original faculty [*ein selbst eigenes Vermögen*]. He who imitates a model shows no doubt, in so far as he attains to it, skill; but only shows taste in so far as he can judge of this model itself" (68). In other words, just as mankind's shared views of good taste signify a deep-lying reason for such an agreement, so the agreement by all peoples that certain products of taste are exemplary is empirical evidence of an equally deep-lying standard for judging models of taste. In estimating certain products of taste to be exemplary, individuals and peoples alike demonstrate that they are capable of judging the forms of these products universally, and furthermore that they are capable of judgments that discriminate between beautiful forms on the basis of some rule. The faculty of taste is an original faculty, in the sense that it is entirely one's own and is not acquired through imitation. As such, it shows two distinct (but interlinked) components: a capacity to judge the forms under which objects are given, and a capacity to judge them with respect to some kind of standard. It is this latter aspect of the judgment of taste that will concern us. Let us allow that, in a judgment of taste, the intuitive manifold of an undetermined object is collected by the imagination such that it exhibits the mere form of an object, and that this form is felt to be the presentation of a concept in general. The question then arises as to the possible role played, in such a presentation, by the second essential aspect of the faculty of taste: namely, the ability to judge the forms of objects according to a rule.

Given that taste is an original faculty, and that the rule for judging a model cannot be borrowed from others, it follows, according to Kant, "that the highest model, the archetype of taste, is a mere idea, which everyone must produce in himself [*in sich selbst hervorbringen muss*] and according to which he must judge every object of taste, every example of judgment by taste, and even the taste of everyone" (68–69). Kant's claim is that having taste means not only being able to estimate the beauty of an object but also possessing the ability to judge which beautiful forms are exemplary—including the ability to judge exemplary models in terms of still more exemplary ones. It follows that, as an inborn faculty, taste must have an inherent standard: a standard not to be found outside, that is, one that is not just another, even higher "object of taste." According to Kant, "every one must produce in himself" such an ultimate standard. This archetype of taste, which is to be brought forward spontaneously and to be activated by everyone individually, must be of the order of the ideas. Yet if this is true, then reason must also have an essential role to play in judgments about the mere form of beautiful things. To put it differently, in such judgments the imagination must relate *in some way* to reason as the faculty of ideas in addition to freely relating to the understanding. As a consequence, "mere form," rather than being a merely formal or even formalistic conception, could be thought only by acknowledging within it the presence of a rational element. In the following, I intend to trace out as clearly as possible the exact status of this relation to reason in judgments about mere form.

Kant claims that the highest model of taste can only be a "mere idea" or an "indeterminate idea that reason has of a maximum"; this statement alone indicates the complexity of the imagination's commerce with reason in pure judgments of taste. He explains:

Idea properly means a rational concept, and *ideal* the representation of an individual being, regarded as adequate to an idea [*die Vorstellung eines einzelnen als einer Idee adäquaten Wesens*]. Hence that archetype of taste, which certainly rests on the indeterminate idea that reason has of a maximum, but which cannot be represented by concepts but only in an individual presentation [*nur in einzelner Darstellung kann vorgestellt werden*], is better called the ideal of the beautiful. (69)

Let us keep in mind that the archetype of taste concerns the mere forms of objects that are judged to be beautiful. The archetype serves to judge some of the products of taste as being exemplary, and to compare the exemplars themselves. In other words, the standard in question bears upon the unity of the manifold, which the imagination collects with a view to offering this unity as a presentation of a concept in general. The mere idea that constitutes the archetype of taste is thus a measure for evaluating, as it were, how successfully an intuitive manifold has been collected into the unity of mere form.

In order to clearly face the stakes of the present analysis, I wish to draw out some implications of what we have seen so far, before expounding on this "mere" or "indeterminate idea," which is required to judge the "mere form" that is to present an indeterminate concept. Kant holds that taste not only judges the forms of objects but also requires a standard by which to estimate the products of taste themselves. He thereby makes it plain that already in a pure judgment of taste—which concerns solely the mere form of an object—presentation is twofold. In other words, the two different kinds of hypotyposes that will be explicitly distinguished only in chapter 59 are already both at work in a judgment of taste. Not only is the presentation involved in such judgments schematic (as the direct sensible illustration of a concept of the understanding), but also the hypotyposis involved is symbolic (as the indirect presentation of a concept, or an idea thinkable only by reason). In all judgments of taste upon objects lacking determined concepts, an indeterminate idea of a maximum of reason, or an idea of reason in general (as Kant puts it regarding concepts of the understanding), bears upon the judgment. In the form of an individual presentation of itself, the indeterminate idea of a maximum of reason provides the standard against which the intuited manifold is collected into the mere form of an object. What is required is a symbolic presentation, not of a determinate idea of reason, but of the mere idea of a maximum of reason, that is, a presentation of the division and unification of a manifold of the understanding through a principle, in the shape of one individual being. The symbolic presentation is warranted to complete, as it were, the presentation of an indeterminate concept of the understanding whose shape is that of a thing that has the mere form of an object. In addition, since in judgments of taste the imagination "schematizes without any concept" (129) and hence is involved in free presentation, the symbolic presentation of an undetermined maximum of reason must necessarily be free as well.

In a judgment about the mere form of an object, theoretical and practical reason are present only in the shape of the concept in general, and the mere idea. For this reason, the judgment of taste achieves the most elementary intertwining of theoretical and practical reason, in advance of their ordinary, and mutually exclusive, employment. More pointedly, in judgments upon the beautiful a strict distinction no longer obtains between sensible intuition and the ideas that exceed the limits of all intuition. Even though the First Critique, by requiring intuitable schematizations of the categories for theoretical cognition, maintains the primacy of sensible intuition that has determined theoretical thought since antiquity, the Third Critique demotes it.[16] Here, sensible intuition (in the shape of mere form) and ideas (in the shape of mere ideas) appear intimately interconnected in judgments of taste—a point that conforms with Kant's designation of reason as both theoretical and practical. In a pure judgment upon the beautiful, the imagination gathers a manifold into the presentation of cognition in general, using the mere idea of a maximum of reason as a standard for the gathering. This use of the mere idea explains why the beautiful can become a symbol of morality. The impact of this idea upon gathering a manifold also testifies to the bridge that the *Critique of Judgment* builds across the abyss between cognition and morality. Indeed, the interlacing of understanding and reason in judgments of taste follows from everything Kant has established in both introductions to the Third Critique about the power of judgment. This power is restricted to mediating between the cognitive and moral powers. The mediation takes place in the very act of presentation itself insofar as it is simultaneously schematic and symbolic. It is this elemental interrelation of the two kinds of presentation for the benefit of pure judgments of taste, as judgments aside from but also in advance of cognitive and practical judgments, that explains the prominence that presentation enjoys in the last Critique.

Any judgment of beautiful form requires that an undetermined idea of a maximum of reason accompany the act of judging. But the individual who judges does not, strictly speaking, have to create this idea ex nihilo, as it were, in himself or herself. As a rational being, the individual already possesses determinate ideas of reason. Thus, judging beauty would seem to involve only actualizing the power of the ideas as such. But since the archetype of taste "cannot be represented by concepts," the individual has to produce a single and sensible presentation of this mere idea; and following Kant's distinction between idea and ideal, this amounts to an ideal of the undetermined maximum of reason.[17] Kant writes of this ideal, "Although we are not in possession of it, we yet strive to produce it in ourselves." It is the ideal, then, that all who make judgments of taste must aim at producing within themselves. Kant adds: "But it can only be an ideal of the imagination, because it rests on a presentation and not on concepts, and the imagination is the faculty of presentation" (69). The ideal of beauty, the standard for judging how well a beautiful form fits the mere form of an object that presents an undetermined concept of the understanding, comes into being through a symbolic presentation. The mere idea of a maximum of reason is actualized in this symbolic presentation, in the shape of an individual being that (given the nature of ideas) can be only an indirect presentation of it. Just as the mere form of the object is not the general concept of the object but only imagination's presentation of concept in general, so the ideal of beauty is not a (determinate) concept of reason but merely the imagination's presentation of a maximum of reason, or of the mere idea of such a maximum. Imagination fashions the intuited manifold of an object into the presentation of a concept in general by collecting this manifold into the shape of mere form. In the case of the standard of beauty, imagination achieves the presentation by striving to produce an ideal: that is, a representation of an individual being that could be regarded as adequate to the undetermined maximum of reason.

Everything we have seen suggests that no single judgment of taste could do without the intervention of a standard of reason. After all, without a standard, aesthetic judgments would be indistinct from judgments concerning the merely pleasant. But, one might object, if this were correct, and all judgments of taste did indeed require a standard, why, in what remains of chapter 17, would Kant limit the ideal of beauty to one particular species of the beautiful? Kant writes:

> It is well to remark that the beauty for which an ideal is to be sought cannot be *vague* beauty [in other words, free, non-adhering, that is to say, pure beauty], but is *fixed* by a concept of objective purposiveness; and thus it cannot appertain to the object of a quite pure judgment of taste, but to that of a judgment of taste which is in part intellectual. That is, in whatever grounds of judgments an idea is to be found, an idea of reason in accordance with definite concepts must lie at its basis, which determines *a priori* the purpose on which the internal possibility of the object rests. (69)

No ideal would thus obtain for free beauties—such as beautiful flowers—where "purposiveness is . . . free." Only for the human being alone is it possible to conceive of an ideal. "The only being which has the purpose of its existence in itself is *man*, who can determine his purposiveness by reason," Kant emphasizes (69). "Alone of all objects in the world," he maintains (70), the human is susceptible of an ideal. Does it then follow from this that no standard exists for judging free beauty, that is, objects that are freely purposive and that display merely the form of the object? Does no symbolic presentation of concepts of reason, in the shape of some sort of an ideal, enter into pure judgments of taste? Is the whole previous demonstration irrevocably flawed?

Kant has categorically established that everyone "*must* judge *every* object of taste, *every* example of taste, and even the taste of *everyone*" according to the mere idea of an archetype of taste that everyone must bring forth in him or herself (68, emphasis mine). How can Kant suddenly reverse his position by holding that only the human being is susceptible of an ideal of beauty? Or is this perhaps no reversal at all? Needless to say, at this juncture of his argument about purposiveness, Kant's claim that the human being is the exclusive subject of an ideal of beauty (which claim gestures toward the problematic of the human being as a final purpose) would require an extensive discussion.[18] After all, any judgment of human beauty according to the standard of a human ideal would no longer be an aesthetic judgment, properly speaking. Whether this ideal is rooted in the aesthetic *normal idea* or in the *rational idea* of the purposes of humanity, it prevents the judgments that rest upon it from being aesthetic judgments. The aesthetic normal idea represents "the standard of our judgment [upon man] as a thing belonging to a particular animal species" (70), and serves as a primarily theoretical and objective judgmental determination; whereas the rational idea points in the direction of practical judgments.[19] In light of what I have established thus far about symbolic presentation and its status as a necessary ingredient of all judgments of taste, I will limit my discussion concerning the exclusively human ideal of beauty to one point. First, however, I wish to recall that the ultimate standard according to which all products of taste are (without exception) to be judged is one that, as a mere idea, is based on an indeterminate idea of a maximum of reason (for which no concept is available). By contrast, the ideal of beauty that applies to the human being alone is an ideal based on "the *rational idea* [of] . . . purposes of humanity" (70). Far from being a mere idea of a maximum of reason, this "idea of the highest purposiveness" (72) is a determined idea. In other words, if the human being alone is said to be subject to an ideal of beauty, it is because

Kant understands such an ideal to be the sensible presentation of a determined idea or concept of reason. This in no way prevents the standard of an indeterminate concept of a maximum of reason—or rather, the imagination's attempt to produce an ideal of the beautiful—from ministering to pure judgments about the forms in which objects are given. Strictly speaking, an ideal of beauty presupposes a determined concept of reason; however, an indeterminate maximum used as a standard in collecting the manifold of intuition of "something" into the mere form in which an object is given, is also an "ideal" of sorts. For the most part, Kant remains silent, in chapter 17, about how to conceive of such an ideal, apart from stating that everyone who judges products of taste must strive to produce, in himself, an individual presentation of the idea in question; and without the ideal of beauty, as we have seen, no pure judgments of taste are possible.

Is it too far-fetched to look to Kant's somewhat mysterious doctrine about the "aesthetical ideas" for a clue? And can this problematic be related at all to the issue of a standard of an undetermined maximum of reason—a maximum that must accompany the imagination's collection of an intuitive manifold into the mere form of an object? At first sight, at least, contextual constraints seem to make any such relation unlikely. The issue of the aesthetic ideas emerges in a context where establishing what constitutes a judgment of taste, and what such a judgment accomplishes, is no longer a central concern. The title of chapter 49, in which the discussion of the aesthetic ideas occurs—"Of the Faculties of the Mind That Constitute Genius"—makes it amply clear that this discussion is part of an investigation that singles out the beautiful arts and inquires into them as products of genius.[20] Little wonder, therefore, that within the history of aesthetics, Kant's doctrine of aesthetic ideas has been valued as a tool to account for the nature of the work of art. Intimately connected to this appraisal is a dominant trend in Kant criticism: it conceives of the doctrine of aesthetic ideas as the counterpart to what is commonly believed to be Kant's aesthetic formalism, and his understanding of the pleasure in the beautiful as the inherent but inconsequential pleasure of the experience of beautiful forms. Moreover, the theory of aesthetic ideas would in fact seem to show that art serves a "higher and peculiar human end than diversion," and that, indeed, its value derives from its link to morality.[21] Such an interpretation of aesthetic ideas would see the latter only as providing art with the higher—that is to say, moral—values that art itself, as a mere play of forms, would lack. This interpretation would seem to derive support from the fact that the images linked to aesthetic ideas in Kant's text, and the feelings to which they give rise, are mainly of the order of the sublime. Needless to say, all of this makes it somewhat difficult to pry an answer to our question out of Kant's discussion of aesthetic ideas.

The issue of aesthetic ideas emerges during the analysis of the different faculties that make up genius. One part of Kant's concern here is to show that genius must at all times be disciplined and corrected by taste if its products are to be beautiful, and hence capable of eliciting universal assent. In Kant's own words:

Taste, like the judgment in general, is the discipline (or training [*Zucht*]) of genius; it clips its wings, it makes it cultured and polished; but, at the same time, it gives guidance as to where and how far it may extend itself if it is to remain purposive. And while it brings clearness and order into the multitude of the thoughts [of genius], it makes the ideas susceptible of being permanently and, at the same time, universally assented to, and capable of being followed by others, and of an ever progressive culture. (163)[22]

Given that this passage follows the chapter on aesthetic ideas, one can safely assume that the ideas alluded to here are in fact aesthetic ones. Now, the point made in the above passage is that if a genius's art is to be *beautiful*, what matters is not his or her abundance of ideas, that is to say, imagination alone, but judgment, the latter being the "indispensable condition (*conditio sine qua non*)" of art as beautiful art (163). This must be kept in mind for what follows, since, as in the case of the production of a standard of taste, the faculties involved in the creation of aesthetic ideas seem to be imagination and reason. Undoubtedly, to speak of ideas is to conjure the faculty of reason. Yet should not the qualification of these ideas as aesthetic make one wonder why, and in what capacity, reason enters into a relation with the imagination? Does reason itself actively intervene in shaping these ideas? I leave these questions in abeyance. In any case, numerous commentators, assuming that reason helps create the aesthetic ideas at the heart of the products of genius, have concluded that the presence of reason reveals art to be a much more serious game than Kant's elaborations on the judgment of taste upon natural beauty had suggested. But it must be noted right away that this conclusion derives from a formalist and aestheticist misreading of what is at stake in judgments about the mere form of objects. The conclusion rests primarily on the assumption that reason plays no part whatsoever in objects' mere form and in judgments of taste thereupon; it thus betrays a misunderstanding of the nature of judgment. For example, Jens Kulenkampff asserts, in his discussion of genius and aesthetic ideas, that "a judgment of taste about art can neither be the sole nor the last word about art, but at very best the first," and that judgment concerning the mere form of an art object must be supplemented and corrected by other concerns.[23] My objection here is that to approach art in this way is to relinquish from the outset its quality as beautiful art. Admittedly, real or empirical (as opposed to pure) judgments about works of art are not exclusively, and sometimes not even primarily, concerned with their beauty. In addition, real art may always be art in which beauty only adheres. But consequently, these judgments are not judgments of taste, and the art in question is not beautiful art, in the strict sense, to begin with.

Kant emphasizes taste rather than an abundance of ideas in beautiful art, and this focus suggests that the purely beautiful is very much on his mind in the discussion of genius. Rather than abandoning the formal conditions of beauty, the section on genius reveals them to have a powerful function in the formation of art as beautiful art. In the formation of the beautiful, reason, rather than replacing or correcting mere form, must therefore contribute in some way to the very constitution of the mere form of objects that are said to be beautiful. We should keep in mind that Kant develops his theory of aesthetic ideas in chapters that are largely dedicated to elucidating what frames and properly constitutes beautiful art, not to examining the emergence of adherent beauty. It follows that aesthetic ideas, produced by genius and expressed in beautiful artworks, evince the role played by reason in the imagination's forming of the beautiful form itself, for the sake of form alone. As we shall see, the higher principles in accordance with which the imagination fashions aesthetic ideas can be none other than the regulative principles of reason.[24]

Aesthetic ideas, Kant argues in chapter 49, are the material (*Stoff*) by means of which the spirit (*Geist*)—understood in an aesthetic sense—enlivens the mind (*Gemüt*). Such animation (*Belebung*) consists in putting "the mental powers purposively into swing, i.e. into such a play as maintains itself and strengthens the mental powers in their exercise" (157). Thus if one asserts of certain objects, especially those expected to "appear as beautiful art" (156), that they lack spirit, it is because they lack the material to enliven the mind, that is, aesthetic ideas. Thus, although form is the absolute requisite of beauty, form alone is not sufficient. More precisely, for the form of the object to trigger a judgment of taste—a judgment founded upon the purposive play of the faculties of imagination and understanding—it must yield to spirit. Without spirit, no animation of the mind takes place; in other words, without aesthetic ideas, beautiful form is condemned to remaining merely formalistic. This is obvious from Kant's examples of spiritless products of art, which, as he remarks, may be "very neat and elegant," "exact and well arranged," "solid and at the same time elaborate," but ultimately not truly beautiful (156). To be judged beautiful, what form needs is not content—for content is the correlate of what still amounts to a formalistic conception of form—but rather enrichment of a different sort: form itself (that is, qua form) must combine with spirit. The form of a beautiful work of art, in order to be judged beautiful, must be, as it were, full of spirit (*geistvoll*).

In the main, chapter 49 is concerned with the mental faculties involved in genius; it follows that Kant is interested, first and foremost, in teasing out spirit as a subjective principle, or faculty, in the creation of beautiful products by genius. In this context, Kant defines spirit as "the faculty of presenting *aesthetical ideas* [*das Vermögen der Darstellung ästhetischer Ideen*]" (157). Before examining the implications of the need of a *presentation* of aesthetic ideas for an artwork to be considered beautiful, let us first look at the definition of aesthetic ideas that Kant proposes on this occasion. He writes:

By an aesthetical idea I understand that representation of the imagination which occasions much thought [*die viel zu denken veranlasst*], without however any definite thought, i.e. any *concept*, being capable of being adequate to it; it consequently cannot be completely compassed and made intelligible by language. We easily see that it is the counterpart (pendant) of a *rational idea*, which conversely is a concept to which no *intuition* (or representation of the imagination) can be adequate. (157)

In view of what Kant understands by "idea," it is very surprising that besides rational ideas there should also be *aesthetic* ideas, not in the sense of (rational) ideas that have been rendered intuitable, but in the sense of ideas *of* the imagination, ideas that originate in a sensible faculty, even though the highest of the sensible faculties. If aesthetic ideas merit the name *ideas*, it is because even they must first of all be representations of totality, that is, of unity in diversity. They are representations, or more specifically, intuitions that "occasion much thought"; thus they enliven the faculty of thinking, but without reason's conceptual delimitation of the totality in question. Aesthetic ideas, consequently, are indefinite, undetermined ideas; they are, on the level of the sensible, analoga of reason, that is, of the faculty of ideas.[25]

At this point I wish to refer once again to Kant's criticism of Marsden, who held that the regular beauty of a pepper garden is more attractive than the "wild . . . , apparently irregular" beauty of a jungle (80). I have argued in my previous chapter that, as Kant understands it, form concerns not regularity but instead a certain irregularity, especially that of a prodigality bordering on luxuriance. To be beautiful, and capable of sustaining continuous pleasure and entertainment, form must be inhabited by a certain wildness. After all, free beauty is called *pulcritudo vaga*; and as such, as Jacques Derrida has pointed out, it carries with it a sense of indefinite erring.[26] Some of Kant's examples of free beauty—for example, "delineations *à la grecque*, foliage for borders or wall papers" (66)—have been derided and used as evidence that his aesthetics is not based on the experience of great works of art. Yet even these examples seem to point toward such an indefinite quality or open determinateness.[27] Clearly, a formally pleasing and regular arrangement of parts does not suffice for form to be judged beautiful. Only the form that causes a proliferation of thoughts, but that no concept can render fully intelligible, deserves to be called beautiful. Despite the "*restful* contemplation" (85) required for one's having a taste for beauty, the form of an object must have a certain profuse wealth that provokes the mind to a sort of "pensée sauvage," in order for this form to earn the title of beauty. Whether natural or artistic, objects that enliven the faculties in such a manner are objects that display spirit, and so express aesthetic ideas.

With this first rather broad sketch of aesthetic ideas' fundamental involvement in beautiful form, we can now study in more detail the nature of aesthetic ideas, their task, and how they accomplish it. Kant observes that spirit, in an aesthetic sense, is "no other than the faculty of presenting *aesthetical ideas*." Spirit, then, is another name for the faculty of presentation, and more precisely, for that faculty in its productive employment. Yet we may wonder what reason there might be for thus renaming productive imagination. Productive imagination, as distinct from reproductive imagination, is freed from the laws of association, that is, from the laws that govern it in its theoretical or empirical employment. Kant writes: "The imagination (as a productive faculty of cognition) is very powerful in creating another nature, as it were, out of the material that actual nature gives it." By this creation, the material of actual nature is remolded "in accordance with analogical laws, but yet also in accordance with principles which occupy a higher place in reason." As a result, nature as we experience it is "worked up into something different which surpasses nature." This "something different" from nature, or rather something wholly other (*ganz anderem*) than nature, this "other nature, as it were [*gleichsam . . . anderen Natur*]," is of the order of the ideas, Kant concludes. He explains: "Such representations of the imagination we may call *ideas*, partly because they at least strive after something which lies beyond the bounds of experience and so seek to approximate to a presentation of concepts of reason (intellectual ideas), thus giving to the latter the appearance of objective reality, but especially because no concept can be fully adequate to them as internal intuitions" (157). As creations of productive imagination, these ideas are aesthetic ideas; that is to say, they are representations in which material nature has been transformed according to higher principles of reason. Such principles or laws "are just as natural to us as those by which understanding comprehends empirical nature" (157), and consequently they can only be the regulative principles of reason. They are thus representations that create, from within nature, a seemingly altogether different nature. If Kant calls productive imagination spirit, could this not be because the imagination in its productive mode, by processing material nature in accordance with the principles of reason, has become an analogon of reason?

Spirit, in Kant's formulation, is the power of ideas on the level of sensibility; a power of sensibility by way of which sensibility (almost) overcomes its nature as sensibility, under its own power. But these ideas are not, strictly speaking, presentations of the ideas of reason. Kant emphasizes that the ideas of imagination only strive toward something that transcends the bounds of experience, and that they seek to approximate a presentation of intellectual ideas. Undoubtedly, in creating aesthetic ideas, the productive imagination goes beyond the bounds of experience. But the other nature that it thereby creates emulates the realm of the ideas only to the extent that it provokes much thought, without any concept being adequate to it. Aesthetic ideas, therefore, do not have the determinateness of rational ideas but rather are presentations of such ideas only by analogy—that is, insofar as productive imagination proceeds analogously to the rule that governs reason as the power of ideas. Productive imagination transcends nature as it is given to us, by reflecting on it in a manner analogous to the way reason reflects on the manifold empirical laws. In short, if productive imagination independently brings something akin to the principles of reason to bear on the material of nature, and thus employs principles that unify the intuitive manifold and the manifold of nature and its laws, then the productive imagination is using a symbolic mode of presentation. One can here catch a glimpse of why no concept could be fully adequate to imagination's internal intuitions of something that no longer belongs to the order of nature. The wealth and prolific indeterminateness of these intuitions stem from their indirect presentation, not of specific intellectual ideas, but only of the rule of reason. Aesthetic ideas are symbolic exhibitions of reason in general, of reason in a formal sense, if one may venture to express it in this way. This is the primary origin of aesthetic ideas' potential (semantic) wealth. It is also the reason why aesthetic attributes can be connected to objects in the first place; and these attributes, by virtue of the limitless number of additional representations to which they give rise, turn these objects into (indirect) presentations of rational ideas.

The power of aesthetic ideas is "properly only a talent (of the imagination)" (158), or in other words, is a natural gift. It manifests itself in the genius's daring attempts either "to realize to sense, rational ideas of invisible beings," or "to present . . . to sense with a completeness of which there is no example in nature," "things of which there are examples in experience." The imagination that creates representations of this kind is one that, according to Kant, "emulates the play of reason in its quest after a maximum [*die dem Vernunft-Vorspiele in Erreichung eines Grössten nacheifert*]" (157–58). Several different readings of this assertion are possible. First, in that it produces sensible representations of rational ideas, or representations of empirical phenomena in their totality, one might say that the imagination strives to imitate what reason has played or acted out for it in advance. Reason's quest for a maximum would thus be the prelude, or overture, for the imagination's competitive attempt to attain such a maximum itself. Reason's play would be a play that clears the terrain, so that the imagination can strive to do on a representational level what reason does on the level of the ideas. But second, one could argue that since the *Vernunft-Vorspiel* is not yet the (serious) play of reason itself, the imagination measures itself only after the "foreplay" of reason, a play of reason that happens in advance of reason properly speaking. It follows from this that in its representations, the imagination exhibits not a maximum itself but solely a quest for a maximum. In this reading only the initial play of reason, rather than reason proper, would take sensible shape in the imagination's representations. Precisely in striving to achieve a maximum for the natural manifold it has collected and reproduced, the imagination (independently of reason and yet in conformity with its *Vernunft-Vorspiel*) offers a presentation of the faculty of ideas; and this presentation is not one of the faculty of ideas in general but a presentation of reason anterior to its function as practical reason. The imagination actualizes and presents a kind of proto-reason in its search for a maximum. As a result, it is not reason itself that intervenes in the production of aesthetic ideas but only an initial play of reason on the level of the sensible.

This is an appropriate moment at which to inquire whether the doctrine of aesthetic ideas is of any help in understanding the symbolic hypotyposis. This hypotyposis, along with the (free) schematic presentation, has been shown to be necessary for judgments upon the beautiful and hence for the constitution of the mere form of an object (or its representation). To pursue this inquiry, I will first recapitulate what I have established so far, while further narrowing down the distinctive features of aesthetic ideas. Undoubtedly, what Kant is saying in chapter 49 is that in producing the beauty of art, genius must possess spirit, but such spirit must be disciplined by taste. Without some discipline of the strife felt by the imagination as it creates another nature from given nature, beauty would be impossible, just as it would be impossible without the imagination's emulation of a maximum of reason. Works of genius are those in which taste disciplines the imagination without imposing a determinate concept. Discipline does not curtail the productive imagination's quest for a maximum but orders its plenitude of thoughts so that it accords with the understanding's conformity to law. Now, aesthetic ideas are precisely the products of the disciplined imagination and of the imagination's wild attempts nevertheless to go beyond the bounds of what can be experienced. If aesthetic ideas occasion an abundance of thought, without there ever being a definite concept that is adequate to them, such abundance is the product of an already cultivated or educated imagination. The prodigality, if not the luxuriance, of beautiful form presupposes that taste has clipped the wings of the imagination—an imagination that, in seeking to emulate reason, has gone wild. Without such excess on the part of imagination, taste would have nothing to clip. In other words, even though taste is the condition sine qua non of the beautiful, productive imagination, by creating a luxuriant wealth of ideas, must have rivaled reason's demand for totality and unity. From taste's cultivation of the imagination's wild creation of an abundance of ideas, aesthetic ideas emerge.

I would like to repeat here an earlier observation: the archetype of taste that "rests on the indeterminate idea that reason has of a maximum" is an idea that "everyone must produce in himself." More precisely, although we never possess such a standard for the beautiful except when we judge the beauty of a human being, "we yet strive to produce it in ourselves [*der-*

gleichen wir, wenn wir gleich nicht im Besitze desselben sind, doch in uns hervorzubringen streben]." Furthermore, since such a standard of taste "cannot be represented by concepts but only in an individual presentation"—in other words, only as an ideal—such a representation must be a product of the imagination (68–69). As we have seen, aesthetic ideas are evidence of the imagination's striving to equal reason, and its effort to realize independently a maximum of reason. But what has also become plain is that imagination achieves this goal only when it is curtailed by taste. Taste is what gives form to the extravagant productions of the imagination. In chapter 51, when he qualifies the aesthetic idea as an "archetype or original image . . . in the imagination," Kant brings the aesthetic idea's unitary character into relief. Only when they are fashioned into a unifying image do the wild imaginings of productive imagination become aesthetic ideas, and thus become capable of the symbolic presentation of a maximum of reason. From a formal perspective, aesthetic ideas are thus similar to the archetype of taste, or to the mere idea of a maximum of reason that is required in judging any object of taste. But before I elucidate this similarity, let me note that these ideas and archetypes also seem to be involved in very different operations despite the fact that both our striving to produce in ourselves a standard for taste and the imagination's disciplined attempt to accomplish a maximum of reason rest on a play between the imagination and reason. What occurs in the production of aesthetic ideas appears to be the exact reverse of what occurs in judgments of taste. Indeed, in striving to produce aesthetic ideas by emulating reason, the imagination must be curtailed at all times by judgments of taste, whereas in forming judgments of taste, the imagination must vie with reason to produce a standard of taste. And yet, if in both cases the imagination enters into a relation to reason—of which the standard of taste and aesthetic ideas are the indirect or symbolic presentations—this relation itself provides clear evidence, both in judgments about the beautiful and in the creation of beautiful works by genius, of an internal intertwining of schematic and symbolic presentations. On the one hand, schematic presentation proceeds here without concepts and hence is free; on the other hand, symbolic presentation (rather than a presentation of determined ideas) is limited to the imagination's striving to approximate, in its own way and on its own level, the demands of reason. Such intertwining may perhaps gesture toward a fundamental unity of schematic and symbolic hypotyposis, in other words, toward an unheard-of "power" (if it can still be so called) of presentation. Moments when we behold the beautiful of nature and of art would always be the singular occasions upon which this power manifests itself: a power that permits an intuited manifold to exhibit a single form (and hence intelligibility in general), and whose standard is the always individualized presentation by the imagination of a maximum of reason.

If, on the basis of the previous arguments, it is correct to postulate a similarity between aesthetic ideas and the mere idea of the standard of taste, what about the individualization that, Kant has argued, is essential for a standard? Would aesthetic ideas submit to an idealizing individualization? Is their effectiveness also dependent on what Kant, in his discussion of the standard of taste, calls "an individual presentation [*einzelne Darstellung*]" (69)? To answer these questions, we must first clarify further what Kant means by "aesthetical ideas" and examine in particular how it is that, in attaining to a maximum, the imagination vies with what reason has played out in advance for the imagination to emulate. Kant writes:

> If now we place under a concept a representation of the imagination belonging to its presentation, but which occasions in itself more thought than can ever be comprehended in a definite concept and which consequently aesthetically enlarges the concept itself in an unbounded fashion, the imagination is here creative, and it brings the faculty of intellectual ideas (the reason) into movement; i.e. by a representation more thought (which indeed belongs to the concept of the object) is occasioned than can in it be grasped or made clear. (158)

As the subsequent discussion in the chapter on aesthetic attributes shows, the representations in question contain an abundance of "approximate representations [*Nebenvorstellungen*] of the imagination" (158). These are over and above what is required for a presentation of the concepts in question, and by this gesture the concepts in (schematic) presentation are rendered indefinite. The imagination increases their extension in an unlimited fashion. But by thus enlarging the concepts, of which the representations were initially to serve simply as presentations, the imagination has in fact revealed the concepts to be limited. Since there is more to the representations than the concepts are capable of grasping—indeed, there is an unlimited multitude of implied additional representations—ideas are therefore necessary in order to comprehend and unify the multifariousness in question. These indefinitely enlarged concepts result from the proliferation of representations, and according to Kant, these concepts "think" this richness— "although in an undeveloped way" (159)—by adding "to a concept much ineffable thought [*viel Unnennbares hinzu denken lässt*]" (160). These enlarged concepts are none other than aesthetic ideas. In that they embody "more thought than can be expressed in a concept determined by words," aesthetic ideas present not specific ideas of reason but the faculty of rational ideas itself, which I have also referred to as "reason in general." By adding a multitude of additional representations to the single representation that is needed to present a concept, the imagination itself only "brings the faculty of intellectual ideas (the reason) into movement." In other words, it plays at the play of reason, and sets in motion a thinking that thinks more than any concept of the understanding can encompass. Reason as practical reason—that is, reason itself, or reason as the faculty of determined ideas—has no direct role to play either in the creation of art or in the creation of the aesthetic ideas that underlie beautiful art. While he returns to the question of the mental powers that constitute genius, Kant mentions only imagination and understanding. Here the imagination is free from the constraints to which it normally must submit when, in the service of the understanding, it helps foster cognition; and the imagination alone furnishes an "unsought, over and above that agreement with a concept, abundance of undeveloped material for the understanding, to which the understanding paid no regard in its concept but which it applies, though not objectively for cognition, yet subjectively to quicken the cognitive powers and therefore also indirectly to cognitions" (160). In other words, in art, the imagination confronts the understanding with the need to open itself up to the exigencies of reason. Aesthetic ideas, which are the products of a faculty of sense, although the highest such faculty, are then merely a symbolic enactment of the maximum of reason.

As Kant explains it, the "genius properly consists in the happy relation [between these faculties] . . . by which ideas are found for a given concept." Nevertheless, genius still needs to express these aesthetic ideas; one must "find for these ideas the expression [*Ausdruck*] by means of which the subjective state of mind brought about by them, as an accompaniment of the concept, can be communicated to others" (160). If the aesthetic idea is the archetype or original image in the imagination, it needs to be expressed in a figure—a *Gestalt*—which is the ectype, or copy (*Nachbild*), of the original (166). In such expression, the specific subjective state that accompanies aesthetic ideas is busy "thinking," in an undeveloped way, a multitude of representations for which there is no determinate concept; consequently this state of mind is in search of a maximum. Several important questions must now be raised concerning the significance of the expression and communication of this state of mind. Is such expression not an individualization of sorts? And once expressed, is the aesthetic idea not an ideal of some kind? Indeed, in the remaining sections of chapter 49, does Kant not qualify the products of genius as the models by means of which genius outlines the rule for art? At the very least, Kant holds that the genius's talent for expressing and communicating aesthetic ideas

> is properly speaking, what is called spirit; for to express the ineffable element in the state of mind implied by a certain representation and to make it universally communicable—whether the expression be in speech or painting or statuary—this requires a faculty of seizing the quickly passing play of imagination and of unifying it in a concept (which is even on that account original and discloses a new rule that could not have been inferred from any preceding principles or examples) that can be communicated without any constraint [of rules]. (161)

Spirit is thus not only involved in the imagination's production of aesthetic ideas, but also connected to the expression of these ideas. Since such expression requires an original concept, in which the play of the imagination is unified and which opens up a new rule, the production of aesthetic ideas is intimately tied to their individualization. The ideas are individualized in what, qua exemplary models, are unquestionably "ideals" as well.

In retrospect, several issues concerning the standard of taste now become much clearer. The aesthetic idea is analogous to the standard of taste; for the mere idea of the archetype of taste, which everyone must strive to bring forth in himself or herself and which is required for any judgment of taste, is an exclusive product of the imagination as it vies independently with reason. The archetype that is produced cannot be an idea properly speaking, given that, as Kant recalls, "*idea* properly means a rational concept" (69). As a mere idea, the idea that productive imagination brings forth is only a presentation of the need for a standard, or maximum, of reason in general. By means of this presentation, the imagination takes on the schematizing presentation in judgments about the form of an object, and in the process meets the needs of the faculty of concepts (the understanding) in general. According to Kant, an "*ideal* [is] the representation of an individual being, regarded as adequate to an idea" (69). By this definition, the standard of a maximum of reason that is required for judging any kind of object of taste—especially objects of vague beauty—cannot be an ideal either; for as Kant insists, an ideal can be found only for human beauty. However, the standard of taste is an "ideal of the imagination," which everyone must seek to produce in himself by way of his imagination; and this standard is, like an ideal in the rigorous sense, an "individual presentation" (69). Kant calls it an archetype, an original image or *Urbild*. Just as the figures of the expressed aesthetic ideas give the rule to art, so the originary, original, and singular image that constitutes the standard of taste gives the rule to the judgment's free schematizing presentation, that is, to its schematization, which lacks a determined concept yet conforms with the rule of the understanding in general. The *Urbild* is a symbolic presentation of the exigencies of reason, functioning as the power of ideas; and it is the standard required in the production of an image of mere form for an intuitable manifold that has no proper concept.

In concluding, I wish to return briefly to a question left somewhat in abeyance at the beginning of this chapter: namely, the question concerning the exact relation between representation and presentation. In light of what this chapter has ascertained in its examination exclusively of the analytic of the beautiful, the question of representation may be said to concern "mere representation." Such representation, though it lacks the concepts with which to determine objectively a manifold of intuition, nonetheless secures the donation of an object (its being given) by informing this manifold such that it displays the mere form of an object. What is the role of presentation in such a representation? What kind of economy exists between the *Vor* and the *Dar* for an object in general, irrespective of what it is, in order that it should make itself available to the powers of representation? From everything we have seen, the importance of the theme of presentation (*Darstellung*) in the *Critique of Judgment* should be clear. In the account of how the mind, in an aesthetic judgment, wrests a form from an intuitive diversity for which the understanding possesses no concept—in other words, a mere representation of the mere form of an object—presentation reveals itself to be a factor without which no representation as such could occur. What the "Analytic of the Beautiful" teaches us is that without a presentation, no representation of a "something" in general would be possible. Furthermore, as I have shown, presentation is capable of this formidable task only insofar as it is double, and thus combines a schematic presentation of the power of understanding as such with a symbolic presentation of an undetermined maximum of reason.[28]

5

Absolutely Great

The current interest in the sublime, particularly among scholars of the postmodern, is no doubt largely the result of a continuing misinterpretation of Kant's idea of the beautiful. Kant's aesthetics of the beautiful, which is commonly held responsible for the development of modern art, centers on the notion of form and is broadly believed to rest on a formalist and aestheticist conception of beauty. Kant's aesthetics of the beautiful thus seems inadequate to account for the most recent contemporary arts, which have been interpreted as disruptive of classical and especially formalist form. However, the conceptual instruments of what is taken to be the other Kantian aesthetics—the aesthetics of the sublime—seem readily to offer themselves for the task.[1] Once contemporary art is interpreted as antagonistic to traditional conceptions of form, it can easily be accommodated by an aesthetics of the formless, such as Kant seems to provide in his aesthetics of the sublime. Whether such an interpretation does justice to contemporary art will not be my concern here. But the analysis of the sublime that I propose in this chapter will question the legitimacy both of privileging the sublime in Kant's aesthetics and of the possibility of turning the sublime against the beautiful. Needless to say, the interpretation of form outlined in the preceding chapters of this book will serve as the background foil for my discussion of the sublime. As we will see, only such an interpretation of form is capable of making sense of Kant's intriguing claim that the sublime is a mere appendix to the beautiful, a claim by which he invites careful consideration of the place that the "Analytic of the Sublime" occupies within the overall architectonic of the "Analytic of the Aesthetical Judgment." Only by systematically exploring the relation between the beautiful and the sublime is it possible to establish what exactly the Kantian sublime achieves, and hence what it is about in the first place. Such an analysis of the intricate web of interrelations between the beautiful and the sublime will make it much more problematic to construe the aesthetics of the sublime as a simple alternative to Kant's elaborations on the beautiful.

Shortly after the publication of the *Critique of Judgment*, Kant, in the *Anthropology from a Pragmatic Point of View*, reinterpreted the feeling of the sublime as a mere emotion (*Rührung*) devoid of all pretension to universality. Nevertheless, and contrary to what Giorgio Tonelli has asserted, the sublime's very brief fortune as an a priori aesthetic category in no way diminishes the significance of the transcendental inquiry into the sublime in the Third Critique.[2] In the Second Introduction to the *Critique of Judgment*, the analytics of the beautiful and the sublime had been termed the two corresponding and major parts (*Hauptteile*) (29) of the critique of aesthetic judgment. However, Kant's claim at the beginning of his discussion of the sublime that the sublime is merely an appendix to the beautiful would seem to suggest that the sublime is far less important than the beautiful. How, indeed, could the sublime claim any prominence if its analysis amounts to nothing but an addition to the analysis of the beautiful? In this context, one is reminded of Ernst Cassirer's suggestion that only in the "Analytic of the Beautiful" has Kant struck truly new ground: after all, the section on the sublime might be merely a concession to eighteenth-century aesthetic theory. Kant's innovative reinterpretation of the question of the beautiful is evidenced, according to Cassirer, by a certain awkwardness that accompanies the rigor and conceptual refinement of Kant's analyses in the relevant chapters. By contrast, Cassirer describes the case of the sublime as a supreme synthesis between the basic principles of Kant's ethics and aesthetics. He claims that Kant is here "once again on terrain that is personally and genuinely his," and mentions the clarity, even the spotless transparency of the developments on the sublime to sustain his point.[3] The question of the clarity of the section of the sublime is contentious: for example, Jean-François Lyotard contrasts the "Analytic of the Beautiful" to the "overall confusion that reigns in the Analytic of the Sublime and [that] renders its reading and interpretation challenging."[4]

Leaving this debate aside, and without losing sight of the aesthetic and reflective nature of judgment of the sublime (which nature warrants the inclusion of the sublime in the Third Critique), the following reading will begin by approaching the sublime from its characterization as an appendage to the beautiful. By deepening our understanding of the appendicular nature of the sublime, not only will we remain faithful to Kant's text, but we will be able to grasp a dimension of the reflective aesthetic judgment upon the sublime that justifies its characterization in the First Introduction as a major part of the "Analytic," despite the fact that the "Analytic of the Sublime" is a late addition to the critique of taste (as Tonelli has convincingly shown). Kant's analysis of the sublime negotiates "contradictory" theoretical demands and advances seemingly exclusive positions with respect to the sublime. His appendicular treatment of the sublime, I intend to argue, models the sublime according to terms and problems that are completely derived from issues related to the beautiful; and paradoxically, this treatment itself is imposed on Kant because the judgment of the sublime is a reflective judgment of an entirely different nature than the judgment of beauty. Kant's appendicular approach will reveal that the sublime belongs to an aesthetic order quite unlike that of the beautiful, rather than appending and hence forming a possible alternative to the beautiful. At the same time, this essential difference, and even lack of structural parallelism, between the two kinds of judgments does not exclude some kind of interrelation. As a result of this complex commerce between them, any simple recourse to Kant's theory of the sublime that disregards the Kantian beautiful, or intends to displace the aesthetics of mere form as developed through the preceding chapters, remains fundamentally flawed.

I

Kant begins his discussion of the sublime in chapter 23 by providing the rationale for including the "Analytic of the Sublime" in the "Analytic of the Aesthetical Judgment." The rationale takes the form of a list of features that judgment of the sublime, qua reflective aesthetic judgment, shares with judgment of the beautiful. This comparison makes the whole analysis of the sublime, from its outset, dependent upon and derivative from the analysis of the beautiful, given that, in the exposition and deduction of the beautiful, the main characteristics of aesthetic reflective judgment have already been set forward. Both judgments are reflective aesthetic judgments, a point that is demonstrated in two ways: first, both establish the purposiveness of an individual intuition, for which no determined concepts are available, as beneficial for the employment of the powers of cognition or reason in general; and second, in both cases the pleasure that accompanies the feeling of this agreement between the powers of cognition is universally shareable. Like the beautiful, the sublime "neither presuppose[s] a judgment of sense nor a judgment logically determined, but a judgment of reflection," Kant remarks. If the beautiful and the sublime are said to "agree in this that both please in themselves," it is because of the analogous satisfaction on which they are grounded. In each case, satisfaction derives from the fact that on the occasion of a given singular intuition, the faculty of the imagination (the power of presentation), while unable to relate the intuition to determinate (cognitive or rational) concepts, "is [nevertheless] considered as in agreement with the *faculty of concepts* of understanding or reason, regarded as promoting these latter."[5] Both judgments establish a subjective purposiveness of the particular object that stimulates them, a purposiveness that is subjective because it does not rest on a definite concept of the object, and only furthers the powers in play. But since there are two possible kinds of subjective purposiveness, the two kinds of reflective aesthetic judgments—those on the beautiful and those on the sublime—are conceivable. In the First Introduction to the *Critique of Judgment*, Kant notes that all purposiveness (whether subjective or objective) "can be divided into *inner* or *relative*; the first kind is based on the representation of the object as such, the second simply on its contingent *use*." Concerning the subjective purposiveness of reflective aesthetic judgments, Kant explains that inner purposiveness in particular is a purposiveness of representations of objects (the form of the object) that contributes to the very perception or intuition of those objects. This subjective purposiveness of the object is "attributed to the thing and to nature itself." By contrast, relative purposiveness concerns exclusively the "possible purposive *use*" that reflective judgment can make of certain sensible intuitions, in view of "a purposiveness lying a priori in the subject (perhaps the suprasensuous determination of the subject's mental powers)"; thus it is a purposiveness that cannot be attributed to the thing or to nature itself.[6] The attribution of an inner purposiveness of objects that is beneficial to the cognitive powers triggers judgments upon the beautiful. Judgments upon the sublime denote the purposive use of certain representations for the furthering of the faculty of ideas, and thus rest on relative purposiveness.[7] Such relative purposiveness is subjective and, like the purposiveness involved in the beautiful, is not based on the concept of the object. Because it permits the linkage of the singular representation to powers of the mind, in the absence of either concepts or ideas, it must be included in the "Analytic."

What the beautiful and the sublime have in common, as we have seen, is merely that both are reflective aesthetic judgments. Kant himself evokes "remarkable [*namhafte*] differences between the two," and distinguishes the specific characteristics of the sublime from the those of the beautiful; however, given that both are reflective judgments, one might be tempted to conclude that they simply represent alternatives open to reflective aesthetic judgment. But we should not forget that determining the specificity of the sublime by way of demarcating it from the beautiful serves, first of all, to stress the appendicular nature of the sublime. The primary distinguishing trait of the sublime is thereby negatively defined, that is, defined in opposition to the dominant trait of the beautiful:

> The beautiful in nature is connected with the form of the object, which consists in having [definite] boundaries. The sublime, on the other hand [*dagegen auch*], is to be found in a formless object, so far as in it or by occasion of it *boundlessness* is represented, and yet its totality is also present to thought [*und doch Totalität hinzugedacht wird*]. Thus the beautiful seems to be regarded as the presentation of an indefinite concept of understanding, the sublime as that of a like concept of reason. Therefore the satisfaction in the one case is bound up with the representation of *quality*, in the other with that of *quantity*. (82)

The beautiful is the foil against which the sublime is brought into view. The determinations of the first serve as the benchmarks for a contrastive characterization of the latter. At the same time, the sublime appears to have an essence of its own, one that in no way reflects the beautiful. Indeed, the boundless formlessness of the sublime is not the symmetrical opposite of beautiful form; the opposite of beauty is instead mere formlessness, mere absence of form. In other words, when a thing is formless—that is, when it does not manifest itself within the boundaries of the form proper to a thing—no judgment upon its beauty is possible. A formless thing is found ugly. Indeed, simple formlessness meets the judgment's disapproval; but while it does not produce any pleasure, such formlessness in no way suggests sublimity. Only when formlessness is not merely a lack of form or a negative modification of it but instead a formlessness entirely different from a simple opposite of the beautiful is it possible also to find sublimity in it. It is evident that the possibility of the sublime rests on a concept of formlessness that is *not* the other side of beautiful form, not only because this formlessness must be boundless but also because it has a sufficient condition: that formlessness be accompanied by the thought of totality. Boundless chaos is not enough to suggest sublimity; it must be such that it allows thinking to add (*hinzugedacht wird*) totality to it. If Kant's strict terminology did not prohibit it, one would be inclined to say that boundless formlessness must have the "form" of a whole, in order for it to be sublime.

In much of what follows I will inquire how totality is added to boundless formlessness: what is the "mechanism" by which this comes about? Thinking performs this addition in two ways—mathematical and dynamical—and these will serve us as a guide in our inquiry. In following up on the question, it will become clear that although the sublime is repeatedly assessed as distinct from the beautiful and hence as within the horizon of the beautiful, its possibility rests on conditions that are not the symmetric opposite of those of the beautiful but are themselves proper to the sublime. But before we can appreciate this, we need to follow Kant through his demarcation of the sublime from the beautiful. As we have seen in our discussion of the concept of mere form and of the judgment made upon it, the judgment of taste concerned with beauty accomplishes the singular epistemological (or rather, para-epistemological) feat of finding a given thing, for which there is no determined concept, to be in agreement with the faculty of cognition in general. The form of the thing permits this thing to provide the presentation of an undetermined concept of the understanding. In its demarcation from the beautiful, the sublime seems to represent a mental accomplishment similar to the one characteristic of the beautiful, yet different from it. Before he embarks on his discussion of what he calls "the inner and most important distinction" between the beautiful and the sublime—namely that the first is concerned with purposiveness and the second with *Zweckwidrigkeit*—Kant notes, "as we are entitled to do, we only bring under consideration in the first instance the sublime in natural objects, for the sublime in art is always limited by the conditions of agreement with nature" (83). In judgments upon the sublime, as in judgments upon the beautiful, the prime referents are objects of nature, or nature as a whole. It is evident from the "Analytic of the Beautiful" that this concern with nature testifies to the para-epistemological thrust of judgment upon beauty. It is to be expected, therefore, that the "Analytic of the Sublime," which centers on the sublime in natural objects, is equally about cognition in a very broad and elementary sense, and not primarily about morality, as so many commentators are inclined to believe. Its focus on nature evidences that judgment of the sublime represents a singular mental accomplishment that has an elemental intellectual function. This point is verified in the passage quoted above, where Kant claims that the sublime must be regarded as the presentation of an undetermined concept of reason. The sublime is not an aesthetic feeling in common sense but one in which an intellectual task is carried out. This is not, as in the case of the beautiful, a para-cognitive task; rather, it is accomplished by adding the thought of totality (that is, a rational idea) to a representation or intuition whose formlessness is so thorough that it defies all subsumption under the powers of cognition. By finding totality in boundless formlessness, a representation that is infinitely rebellious against all cognition is nonetheless found to agree with the faculty of reason and hence to be minimally intelligible. If the satisfaction found in the beautiful is bound up with the representation of "quality," the satisfaction found in the sublime concerns "quantity." The categories of "quality" and "quantity" refer to the conceptual grid by means of which Kant sought to determine the judgment of taste upon the beautiful in the preceding "Analytic." Under the heading "quality," judgment upon the beautiful was described as being disinterested, concerned not with the existence of an object but only with its mere form. "Quantity" referred to the judgment upon the beautiful in its claim to universality. In the case of the beautiful, it is clear that quality is the defining feature.[8] Classified as "quantity," the sublime seems at first to be an inversion of the beautiful; however the particular achievement that determines it as "quantity" is altogether different from the achievement that characterizes the beautiful. In the sublime, there is a presentation of a power that subtends cognizability and its intelligibility, namely reason. This presentation takes place precisely at moments when a given thing not only cannot be subsumed under given concepts but refuses even to be a presentation of the powers of cognition in general.

Despite being situated in relation to the beautiful, the sublime reveals an additional aspect that further sets it apart from the order of the beautiful and its opposite (the ugly). The satisfaction involved in the sublime "is quite different in kind [*der Art nach . . . gar sehr unterschieden*]" from that brought about by the beautiful (83). The feeling could not be classified as the opposite of the satisfaction in the beautiful, but is rather of a different species. Whereas the feeling of satisfaction in beautiful form immediately animates the powers devoted to cognition and represents "a feeling of the furtherance of life," the satisfaction brought about by the sublime "arises only indirectly; viz. it is produced by the feeling of a momentary checking of the vital powers and a consequent stronger outflow of them." Kant explains that since in the case of the sublime "the mind is not merely attracted by the object but is ever being alternately repelled, the satisfaction in the sublime does not so much involve a positive pleasure as admiration or respect, which deserves to be called negative pleasure" (83). The feeling of the sublime must be regarded as a *Rührung* (Bernard translates this as "emotion"): that is, as a state of mind that involves being inwardly touched, or rather, deeply *moved*. Needless to say, such feeling happens only before something that is grand in all senses of the word. Consequently, Kant links the feeling associated with the sublime to a sense of seriousness or earnestness in the exercise of the imagination, and thereby opposes it to the playfulness associated with the beautiful. But Kant mentions the repulsion resulting from the frustration of the powers of cognition, and the attraction felt toward the boundlessly formless object when it serves as a presentation of the power of reason; these terms demonstrate that the feeling brought on by the sublime is literally characterized by turbulence, agitation, and movement. It refers to an agitation in the mind, resulting from the feeling that even though the formless object thwarts the powers of cognition, it does not bring the mind to a final halt or put it at a complete loss. In other words, it is the feeling that despite a sense of blockage, the mind remains capable of further movement.[9] If Kant calls the satisfaction that the sublime brings with it a negative pleasure, this is because it is only the pleasure involved in feeling that the mind is still in business at all.[10] Despite the surrender of the powers of cognition, the satisfaction in the sublime testifies that the mind, by judging boundless formlessness to be a totality, is still able to master the formlessness that frustrated cognition.

One final distinction between the beautiful and the sublime needs mentioning; indeed, it is the one that Kant calls "the inner and most important distinction." He writes:

Natural beauty which is independent brings with it a purposiveness in its form by which the object seems to be, as it were, preadapted to our judgment, and thus constitutes in itself an object of satisfaction. On the other hand, that which excites in us, without any reasoning about it, but in the mere apprehension of it [*bloss in der Auffassung*], the feeling of the sublime may appear, as regards its form, to violate purpose in respect of the judgment, to be unsuited to our presentative faculty, and as it were to do violence to the imagination; and yet it is judged to be only the more sublime. (83)

The essential distinction is thus between representations that have purposiveness and representations that lack it, or more precisely, that violate it, and that are thus *zweckwidrig*. The beautiful form of an object of nature is pleasurable because its representation fosters a minimal harmony between the powers of cognition and thereby animates them. By contrast, the boundless formlessness of nature encountered in the sublime does not facilitate any agreement between the imagination and the understanding. It is a representation that remains adverse to cognition in general, because it infinitely lacks form. Yet the very untowardness of such a representation is what is judged sublime. Like the beautiful, the sublime arises on the occasion of "the mere apprehension" of an object. In the case of a judgment upon the sublime, such an apprehension implies that no definite rational concepts are involved. But more important is the fact that a mere apprehension is possible at all under the circumstances; which is to say not only in the absence of form but also in the face of a representation that is infinitely adverse to form and to purposiveness. Even though it defies the power of presentation, and hence the possibility of the minimal objectification that makes beautiful natural form so pleasurable, the boundless formlessness that excites the feeling of sublimity allows itself to be apprehended. Indeed, the feeling of the sublime, along with the complex satisfaction that it brings, can basically be defined as follows: it is the satisfaction of being able to apprehend in one representation that which defies objectification in the first place, that which is definitely adverse to form as such. With this definition we touch upon the singular achievement of judgment of the sublime. In the sublime, the mind secures a minimal (or mere) apprehension of the boundless formlessness of certain objects of nature, by adding the undetermined rational idea of totality to these representations.

From what we have just elucidated, it is clear that judgment upon the sublime must be of a kind different from judgment upon the beautiful. Kant implicitly advances as much when he points out that it is in fact incorrect to "call any *object of nature* sublime, although we can quite correctly call many objects of nature beautiful" (83). If judgments upon the beautiful of nature are judgments about the form of a natural object, judgments on the sublime of nature do not target natural formlessness. They are not *about* the formlessness of nature in the way that judgments upon natural beauty are about purposive form. Indeed, judgments on the sublime cannot be *about* formlessness because the latter defies "aboutness"—that is, objectification—by its very definition. Rather, boundless formlessness is the pretext or occasion on which sublimity is predicated, and "which can [only] be found in the mind" (83). What is judged sublime is the mind's capacity to form an apprehension of something that thwarts even the possibility of minimal objectification, and that, like "the wide ocean, disturbed by the storm . . . is [just] horrible" (84). If such a boundlessly formless object can be made into a presentation of an indefinite concept of reason, this is due to the mind's ability to muster an apprehension of this object; thus it demonstrates that the mind possesses the supersensible faculty of totalization. The judgment that arises in perceived formlessness, if such formlessness is truly boundless, is structurally distinct from the judgment of beauty, for in it nothing is predicated of any object.

The insight resulting from the comparison of the judgments upon the sublime and upon the beautiful culminates in the recognition that, qua reflective judgment, the sublime is not a judgment upon nature, and consequently that it represents another species of judgment. Although this is not the sole difference between the sublime and the beautiful, it explains Kant's conclusion that the "Analytic of the Sublime" is an appendix to the beautiful. When we encounter beautiful form in nature, we judge nature as if its productions revealed a design in its being that would be adequate to our faculties of understanding. The mere form predicated in mere apprehension of a beautiful natural object does not extend our knowledge of the object itself; all it tells us is the precognitive "fact" that it has the form of an object. Nevertheless, it expands our notion of nature by suggesting that nature is technical—an art in the sense of *téchnē*, whose principle we are unable to fathom. The judgmental discovery that some natural objects, for which we have no concepts, are nonetheless possessed of form—and hence are suitable for the exercise of our faculties of cognition—opens up an unexpected dimension of natural form. As Kant writes: "This leads to profound investigations as to the possibility of such a form." In spite of the fact that judging beautiful form does nothing to extend our knowledge of nature, it is the basis for a deepening reflection on form, that is to say, on the conditions of objectivity, and on nature's (active) suitability to cognition. But, writes Kant,

> in what we are accustomed to call sublime there is nothing at all that leads to particular objective principles and forms of nature corresponding to them; so far from it that, for the most part, nature excites the ideas of the sublime in its chaos or in its wildest and most irregular disorder and desolation, provided size and might are perceived. Hence, we see that the concept of the sublime is not nearly so important or rich in consequences as the concept of the beautiful; and that, in general, it displays nothing purposive in nature itself, but only in that possible use of our intuitions of it by which there is produced in us a feeling of a purposiveness quite independent of nature. (84)

In principle, natural beauty can be predicated only of objects in the wild, that is to say, of objects whose determinability is still open, but which are found beautiful because they at least have the form of objects. The sublime is predicated where nature is "in its wildest and most irregular [*regellos*] disorder and desolation," and thus where any possible objectification is completely excluded. Nothing objective, nothing concerning form and cognition, can therefore be associated with the sublime. Its possibility presents itself only when and where cognizability is utterly thwarted. Yet whatever judgments upon the sublime may accomplish, they are few by comparison with the achievements of the reflective aesthetic judgment about beauty. In being evaluated and even conceptualized over and against the beautiful, the sublime and its achievements are measured against the standard of empirical cognition in all its power and prestige, more precisely, the standard of cognition in general, as it is actualized and felt pleasurable in the beautiful. Whereas judgment about beautiful form motivates the expansion of our concept of nature and encourages a deepening reflection on cognizability in general, judgment about the sublime does not concern anything about nature and exhibits no innate purposiveness of nature. Rather, it arises in circumstances where even the minimal conditions of cognizability—of a unified formal representation of something as an object—have become impossible. With respect to the cognition of nature, or the totality of what is knowable, the insights gained through the sublime are therefore of little bearing, and have few consequences for cognition itself. Since judgments on the sublime do not concern anything about nature but only predicate something about our attitude of thought, the ideas of the sublime, according to Kant, are completely separated (*ganz abtrennt*) "from [those] of a purposiveness of *nature*." Kant goes on to explain that this "makes the theory of the sublime a mere appendix to the aesthetical judging of that purposiveness, because by means of it no particular form is presented in nature, but there is only developed a purposive use which the imagination makes of its representation" (84–85). In Kant's emphasis on thought in the judgment upon the sublime, one can already sense that this kind of aesthetic reflective judgment must inevitably be quite different from the one concerned with the beautiful. Throughout the "Analytic of the Beautiful," the guiding thread had been the purposiveness of nature. In the absence of all such purposiveness, the sublime is limited to making a purposive use of a representation of nature—one that, moreover, defies all consideration of purposiveness—and can therefore be only an appendage to the beautiful.

One could, of course, understand the appendicular status of the sublime as implying that the sublime is merely a liminal possibility of the beautiful. After all, is not formlessness a possibility opened by the beautiful itself? Once one is given beautiful form, one is also given the possibility of an absence of form, that is, the possibility of formlessness. But, as Kant has made clear from the outset, the sublime has its inception in boundless formlessness. Furthermore, if one is to make use of such formlessness with a view to a purpose higher than the purposiveness of nature, one must "introduce [*hineinbringen*]" considerations that are entirely separate from nature into the representation of formlessness. Devoid of boundlessness, and lacking the introduction of something completely separated from nature, the representation of formlessness would be judged only as ugly and horrible. By this observation, however, we have brought to light another sense of what it means to say that the sublime is appendicular to the beautiful. Undoubtedly, the sublime can be an appendix to the beautiful only if it is evaluated in light of the specific para-epistemological achievement of the judgment upon beautiful form. But it must be recalled that up to this point in the "Analytic," the judgment upon the beautiful has served as the template and the standard of the reflective aesthetic judgment. By introducing the supersensible in its bearing on a representation of infinite formlessness, Kant demonstrates the involvement in reflective aesthetic judgments of a dimension of the mind that, at least initially, was not explicit in the judgment upon beautiful form. The appendicular nature of "The Analytic of the Sublime" thus consists also in this: that it adds the problematic of reason, that is, the problematic of the power of the ideas, to the analytic of the reflective aesthetic judgment that has been illustrated by privileging the beautiful. In the discussion of the sublime, it becomes clear that there is an autonomous kind of reflective judgment in which reason, rather than the understanding, plays the major role. At the same time, by this treatment of the sublime Kant also insinuates that reflective aesthetic judgment, whether upon the beautiful or upon the sublime, requires the intervention of reason in one way or another. In its status as an appendix, the sublime is thus also treated as a positive addition: one that causes the "mere appendix" to the "Analytic of the Beautiful" to emerge as a major part of the "Analytic of the Aesthetical Judgment."

II

Given that the feeling of the sublime is a judgment, its analysis must obey the same methodological division of the judgmental moments that guides the analysis of judgment of taste about the beautiful. Kant explains:

"For as an act of the aesthetical reflective judgment, the satisfaction in the sublime must be represented just as in the case of the beautiful—according to *quantity* as universally valid, according to *quality* as devoid of *interest*, according to *relation* as subjective purposiveness, and according to *modality* as necessary" (85). Even the fact that the analysis of the sublime begins with quantity, rather than with quality as in the case of the beautiful, does not tarnish the profound continuity of the methodology between the analyses. After all, the sublime is an aesthetic reflective judgment. But, writes Kant, "the analysis of the sublime involves [*hat nötig*] a division not needed in the case of the beautiful, viz. a division into the *mathematically* and *dynamically sublime*" (85). Let me emphasize right away that this division does not mean that there are two different kinds of sublimity. In Kant's words, the distinction between the mathematical and the dynamical refers to a "twofold way of representing the sublime" of an "object" (86). The mathematical and the dynamical dimensions simply concern two different aspects of the sublime. Indeed, these two terms refer to the groupings of the judgmental moments that guide the analysis of the judgment of the sublime insofar as it is a judgment. The mathematical comprises the categories of quantity and quality (and thus, one might conjecture, concerns the possibility of the intuition of a sublime phenomenon), whereas the dynamical comprises relation and modality (and thus might be said to concern the existence of the sublime phenomenon). At first sight, this division seems to amount to little more than a regrouping of the judgmental moments involved in the methodological approach to the sublime, a regrouping that will not affect the basic continuity between the beautiful and the sublime insofar as both are reflective judgments. However, this division, which the sublime requires, is in truth the sign of an essential difference between the two reflective aesthetic judgments. As will become evident in the following discussion of the two aspects of the sublime, the difference is one in nature, one that demarcates a different species of reflective aesthetic judgment. We will see this most clearly in the significantly more elaborate treatment of the mathematical sublime. But let us first take up the reasons that Kant advances for the division in question.

Kant explains the need to divide the analysis of the sublime into mathematical and dynamical on the grounds that the feeling of the sublime is different in kind from the feeling associated with the beautiful. He writes: "For the feeling of the sublime brings with it as its characteristic feature a *movement* of the mind bound up with the judging of the object, while in the case of the beautiful taste presupposes and maintains the mind in *restful* contemplation" (85). As we have seen, the feeling of the sublime is a feeling of being moved—a *Rührung*. The division of the sublime into its mathematical and dynamical features is necessitated by this quality of movement that distinguishes the sublime from the restful state of mind that characterizes the beautiful. The movement of the mind experienced in the sublime is felt as "subjectively purposive," because it awakens in us the power of reason; as a result, it is judged to be pleasant. But the movement can be judged to be subjectively purposive in two respects: in relation to the powers of cognition or in relation to the powers of desire, that is to say, reason. The movement of the mind that is felt in the sublime, understood literally as a movement, benefits the undetermined employment of both understanding and reason. When referred to the powers of cognition, the purposiveness of a given representation of boundless formlessness "derives from the imagination's *mathematical attunement* [*Stimmung*], which it ascribes to the object, whereas, when the movement of the mind is referred to the power of desire, it derives from a *dynamical attunement* of the imagination" (86, trans. modified). It should be recalled that, whereas in the case of the beautiful the imagination refers to the understanding, in the case of the sublime it refers to reason. Thus the division between the mathematical and the dynamical sublime concerns the twofold way in which the undetermined ideas involved in judgments upon the sublime bear upon the powers of cognition and desire. The ideas of reason that are awakened in the face of a boundlessly disordered nature are therefore relevant to both theoretical and practical reason. Furthermore, with the introduction of the mathematical sublime, Kant brings to light an involvement of reason in cognition that he had barely touched in his treatment of judgment upon the beautiful, a point that may in part explain the substantial treatment Kant devotes to this kind of the sublime in the Third Critique.[11]

III

Before elaborating on the mathematical sublime, Kant offers a nominal explanation of the sublime in general: "We call that *sublime* which is *absolutely great* [*schlechthin gross*]. To be great and to be a great something [*eine Grösse*] are quite different concepts (*magnitudo* and *quantitas*). In like manner to say simply [*schlechtweg . . . sagen*] (*simpliciter*) that something is *great* is quite different from saying that it is *absolutely great* (*absolute, non comparative magnum*). The latter is *what is great beyond all comparison*" (86).

Whereas what pleases in judgments upon the beautiful is mere (*blosse*) form, the judgment upon the sublime concerns exclusively what is absolutely (*schlechthin*) great. The adverb *schlechthin*, in philosophical language, is synonymous with "absolutely," but also signifies "pure and simple," "entirely," "unlimitedly," "unconditionally"; like the restrictive adverb "mere," it has a discriminating function. But while the designation of the "mere" determines something through restriction, the adverb *schlechthin* achieves a similar determination by way of a radicalization, ab-solutization, or even a certain elevation, of its object. The restrictive definition of mere form, which excludes notions of charm or concept, makes mere form a rare commodity; and similarly the "objects" of a sublime judgment must be extremely limited in accordance with the nominal definition of sublimity. Because it requires absoluteness, the sublime excludes everything that is a *quantum*. Claiming that something is simply great does not make it sublime, for sublimity can be predicated only of something that is great beyond measure, whose greatness cannot be converted, by way of comparison, to a great something. But even though it must be great beyond measure, the sublime clearly concerns magnitude in that it demarcates the absolutely great from anything that is simply qualified as great. By its nominal definition, the sublime is situated on a level that is entirely heterogeneous to the one that characterizes beauty, for what is at stake with the sublime is not form, not even negatively as the absence of form. The reflective aesthetic judgment upon the sublime is about something entirely different—magnitude—and hence it is most likely a judgment of a type different from the judgment upon the beautiful. The sublime is a reflective judgment about measurement in spite of the fact—or precisely because of it—that it refers to a greatness beyond comparison. It is a reflective judgment because it must find a measure for a magnitude that defies all measurement; and it is an aesthetic judgment because that measure can be felt only subjectively. But precisely because it is a judgment involving magnitudes and standards, it remains on a plane different from that of the beautiful.

In order to delimit the meaning of the absolutely great, it is necessary to expound, however summarily, on what Kant advances about the measurement of size. But first, it is crucial to point out a certain chronology in the definition of judgments on the sublime. In chapter 26, Kant demarcates the judgment of absolute greatness from judgments about size in mathematically definite judgments—judgments that are theoretical, cognitive, or logical, and that proceed by way of pure concepts of the understanding.

However, in chapter 25 Kant had already distinguished judgments of the absolutely great from judgments that state that something is simply (*schlechtweg*) great (or small or medium sized). Since such judgments signify neither an intuition of sense nor a concept of the understanding or of reason, "a subjective purposiveness of the representation in reference to the judgment must lie at its basis" (66). These judgments that state that something is simply great are thus unmistakably designated as aesthetic reflective judgments. They represent a brand of judgments of taste that receive their first mention in the "Analytic of the Aesthetical Judgment." They are judgments neither upon the beautiful nor upon the sublime, even though they may occur when an object is considered to be formless (87). Significantly enough, judgments upon the sublime derive from this latter kind of judgment. Judgments upon the sublime do not owe their existence to the judgments' failure to predicate beautiful form; instead they are limit cases of an entirely different family of reflective aesthetic judgments: ones that estimate something to be great, small, or medium.

I would like to highlight this additional class of reflective aesthetic judgments, to which Kant devotes only one chapter of the Third Critique and on which he expounds just long enough to prevent any confusion between these judgments and judgments upon the sublime.[12] To estimate the greatness of a phenomenon's magnitude, another magnitude has to be held up against it. It has to be compared to a standard; moreover, the magnitude of this standard unit itself requires a comparison and thus yields (only) a comparative concept of magnitude. But if "I say simply [*schlechtweg*] that anything is great, it appears that I have no comparison in view" since I do not in any way objectively determine how great the thing in question is. This statement is not at all a logical judgment about size. At the same time, in simply saying that something is great, I intimate that its "magnitude is superior to that of many objects of the same kind, without, however, any exact determination of this superiority." Consequently, there must be a standard at the basis of such a judgment, and given that all objective standard is excluded, this standard can only be subjective. But, according to Kant, although this "standard of comparison is merely subjective, yet the judgment nonetheless claims universal assent." At the basis of judgments that simply state that something is great, there is thus "a standard which we assume as the same for everyone; this, however, is not available for any logical (mathematically definite) judging of magnitude, but only for aesthetical judging of the same, because it is a merely subjective standard lying at the basis of the reflective judgment upon magnitude" (87). Like judgments upon the beautiful, these judgments are not cognitive; and yet like theoretical judgments, they demand universal assent—although in this case on the grounds of a standard that is merely subjective. These judgments that designate something as simply great or small are thus clearly reflective aesthetic judgments, in the same way that judgments of taste about the beautiful are. But judgments that declare something to be simply great are not reflective aesthetic judgments upon beauty, since they are not about the form of something or about the form's subjective purposiveness for cognition in general. Rather, they predicate greatness, and are thus judgments involved in measuring magnitude.

Before further distinguishing the judgments that establish that something is simply great from those about mere form, I wish again to emphasize the aesthetic reflective nature of the former. Indeed, their concern with simple greatness makes these judgments as disinterested as are those about pure beauty. Kant writes: "it is remarkable that, although we have no interest whatever in an object—i.e. its existence is indifferent to us—yet its mere size [*blosse Grösse*], even if it is considered as formless, may bring a satisfaction with it that is universally communicable and that consequently involves the consciousness of a subjective purposiveness in the use of our cognitive faculty" (87). Judgments about the "mere size" of something, that estimate something to be simply great, are like judgments about the "mere form" of an object, in that both are accompanied by pleasure and hence are aesthetic. If "mere size" elicits satisfaction, it does so for reasons similar to those that cause "mere form" to induce pleasure. The representation of "mere size" is felt to be beneficial to the powers of the mind. However, in this context a further difference between judgments about mere magnitude and those about mere form comes to light; for whereas with beautiful form the imagination "finds itself purposively determined in reference to cognition in general," with the mere size of an object the imagination becomes extended by itself (*Erweiterung der Einbildungskraft an sich selbst*) (87). What is felt as pleasurable in the latter case is that mere size leads to an expansion of the imagination, and as we will see, this brings the imagination into a (complex) relation with reason. Still, despite this relation of the imagination to reason in the reflective aesthetic judgments in question, and despite the fact that this relation differentiates them solidly from judgments upon the beautiful, they are not yet judgments upon the sublime.

There is an additional characteristic of judgment upon mere size—

judgment that is "no mathematically definite judgment, but a mere judgment of reflection"—that requires our attention. In a sort of aside, Kant points out that "the judging of things as great or small extends to everything, even to all their characteristics; thus we describe beauty as great or small. The reason of this is to be sought in the fact that whatever we present in intuition according to the precept of the judgment (and thus represent aesthetically) is always a phenomenon, and thus a quantum" (88). Distinct as they are from judgments about pure form and also from the sublime, judgments upon mere size are said to be possible of everything; their extension has no limits. In order to understand how judgments upon the sublime differ from them, and what exactly the boundless formlessness implies that makes them both possible and necessary, we must grasp the following paradoxical point: phenomenality (i.e., *all* that is) is the limit beyond which these judgments upon mere size cannot extend. Indeed, Kant explains the universality of these judgments by pointing out that it is always the representation of a phenomenon that leads to a reflective aesthetic judgment (whether on size or on form). Being a phenomenon, being a thing in space and time, by definition implies having magnitude. As Kant notes: "That anything is a magnitude (*quantum*) may be cognized from the thing itself, without any comparison of it with other things, viz. if there is a multiplicity of the homogeneous constituting one thing" (86).[13] Since all things are phenomenal, they can lend themselves in all cases to reflective aesthetic judgments concerning their mere size. Since they lack determined concepts, they are in a way anterior to determining judgments about the exact size of things. But if judgments upon the sublime are distinct from judgments upon mere size, notwithstanding the fact that they derive from the latter, we may still ask: on what conditions do they become possible? From what we have seen so far, judgments upon the sublime must be concerned with instances in which the possibility of phenomenality, and hence of the quantum of something, is somehow in question.

IV

To the extent that all phenomena have magnitude, they can give rise to judgments that simply state that they are great (or small). But for the same reason, they also lend themselves to a logical determination of their size. In that they are reflective aesthetic judgments, judgments upon the sublime are wholly distinct from theoretical or logical judgments of magnitude; thus if Kant addresses the mathematical estimation of magnitude in chapter 26, he does not do so in order to bring this obvious point home one more time. Rather, Kant's discussion of the cognitive judgment about mathematical size serves a different purpose. Just as the discussion of judgments that simply establish something as great served to illuminate the specificity of the judgment upon the sublime, so now the demarcation of these latter judgments from cognitive judgments concerning the magnitude of a phenomenon aims to define the exact point at which judgments upon the sublime become possible.

At the beginning of this chapter, Kant introduces a crucial distinction between the mathematical estimation of magnitude—which proceeds by numbers—and an aesthetic estimation of magnitude—which is performed "by mere intuition (by the measurement of the eye)." The first or fundamental measure (*Grundmass*) is one that logical or mathematical estimations of magnitude need in order to reach a definite concept of the size of a given magnitude, but Kant holds that this measure is ultimately a product of a mere intuition of size. If the unit of the measure is itself measured by numbers, and the unit of these must be another smaller measure, such units become caught up in an infinite regress that never reaches a final standard. Kant therefore concludes that "the estimation of the magnitude of the fundamental measure must consist in this, that we can immediately apprehend it in intuition and use it by the imagination for the presentation of concepts of number. That is, all estimation of the magnitude of the objects of nature is in the end aesthetical (i.e. subjectively and not objectively determined)" (89). If numbers, which are concepts, are not presented or rendered intuitable by way of a fundamental aesthetic measure, no determinate cognition of size is conceivable. In short, any definite estimation of magnitude hinges on the possibility of a fundamental aesthetic measure; in other words, on an intuitive apprehension of magnitude.

While reflecting on the difference between the two kinds of estimation of magnitude, Kant observes that the mathematical estimation of magnitude never reaches a maximum, because the power of the imagination to produce numbers is infinite. The imagination, according to Kant, proceeds to infinity without obstacles. The imagination is fully up to the task, and feels no inadequacy whatsoever with respect to this line of work. However, "for its aesthetical estimation there is indeed a maximum [*ein Grösstes*], and of this I say that, if it is judged as the absolute measure than which no greater is possible subjectively (for the judging subject), it brings with it the idea of the sublime" (89–90; trans. modified). Unlike the mathematical estimation of greatness, the aesthetic estimation cannot proceed *ad infinitum*, for the imagination is not (always) equal to the task that such an estimation requires. The imagination is intent on seeking to comprehend objects in one intuition, so as to provide a fundamental measure for the logical estimation of magnitude. But faced with certain objects, it encounters a maximum, or limit beyond which it cannot go. This is a limit of the imagination's power to judge magnitude aesthetically. However, as we will see, it is precisely at the moment where the imagination is incapable of an aesthetic estimation of magnitude that a feeling of the sublime—that is, of the absolutely great—arises.

Kant states:

> In receiving a quantum into the imagination by intuition, in order to be able to use it for a measure or as a unit for the estimation of magnitude by means of numbers, there are two operations of the imagination involved: *apprehension (apprehensio)* and *comprehension (comprehensio aesthetica)*. As to apprehension there is no difficulty, for it can go on *ad infinitum*, but comprehension becomes harder the further apprehension advances, and soon attains to its maximum, viz. the greatest possible aesthetical fundamental measure for the estimation of magnitude. (90)

Comprehension promptly reaches this insurmountable maximum because the imagination cannot keep up with the apprehension's progressive intake of the partial representations of a sense intuition concerning magnitude. What has been apprehended first soon vanishes after the impact of new partial representations. The full rationale for this argument (which I will take up in the next section) will be fully given only in chapter 27. In this later chapter, Kant explains that all measurement of magnitude does violence to inner sense. By this insight, the imagination's failure to produce a fundamental aesthetic measure for certain phenomena is linked to the structural peculiarities of the human mind. Kant resorts to the examples of the Egyptian pyramids and St. Peter's in Rome in order to illustrate the different paces of the imagination's apprehension and its comprehension. Let me stress right away that these are not just examples of ordinary magnitudes or everyday estimations of size; certainly they were not ordinary in Kant's time. Both illustrations are exemplary in that "the comprehension of them is never complete" (90). Before them, the spectator feels "the inadequacy of his imagination for presenting the ideas of a whole, wherein the imagination reaches its maximum, and, in striving to surpass it, sinks back into itself, by which, however, a kind of emotional satisfaction is produced" (91).

This satisfaction is none other than the feeling of the sublime.[14] These examples concern the aesthetic estimation of the size of very particular objects, objects that are out of the ordinary; and here the imagination, in seeking to produce an aesthetic intuition of them as a whole that could serve as a fundamental measure, soon reaches its maximum. In other words, the maximum reached by the imagination is an obstacle to its comprehending the magnitude as a whole. But if the failure of the imagination produces a feeling of sublimity, this feeling is precisely a response to the imagination's incapacity to produce a fundamental aesthetic standard (one that would allow us to determine its size mathematically). Undoubtedly, in seeking to grasp the whole of such a grand object in one intuitive glance, the imagination quickly reaches its limit; yet, as the examples illustrate, this is not something that happens frequently to the imagination. It will become increasingly clear that only certain phenomena radically inhibit the imagination's effort at comprehending them; therefore, the feeling of the sublime is not very common. The idea of such a maximum subtends the remaining part of chapter 26, demarcating a limit at which the imagination fails in its attempt at merely—that is, aesthetically—comprehending the apprehended representations of certain magnitudes. The chapter is otherwise mainly devoted to elucidating the particular kind of subjective purposiveness of the mere estimation of a magnitude: a kind for which our faculty of imagination is inadequate, yet which is accompanied by universally valid satisfaction. The question this raises concerns the grounds of the satisfaction that is bound up with certain representations, ones in which not only is no form involved, but the imagination's attempt to grasp them in their phenomenal entirety (as wholes) is made to sink back into itself.

In this discussion of magnitude, Kant returns first to the mechanics of the mathematical estimation of size. He recalls that in the logical estimation of magnitude, the imagination proceeds to infinity, guided by the understanding to which it furnishes the schema for the concepts of number. But in providing schemas for the numbers, that is, in providing an intuition for any unit of measurement such as "a foot or rod, or a German mile or even the earth's diameter," the imagination is not forced "to push the magnitude of the measure, and consequently the *comprehension* of the manifold in an intuition, to the bounds of the faculty of imagination, or as far as ever this can reach in its presentations" (92). Whether or not one can apprehend the unit in one glance, Kant explains, the understanding is satisfied: for in its estimation of magnitude, the understanding requires only a combination that proceeds merely by way of progression. However, satisfied or not, the understanding is not the only faculty that makes its demands upon the mind. Kant writes:

> But now the mind listens to the voice of reason which, for every given magnitude—even for those that can never be entirely apprehended, although (in sensible representation) they are judged as entirely given—requires totality. Reason consequently desires comprehension in *one* intuition, and so the [joint] *presentation* of all these members of a progressively increasing series. It does not even exempt the infinite (space and past time) from this requirement; it rather renders it unavoidable to think the infinite (in the judgment of common reason) as *entirely given* (according to its totality). (93)

Even though the understanding is content with estimating a magnitude numerically, that is, by way of a "progression (not of comprehension) in accordance with an assumed principle of progression" (92), the mind requires additionally that the magnitude be apprehended in its totality. Since all phenomena of a magnitude that is given in a sensible representation are given in their entirety—including those phenomena that cannot be entirely apprehended (such as rude nature)—reason submits that they must be taken together in one intuition. Nor is the infinite exempt from this demand, even though it is not an object of the senses and thus excludes intuitive comprehension. However, no standard of the senses is capable of achieving totalization of what is infinite, or in other words, what is absolutely great. Reason's demand must therefore be met in another, specifically nonsensible, way. The infinite requires that it be *thought* in its entirety. Even though success in meeting such a demand is not self-evident, precisely because the infinite is great beyond comparison, the mind's ability to conceive of the infinite thinkingly, according to its totality, reveals that the mind is capable of a nonsensible or "pure intellectual estimation of magnitude" (93), and that it possesses a standard that is purely intellectual. This is why Kant can write that "to be able only to think it as *a whole* indicates a faculty of the mind which surpasses every standard of sense." Indeed, he adds, "*the bare capability of thinking* this infinite" testifies to a supersensible faculty in the human mind or reason. Thanks to this intellectual estimation of magnitude, it becomes possible to "*completely* comprehend *under* one concept" "the infinite of the world of sense" (93). For its part, the understanding meets this rational request by seeking to account for this infinite in the never-ending process of the mathematical estimation of magnitude, by means of *concepts of number*.[15]

"In mathematical estimation of magnitude, the imagination is equal to providing a sufficient measure for every object, because the numerical concepts of the understanding, by means of progression, can make any measure adequate to any given magnitude" (94). However grand and great a natural phenomenon may be, the imagination is up to the task of measuring it as long as its size is numerically calculable. The imagination can go on and on, if needs be. Infinity does not pose a problem for the imagination in such cases; consequently, such progression to infinity is not conducive to judgments upon the sublime. The infinite of sense carries with it a feeling of the sublime only when the size of the natural phenomenon compels the mind to activate the intellectual standard of which it is capable. Kant writes that nature is sublime "in those of its phenomena whose intuition brings with it the idea of infinity," that is, in those phenomena that activate the intellectual standard of magnitude we have just discussed. Such infinity, Kant adds, "can only come by the inadequacy of the greatest effort of our estimation to estimate the magnitude of an object." And only in the case of such inadequacy does infinity provoke reason into thinking its totality according to reason's intellectual standard of magnitude. It follows clearly from this that in "the mere estimation of magnitude" (92), the imagination must fail in its effort to take a natural object together into one intuition if it is to suggest the infinity indicative of a supersensible standard. Since this never arises in the imagination's numerical assessment of the magnitude of an object,

> it must be the *aesthetical* estimation of magnitude in which the effort toward comprehension surpasses the power of the imagination. Here it is felt that we can comprehend in a whole of intuition the progressive apprehension, and at the same time perceive the inadequacy of this faculty, unbounded in its progress, for grasping and using any fundamental measure available for the estimation of magnitude with the easiest application of the understanding. (94)

Only when the imagination fails in the task of comprehending a natural phenomenon in one intuition—having intended to use the intuited manifold either as a measure or as the unit for measuring its magnitude—in short, when it fails to establish a fundamental aesthetic measure, then and only then does the object of nature suggest infinity and hence the intellectual standard of reason. In short, on condition that the imagination fails in the *comprehensio aesthetica* of a phenomenon of nature, the mind becomes aware that it possesses a purely intellectual standard with which it can estimate magnitude and thinkingly comprehend the object in its totality. Only when it is unsuccessful at aesthetically comprehending an object of nature does the imagination become aware of another, nonsensible standard for measurement in the mind; and the phenomenon of nature that caused the imagination to fail then becomes the indirect presentation of that standard.

The distinction between the logical and the aesthetic estimation of magnitude has revealed that judgment upon the sublime is a limit case of the "mere estimation of magnitude" (92), a reflexive mode of judgment upon magnitude that serves as the foundation for logical measurement. It is a limit case of the aesthetic estimation of magnitude since sublimity is suggested only in cases where the imagination fails to comprehend the size of a phenomenon in one intuition. The judgment of the sublime is an aesthetic reflective judgment for at least two reasons. First, it derives from judgments about the mere size of a phenomenon. Second, in a judgment upon the sublime the mind relates or subsumes a phenomenon of nature, one that the imagination cannot comprehend under the discovered nonsensible substratum of totality; the phenomenon is thus subjectively purposive in that it expands the mind and gives it a practical bent. In sum, then, whereas the mathematical estimation of magnitude is logical and based on determining judgments, the judgment upon the sublime is a reflective judgment: it is rooted in a limit situation of the aesthetic and reflective estimation of magnitude, and its effort to produce a fundamental measure for the logical estimation of magnitude.

At the conclusion of chapter 26, Kant reasserts the subjective nature of sublimity. The sublime lies not in the magnitude of the natural object that the imagination vainly attempts to comprehend aesthetically, but rather in the "supersensible substrate" that is awakened in the mind during its estimation of this magnitude. Returning for a moment to the difference between the beautiful and the sublime, Kant remarks:

> Just as the aesthetical judgment in judging the beautiful refers the imagination in its free play to the *understanding*, in order to harmonize it with the *concepts* of the latter in general (without any determination of them), so does the same faculty, when judging a thing as sublime, refer itself to the *reason*, in order that it may subjectively be in accordance with its *ideas* (no matter what they are)—i.e. that it may produce a state of mind conformable to them and compatible with that brought about by the influence of definite (practical) ideas upon feeling. (94–95)

It is not the "shapeless mountain masses piled in wild disorder upon one another with their pyramids of ice" (95) that are sublime, but rather the intelligent substrate "great beyond all standards of sense" that they inevitably invoke and that causes the representation of unbound nature to benefit the practical employment of reason. As a result of the failure of an intuitive comprehension of a magnitude, a subject discovers within itself the intellectual standard for measuring magnitude; the state of mind that arises at that moment raises the subject above itself, above itself as a merely sensible being. "The mind feels itself raised [*gehoben*] in its own judgment if, while contemplating them [the mountains of ice] without any reference to their form, and abandoning itself to the imagination and to the reason—which, although placed in combination with the imagination without definite purpose, merely extends it—it yet finds the whole power of the imagination inadequate to its ideas" (95). In the judgment upon the sublime, sublimity designates only the mind's being raised to a higher level because it is able to judge according to the nonsensible standard of the ideas, even though the imagination proves inadequate to this standard. I should point out here that *Erhabenheit* (sublimity) suggests *Gehobenheit* (elevation, elatedness). The latter, significantly, cannot be predicated of objects of nature but refers to the position of the human being as a social and moral being, as well as to the position of the mind.

V

Judgment upon the sublime is thoroughly dependent on the failure of the imagination with respect to the very specific task of aesthetic estimation of magnitude. The imagination's inability to comprehend intuitively the size of certain objects of nature activates a purely intellectual standard of measurement in the mind, which in turn leads us to judge these objects as sublime.[16] It remains to be seen how exactly this inadequacy on the part of the imagination, even in its greatest efforts to comprehend certain phenomena of nature into a unified whole of intuition, becomes construed as an achievement. Since the sensible faculty of the imagination must be pushed to its limits in order for the intellectual standard to manifest itself, the feeling of the sublime is distinct from the satisfaction that comes with the beautiful. It is a double feeling, one in which pleasure and pain are intrinsically linked together. Concerning this element of pain, Kant explains: "The feeling of the sublime is therefore a feeling of pain arising from the want of accordance between the aesthetical estimation of magnitude formed by the imagination and the estimation of the same formed by reason" (96). The pain suffered by the imagination in judgments upon the sublime has led some critics of Kant to denounce the tyranny of reason, to which the imagination submits itself in judgments upon the sublime. Undoubtedly, Kant's references in this context to subjection (*Unterwerfung*), violence (*Gewalt*), deprivation (*Beraubung*), and sacrifice (*Aufopferung*) encourage such an interpretation. The notion of *Beraubung* is particularly significant here, since in addition to its usual meaning of "being robbed," it can also suggest rape. But we must still ask whether it is permissible, in discussing the sublime, to characterize the relation between imagination and reason as one in which the imagination is simply the object of a violent assault by domineering reason. Such a representation presupposes both that the imagination is in its very essence hostile to reason and that reason has no legitimate demands to make on the imagination as imagination. However, not only would this completely misrepresent the nature of these Kantian faculties, it would also destroy the means of explaining the very origin of the feeling of the sublime. Indeed, without some agreement to the demands of reason on the part of the imagination, and without reason's legitimate right to demand the submission of the faculty of the senses, no feeling of the sublime would ever take place. As Lyotard has pointed out,

> if the thought that imagines (always in Kant's sense: that presents here and now) opposed the thought that conceives of the absolute with a pure and simple refusal, there would be no sublime feeling. The same would be true if reason demanded nothing, that is, if thought were not available, "liable," did not have the necessary *Empfänglichkeit* to the Ideas of reason for them to "arise" on the occasion of this almost impossible presentation.[17]

Kant occasionally notes that this violence is not actual, especially during his discussion of the dynamical sublime. Although I will linger hereafter on the seeming violence done to the imagination by reason, my primary concern is not to engage the accusation that reason bullies the imagination into submission. Rather, my goal is to gain a more precise understanding of how the imagination's inadequacy in the face of certain magnitudes brings on the intellectual standard, and thus the judgment upon the sublime. An investigation of the pain that accompanies the imagination's failure in comprehending certain magnitudes will provide a more precise insight into how the relation to reason comes about in aesthetic judgments upon the sublime; an event in which, qua aesthetic judgment, reason as such cannot be present itself.

Let us begin by asking why the imagination feels pain when it proves unable to comprehend the magnitude of an object of nature aesthetically? Is such pain merely the result of an outside imposition on the imagination? Kant reminds us in chapter 27:

The idea of the comprehension of every phenomenon that can be given to us in the intuition as a whole is an idea prescribed to us by the law of reason, which recognizes no other measure, definite, valid for everyone, and invariable, than the absolute whole. But our imagination, even in its greatest efforts, in respect of that comprehension which we expect from it of a given object in a whole of intuition (and thus with reference to the presentation of the idea of reason) exhibits its own limits and inadequacy, although at the same time it shows that its destination is to make itself adequate to this idea regarded as law. (96)

Thus *within* the highest sensible faculty, the imagination's effort to provide a fundamental aesthetic measure for the logical estimation of magnitude is "a reference to something *absolutely great*, and consequently a reference to the law of reason, which bids us take this alone as our highest measure of magnitude" (96–97). The imagination seeks to achieve the task that is properly its own, by virtue of its status as the highest sensible faculty. By intuiting a given magnitude into a whole, the imagination is thus by definition *already* yielding to the law of reason. More important, the pain that it suffers in not being up to that task, when it is confronted with certain magnitudes of nature, is a pain that it can feel only because it obeys the laws of reason from the very outset. In its failed quest for a fundamental aesthetic measure, the imagination already seeks to realize the law of reason; and only because of this can the imagination experience its inadequacy as a sensible faculty. This pain is therefore not simply pain; it is inextricably linked with the realization of the imagination's supersensible destination. Kant writes: "the inner perception of the inadequacy of all sensible standards for rational estimation of magnitude indicates a correspondence with rational laws; it involves a pain, which arouses in us a feeling of our supersensible destination, according to which it is purposive and therefore pleasurable to find every standard of sensibility inadequate to the ideas of reason" (97, trans. modified). The very possibility of suffering pain shows that the imagination is in a constitutive bond with reason. After all, the imagination is only another faculty of the mind.

Further evidence of the intimate connection, or rather complicity, between the imagination and reason comes to light in the sublime's nature as a feeling of *Rührung*. Kant writes: "The mind feels itself *moved* in the representation of the sublime in nature, while in aesthetical judgments about the beautiful it is in *restful* contemplation. This movement may (especially in its beginnings) be compared to a vibration [*Erschütterung*], i.e. to a quickly alternating attraction toward, and repulsion from, the same object" (97). The movement that characterizes the feeling of the sublime, in contrast to the restful state of the feeling of the beautiful, is an inner agitation in which the mind is shaken by being thrown to and fro.

> The transcendent [*Überschwengliche*, the exuberant, rapturous, effusive] (toward which the imagination is impelled in the apprehension of intuition) is for the imagination like an abyss in which it fears to lose itself; but for the rational idea of the supersensible it is not transcendent [*überschwenglich*], but in conformity with law to bring about such an effort of the imagination, and consequently there is the same amount of attraction as there was of repulsion for the mere sensibility. (97)

A sublime representation threatens the imagination with loss of itself. This faculty is one of "mere sensibility," and the magnitude that demands measurement in the sublime is excessive; hence the imagination is repulsed by it. However, the sublime representation holds nothing excessive for reason, in that the magnitude in question is indicative of the law. The imagination's failing effort to approximate it is therefore in line with the demand of reason, and consequently, the sublime representation is also attractive. Kant emphasizes that the amount of attraction involved in the feeling of the sublime is equal to the amount of repulsion, and this is clear evidence that reason is present in the judgment in question as an equal of sorts of the imagination, rather than as a domineering power over it. Indeed, without such equality it would be difficult to see how the mind could be moved in the sublime, given that movement here refers to an inner agitation. Reason is not involved in the judgment upon the sublime in the guise of a determined power, that is to say, as a rational or moral judgment properly speaking. Kant reminds us at this point that the judgment upon the sublime remains aesthetic rather than becoming rational or moral.

> The judgment itself always remains in this case only aesthetical, because, without having any determinate concept of the object at its basis, it merely represents the subjective play of the mental powers (imagination and reason) as harmonious through their very contrast. For just as imagination and *understanding*, in judging of the beautiful, generate a subjective purposiveness of the mental powers by means of their harmony, so [in this case] imagination and *reason* do so by means of their conflict. That is, they bring about a feeling that we possess pure self-subsistent reason, or a faculty for the estimation of magnitude, whose superiority can be made intuitively evident only by the inadequacy of that faculty [imagination] which is itself unbounded in the presentation of magnitudes (of sensible objects). (97)

As a purposive play of faculties, the feeling of the sublime disallows the presence of reason in its usual determining role. In fact, reason is present in this play only insofar as the painful inadequacy of the imagination is felt to be purposive. By experiencing the imagination's inability to comprehend certain magnitudes of nature as a failure, the mind reveals itself to possess a higher standard of estimation. How otherwise could the imagination judge its struggle to be a failure, and suffer a resulting sense of pain? Furthermore, since reason cannot be present in its determined form in aesthetic judgment upon the sublime, the feeling of the sublime must arise within the imagination. More precisely, it must arise between the imagination as a mere sensible faculty and the imagination as the highest faculty of the senses. As we will see, it is only in this sense that the imagination's self-sacrifice can be understood. In the sublime, the imagination itself, in its quality as the highest sensible faculty, is attracted by its own failure to comprehend aesthetically a magnitude of nature that is absolutely great, attracted because this failure reveals that it is susceptible (even as a sensible faculty) to a kind of standard other than the standard of sense.

Much more remains to be said about the question of the pain that the imagination feels when it realizes its inadequacy for the task of intuiting certain magnitudes of the natural sublime in one whole. This pain is triggered in the face of reason's demand that the imagination comprehend a given magnitude in its totality; however the imagination is subjected to such pain not exclusively in the sublime but in any measurement of magnitude where, in addition to the progressive apprehension of a magnitude, there is a demand for the comprehension of the manifold in the unity of intuition. In chapter 27, Kant recalls that all measurement of magnitude, including ordinary, everyday estimation of magnitude, does violence to inner sense. Indeed,

the comprehension of the successively apprehended [elements] in one glance is a regress which annihilates the condition of time in this progress of the imagination and makes *coexistence* intuitable. It is therefore (since the time series is a condition of the internal sense and of an intuition) a subjective movement of the imagination, by which it does violence to the internal sense; this must be more noticeable, the greater the quantum is which the imagination comprehends in one intuition. (98)

Kant's remarks here echo the discussions of the measurement of space in the *Critique of Pure Reason*;[18] they clearly establish that in the measurement of magnitudes, apprehension's taking in of something (the first moment in measuring) is progressive and obeys the form of time that is constitutive of inner sense. But invoking measurement implies not only apprehension's first moment but also the second moment of representing the apprehended manifold in its simultaneity. Such comprehension, however, is regressive, in that it abolishes the condition of time in the progress of the imagination. This annihilation of time is violence done to the form of inner sense, which guides the imagination in its apprehension of the manifold.[19] But it is violence without which no determinate measurement of magnitudes would be possible, to the extent that such measurement requires a fundamental aesthetic standard. The imagination, by inflicting violence upon the form of inner sense in a move to apprehend and measure a manifold, reveals its complicity with reason, a complicity that is already operative in such ordinary activities of the mind as the estimation of the size of a quantum. As Kant observes, the intensity of this violence is a function of the size of the quantum to be estimated, and since no measurement of size could take place without doing violence to the form of inner sense, it is violence that is judged purposive. Kant concludes:

> The effort, therefore, to receive in one single intuition a measure for magnitude that requires a considerable time to apprehend is a kind of representation which, subjectively considered, is contrary to purpose; but objectively, as requisite for the estimation of magnitude, it is purposive. Thus that very violence which is done to the subject through the imagination is judged purposive *in reference to the whole determination* of the mind. (98)

As I argued earlier, the judgment upon the sublime derives from judgments that concern magnitude. More precisely, it is a limit case of the aesthetic estimation of magnitude, in that it presupposes the imagination's inability to arrive at a fundamental aesthetic measure for a given quantum. In other words, judgment upon the sublime is somewhat paradoxical, in that the imagination is pained by its inability to enact the violence that is required to freeze an apprehended manifold into one intuition. In the sublime, the imagination suffers from an inability to perform aesthetically its usual—and habitually painful—job of meeting the demands of reason, and we should recall that the imagination by definition seeks to dispatch these demands. In the face of objects so great that no time, however extensive, would suffice to apprehend them, the imagination feels pain because it is unable to perform its usual painful job on the form of inner sense. At the same time, through "the very incapacity in question [it] discovers the consciousness of an unlimited faculty of the subject, and that the mind can only judge of the latter aesthetically by means of the former" (98).

Some of Kant's observations in the "General Remark upon the Exposition of the Aesthetical Reflective Judgment" about the negative pleasure involved in the sublime can further highlight what I have said so far about the imagination's pain. We have already seen that in his discussion of the difference between a moral judgment and a judgment upon the sublime, Kant emphasizes that reason is not present *in propria persona* in judgments upon the sublime, although in such judgments the imagination still relates to reason. Whereas "law-directed *occupation* ... is the genuine characteristic of human morality, in which reason must exercise dominion over sensibility ... in aesthetical judgments upon the sublime this dominion is represented as exercised by the imagination, regarded as an instrument of reason" (109). Furthermore, Kant elaborates on the satisfaction in the sublime by attributing its merely negative character to the fact that "the imagination is depriving itself of its freedom [*Beraubung der Freiheit der Einbildungskraft durch sich selbst*], while it is purposively determined according to a different law from that of its empirical employment" (109). Sublimity is precisely the result of a state of mind in which, in the absence of reason proper, the imagination sacrifices itself. Indeed, any contention that reason itself coerces the imagination into this act of violence against itself mistakes the judgment upon the sublime for a moral judgment. Now, Kant describes this self-sacrifice as the imagination's depriving itself of the freedom that it has in its ordinary, empirical employment; yet in its ordinary employment, the imagination is not free at all. It operates under the strict rules of the understanding. It has no identity of its own, so to speak, in its empirical employment. The apparent consequence is this: that only by ridding itself of its merely sensible nature and turning itself into an the instrument of reason can the imagination become the highest sensible faculty, and secure for itself a self. The imagination subjects itself to a law other than that of the understanding and thereby deprives itself of its merely sensible nature in a sensible way; but only by way of such violence does the imagination realize—though only aesthetically, of course—the rational idea of self and the concomitant notion of freedom. One could even say that this self-sacrifice is the only occasion upon which the imagination is raised to the status of a faculty, with an identity of its own.[20]

VI

Standing in its complex relation to reason, the imagination passes its judgment on the boundlessly formless objects of nature in one of two ways. When the harmonious conflict of imagination and reason is beneficial for the powers of cognition, the objects before the imagination are judged to be mathematically sublime. But the mental agitation caused by these objects can also elicit the powers of desire, that is, of reason, and in this case the sublime is judged to be dynamically sublime. This second, dynamical aspect of the sublime requires that nature be experienced as an irresistible power over our sensible forces and faculties, rather than as a magnitude that surpasses the imagination's capacity to comprehend it (as in the mathematically sublime). We have seen that a higher power of comprehension was awakened in the mind by the imagination's failure to intuit the magnitude of nature as one entirety. Similarly, as the imagination realizes that it is no match for the might of nature, a higher power of resistance is brought onto the scene. Kant explains as follows: "*Might* is that which is superior to great hindrances. It is called *dominion* [*Gewalt*] if it is superior to the resistance of that which itself possesses might. Nature, considered in an aesthetical judgment as might that has no dominion over us, is *dynamically sublime*" (99). If it is to be judged sublime in this second perspective, the might of nature must *not* be a dominion; that is, it must not be superior to all resistance that we can muster against it. But nature must be represented as exciting fear in us before we can judge it as sublime and consequently as having no dominion over us. Even though our fear is not a sufficient reason to call an object of nature sublime, it is a necessary condition for judging something to be sublime.[21] As we will see, sublimity refers only to the mental power that is superior to nature and that is called up by the fearsome object. If nature must be experienced as fearsome in order for a judgment upon the sublime to be possible, this is because "in aesthetical judgments (without the aid of concepts) superiority to hindrances can only be judged according to the greatness of the resistance" (99–100). The fear in question, however, must not amount to actual fear. It must not imply being afraid. Indeed, as Kant remarks, "he who fears [in the sense of being afraid] can form no judgment about the sublime of nature, just as he who is seduced by inclination and appetite can form no judgment about the beautiful" (100). No disinterested aesthetic judgment could ever come into being in the face of an object that literally threatened us in our natural existence. "It is impossible to find satisfaction in a terror that is seriously felt" (100), Kant remarks. It follows that the nature that inspires fear in us and leads to the mind's discovery within itself of a nonsensible power of resistance must be of such a kind that the mind is not actually afraid of it. Otherwise, nature could not be judged to be sublime. The mental experiment in which we imagine our resistance to the might of nature and then our subsequent failure to overcome that might provides the paradigm for the experience of nature that incites a judgment upon the sublime.[22] "We can regard an object as *fearful* without being afraid *of* it, viz. if we judge of it in such a way that we merely *think* a case in which we would resist it and yet in which all resistance would be altogether vain" (100). If we are to attribute sublimity to objects over which our natural capabilities are powerless—for example, "bold, overhanging, and as it were [*gleichsam*] threatening rocks" (100)—these objects must not be truly menacing. One must be secure from any actual danger that they might represent. Only under such conditions is it possible to reflect upon them and perform a judgment about them.

Kant claims of objects that "exhibit our faculty of resistance as insignificantly small in comparison with their might," that "we willingly [*gern*, readily] call these objects sublime." If this is so, it is because "they raise the energies of the mind [*Seelenstärke*] above their accustomed height [*Mittelmass*, average]," in other words, because they dynamically expand the mind (100). The imagination, in its experimentation, realizes that as a sensible faculty it is entirely at the mercy of nature and has nothing with which to oppose nature; and this realization in turn makes us "discover in [ourselves] a faculty of resistance of a quite different kind, which gives us courage to measure ourselves against the apparent almightiness of nature" (100–101). Needless to say, the power over the realm of the senses that the mind thus discovers within itself is the power of reason. And because nature therefore has no dominion [*Gewalt*] over us, in spite of its superiority over us insofar as we are natural beings, it is judged sublime insofar as it makes us aware of our supersensible determination and destination.

In terms of their structure, judgments about the mathematical and the dynamical sublime are isomorphic. As we have seen, the inability of the imagination to provide a standard for aesthetically measuring the immensity of nature reveals in us a purely intellectual standard, and hence a rational ability to estimate magnitude. In the same way, "the irresistibility of [nature's] might, while making us recognize our own [physical] impotence, considered as beings of nature, disclose(s) to us a faculty of judging independently of and a superiority over nature, on which is based a kind of self-preservation entirely different from that which can be attacked and brought into danger by external nature" (101). In distinction from the mathematical sublime, in which the imagination is faced with the impossibility of comprehending natural magnitude, the dynamical sublime concerns the imagination's powerlessness to contain nature experienced, or thought, as power or might. Whereas in the mathematical sublime the mind is made aware of a purely intellectual standard for measuring magnitude, in the dynamical sublime the mind is made to realize that it has a force of resistance that is not sensible but purely intellectual. Kant adds that this force of resistance that is called up in the mind by the might of nature is the idea of our humanity, that is, of our moral destination. The intellectual standard of which we become aware in the mathematical sublime consists in the theoretically relevant idea of totality; by contrast, the intellectual power of resistance that we discover in the dynamical sublime concerns the practically relevant moral idea of humanity as an end in itself. We should recall here that the discovery of an intellectual standard is not a mathematical or theoretical estimation of a magnitude, and contributes nothing specific to either, but instead only extends and legitimizes the mind in its ability to go beyond the limits of sensibility. Similarly, the disclosure to us of a moral force of resistance does not yet imply that our actions are moral. After all, in the dynamical sublime the subject discovers "only the *destination* of our faculty which discloses itself in such a case, so far as the tendency to this destination lies in our nature [*nur die sich in solchem Falle entdeckende* Bestimmung *unseres Vermögens, so wie die Anlage zu demselben in unserer Natur*], while its development and exercise remain incumbent and obligatory" (101–2). The satisfaction felt in the sublime does not concern any satisfaction over moral action (satisfaction, in fact, is not moral at all) but pertains to the mere discovery that we are capable of action according to moral principles.

As the preceding analysis of the two ways of approaching the sublime has shown, the aesthetic reflective judgment on which the sublime rests is quite different in kind from the one that characterizes the beautiful. The boundless formlessness of nature that gives rise to the judgment upon the sublime is a formlessness so radical as to exclude all formal considerations, including the possibility of judging it to be ugly. In response to such formlessness, another kind of reflective aesthetic judgment becomes both possible and necessary: namely, a judgment involved in the estimation of the magnitude or the might of an object. More precisely, when the imagination is presented with boundless formlessness in nature, and hence with the aesthetic impossibility of bringing the latter under the form of the concept in general in order to ensure a minimal objectification, the resulting judgment of sublimity secures a minimal mastery by imposing a thinkable totality on this infinite formlessness and by resisting its destructive might with the power of rational ideas. This concern with either magnitude or might sets the judgment upon the sublime entirely apart from the judgment upon the beautiful, and for more reasons than the simple fact that the latter is about the form of the object whereas the sublime is about totality and a might of another kind. Judgments upon the sublime also differ from judgments upon the beautiful because, as we have seen, the "mechanics" of reflective aesthetic judgments upon form are distinct from the "mechanics" of judgments upon magnitude or force. Unlike judgments upon the beautiful, judgments upon the sublime are not "about" nature. They arise in response to spectacles that inhibit all possible objectification, and they testify only to the intellectual standard and destination of the mind, which is the only meaningful context for something like displeasure with the boundlessness of nature. In other words, whereas judgments upon form predicate the minimal conformity of a "something" with the form proper to a thing or object, judgments upon the sublime infer only an intellectual standard: the standard that is implied, and presupposed, in judging a formlessness that prohibits any objective relation, including an aesthetic one.

These differences go to the core of what judgment means in the case of either the beautiful or the sublime, yet they are not symmetrical with each other. Judgment upon the beautiful, that is, judgment of mere form, is motivated by objects that lack definite concepts; and the subsumption of such objects under concept in general in judgments of taste secures a minimal objectification, and thus the possible success of the most common kind of employment of the mind, namely cognition. Judgment upon the sublime, by contrast, comes into play only where the formlessness of the object thwarts even aesthetic objectification. The sublime is thus a secondary possibility, or as Kant holds, an appendix to the beautiful. The fact that the "Analytic of the Aesthetical Judgment" is positioned after the "Analytic of the Beautiful" is not accidental or trivial, as we have seen. It is in the "Analytic of the Beautiful" that Kant develops the specifics of reflective aesthetic judgment, which subsequently become the point of reference for his discussion of the sublime. But this sequential order is significant in still another sense; for with the judgment upon the sublime, Kant sketches out a species of aesthetic reflective judgments that, while still within sensibility, moves away from the sensible and hence beyond the aesthetic. This resistance to the aesthetic within the aesthetic highlights the role of reason in aesthetic reflective judgment upon the sublime. But not only the sublime is at issue; as I have suggested, the discussion of the sublime also brings to light a constitutive "presence" of reason in judgments upon the beautiful. Working backward from the appendix on the sublime, it becomes possible to isolate and thematize the essential contribution of reason to those judgments in which only the imagination and the understanding seem initially to be at play. But even though the "Analytic of the Sublime" allows this crucial insight into the mechanics of the beautiful, this is still no reason to privilege it. The insight is only one more facet of the appendicular nature of the "Analytic of the Sublime."

Judgment upon the sublime is quite distinct in scope and kind from the judgment upon the beautiful. It has its own judgmental structure and task that cannot be exchanged for those of judgment upon the beautiful. The sublime is not simply an alternative to the beautiful. However, the order in which the exposition of the beautiful and the sublime proceeds can be viewed from yet another angle. Indeed, since the aesthetic judgment upon the sublime constitutes an aesthetic judgment at the very limits of aesthetics, it is only natural that it should follow the exposition of the beautiful. Even though the sublime remains within aesthetics—and as one of its main parts, according to Kant—it gestures toward something else, namely, practical reason and morality. Nevertheless, privileging the sublime on these grounds would do violence to the Kantian conceptuality and uproot the sublime from the aesthetics to which it belongs. In fact, conceiving of the sublime as an alternative to the beautiful would privilege something that is finally not Kantian at all.

6

Interest and Disinterestedness

Just as Kant is about to engage the beautiful arts in *Critique of Judgment*—a work whose analysis of beauty has been based essentially, if not exclusively, on the beautiful of nature—he recalls that for a judgment of taste to be pure, that is, to be such a judgment in the first place, it "must have no interest [whatsoever] *as its determining ground*."[1] Judgment upon the beautiful arts is not to be exempted from this basic requirement established in the "Analytic of the Beautiful," if it is to be pure judgment concerning their beauty. As Kant argued at the beginning of the Third Critique, with regard to quality, that is, with regard to what distinguishes the judgment of taste from other judgments involving a feeling in the subject, it must be disinterested in—that is, entirely free of satisfaction deriving from—the representation of the existence of the object.[2] Since "such satisfaction always [has] reference to the faculty of desire, either as its determining ground or as necessarily connected with its determining ground" (38), a pure judgment of taste must be free of partiality toward the existence of objects that cause the respective pleasures of the sensibly pleasant and the morally good, a partiality that is characteristic of the senses and the will. A pure judgment of taste, by contrast, comes into being only when all such concern with the existence of the object is excluded, and when that which is judged beautiful (rather than pleasant or good) pleases independently of "whether anything depends or can depend on the existence of the thing, either for myself or for any one else" (38). Undoubtedly, a judgment of the senses is also aesthetic in that its ground of determination is "no other than subjective" (37), and a moral judgment can also be aesthetic, because it derives pleasure from its object, just as a judgment of the senses does. But the satisfactions involved in these types of judgment are intimately tied to the existence of the object as well as to its continued desirability. Distinct from such judgments is the pure reflective aesthetic judgment, or judgment of taste. For it to be possible at all—that is, for it to derive satisfaction from the fact that a thing for which one has no concept (nor any use) still has the mere form of an object—this condition of disinterestedness in the existence of the object must obtain. Otherwise, the judgment will be either a judgment of the senses or a moral judgment, but certainly not a pure aesthetic judgment. With "disinterestedness," Kant manages to exhibit a category of aesthetic judgments that, rather than being grounded on the pleasure from the existence of the object, finds satisfaction with the possibility that a thing for which no determined concept is available has, nonetheless, the form of an object and consequently meets the minimal condition of cognizability, namely, representability. Within the broad domain of aesthetic judgments, the judgments based on disinterested pleasure constitute a sphere of judgments that are not private and incommunicable, as judgments of the senses are, but that are not universal in the same way that moral judgments are, either, because they do not rest on the pregiven and universally shared concept of the good. Within the general domain of aesthetic judgments, "disinterestedness" is the index of one particular area of judgments that can lay claim to universality without any pregiven concepts, because disinterested pleasure stems from the discovery that the objects under consideration have form, more precisely, the mere form of an object, rather than no form (in which case the objects would refuse representation). Since the pleasure in question concerns the very possibility of cognition when the latter is faced with objects for which the understanding cannot provide concepts, we can safely assume that anyone could, in principle, enter into agreement with such a judgment. Disinterestedness thus constitutes pure aesthetic judgments as judgments that establish the possibility that certain things are objects, and that thus secure the possibility of cognition for these objects even if cognition does not necessarily give rise to determined judgments. Disinterestedness is the condition under which a very specific, if not singular, kind of epistemological accomplishment comes to light; and it is with this accomplishment, and this alone, that Kant's aesthetics is concerned.

Kant's reminder that the requirement of disinterestedness for judgment upon the beautiful remains fully valid, and will not be rescinded in his analysis of the beautiful arts, becomes all the more crucial as this analysis explores a possible relation between the beautiful and the morally good. Indeed, one of the more persistent misunderstandings of Kant's aesthetics is the belief that disinterestedness in judgments of beauty excludes any possible linkage of beauty to the morally good. A linkage to the morally good, to a concept that is at our disposal insofar as we are rational beings and that we cannot but wish, and will, to become reality, would suggest interest. Even though interest can be attributed to all powers of the mind, the morally good warrants interest because interest itself is intimately and essentially tied up with the faculty of reason as a faculty of principles.[3] The question concerning a possible interest in the beautiful—the question that guides and perhaps even motivates Kant's discussion of the beautiful arts—is thus a question of the moral and rational relevance of the beautiful. By turning to the beautiful arts and to this question of a possible interest stirred by their beauty, Kant's aesthetics of the beautiful would thus seem to take a turn, leaving behind what numerous commentators consider a frivolous concern with mere form to pursue more serious issues. Adding fuel to such a view, Kant also admits to a connection of the moral to the beautiful of nature. So although the mere form at stake in a pure disinterested judgment of taste is demonstrably not a frivolous concern—after all, mere form is found pleasurable because it signifies that the object is attuned to the powers of cognition—nonetheless, the introduction of the question of interest suggests a kind of turning point in Kant's thinking about the beautiful. What are the reasons for having the question of interest return after everything that has been established with regard to disinterestedness as being essential to the pure judgment of the beautiful? Has Kant relaxed his standards? Has he abandoned pure judgments of taste to take up aesthetic judgments upon the morally good, which, because they presuppose concepts, are impure judgments of taste? Why does Kant broach the question of interest at the moment he resorts to the analysis of artificial beauty? And finally, given Kant's reminder that the principles set forth by the "Analytic of the Beautiful" are not to be rescinded when considering the beautiful arts, how does interest link to disinterestedness? What kind of form does the articulation take? These are among the questions we must ask at this undoubtedly crucial juncture of Kant's text.

Before seeking answers, I need to point out that the theme of interest brought up in the chapters concerning artificial beauty (and seemingly for the first time in relation to beauty) had already been at issue in Kant's discussion of the sublime. Notwithstanding that Kant broaches this issue, in the "General Remark upon the Exposition of the Aesthetical Reflective Judgment," almost exclusively with respect to the sublime, a discussion of this chapter should help us understand what Kant means by interest, and how it is linked to disinterested judgments of taste. Furthermore, since it is certainly not by accident that the question of an interest in the sublime precedes the discussion of an interest in the beautiful, we can also expect this chapter to suggest why the interest in the beautiful could be properly discussed only in the wake of what has been established about the interest in the sublime.

Returning to the different kinds of feeling that ground the different kinds of aesthetic judgment and determine whether an object, or its representation, is classified as pleasant, beautiful, sublime, or good, Kant remarks:

> The *absolutely good*, subjectively judged according to the feeling that it inspires (the object of the moral feeling), as capable of determining the powers of the subject through the representation of an *absolutely compelling* law, is specially distinguished by the *modality* of a necessity that rests *a priori* upon concepts. This necessity involves, not merely a *claim*, but a *command* for the assent of everyone and belongs in itself to the pure intellectual rather than to the aesthetical judgment, and is by a determinant and not a mere reflective judgment ascribed, not to nature, but to freedom. (107)

It follows from all this that the pleasure, or satisfaction, inspired by the morally good cannot be part of an investigation into pure aesthetic reflective judgments. Satisfaction with the good should be set aside just as the feeling of the pleasant is, though not because it is based on a judgment of the senses as is the latter, but because it rests on an intellectual judgment rather than on a merely reflective one. Yet while judgment of taste bars all "natural combination with the feeling of the pleasant" (107), its relation to satisfaction with the morally good is more complex. Indeed, as Kant argues, even though judgment upon the absolutely good is clearly a determining judgment by which the idea of the good is ascribed to the subject, the *"modification of [the subject's] state"* to which this determination *can* give rise—a modification consisting in the subject's feeling of *"hindrances* in sensibility and at the same time [the subject's feeling of] its superiority to them by their subjugation"—shows the moral feeling to be "cognate [*verwandt*] to the aesthetical judgment and its formal conditions" (107). Thanks to this formal resemblance to aesthetic judgment, the moral feeling can even "serve to represent [*vorstellig zu machen*] the conformity to law of action from duty as aesthetical, i.e. as sublime or even as beautiful, without losing purity" (107). In other words, while pleasure in the good results from an intellectual determination of the will—an intellectual pleasure, as it were, no doubt entirely distinct from the pleasure of the senses, but also from that of the beautiful and the sublime—the need to overcome hindrances of sensibility in the process of that determination, and the superiority the subject feels when those hindrances are vanquished, also predisposes moral feeling to serve as an aesthetic representation of moral action. Moral feeling as satisfaction with the absolutely good thus seems to warrant inclusion in Kantian aesthetics. At the same time, it is necessary to emphasize the modalities of this recognition. If the moral feeling does not lose its intellectual purity in this process—that is, if no confusion whatsoever takes place between the feeling that derives from the subject's intellectual determination and what predisposes that feeling to become an aesthetic representation of the morally good —this is so basically for two reasons. First, the moral feeling's ability to serve as an aesthetic representation is (only) added to the subjective judgment about the absolutely good. Second, what explains that ability is only a formal similarity, or isomorphism, between the modification of the subject's state by the moral law and the modification of the subject's state in aesthetic judgment of the sublime and the beautiful. In no way is the moral feeling itself to be confused with an aesthetic representation of the absolutely good. Only because the moral feeling can lead to a modification of the subject's state akin to the modification brought about in the judgment of the sublime and the beautiful can this feeling, in addition to being what it is, also assume the function of aesthetically rendering the law present. If the moral feeling's aesthetic credentials have thus been acknowledged, its aesthetic function is, nonetheless, an indirect, oblique, if not also contingent, possibility since it is based on a feeling that the subject *can* have in addition to the feeling that the morally good produces in him. It is therefore a rather intricate and precarious possibility.

Kant has thus made room for an aesthetic function of moral feeling in conformity with the principles of the power of judgment. Undoubtedly, it remains to be seen how we must understand such aesthetic representation if we are not to contradict Kant's claim that the purely intellectual warrants no sensible presentation. We will return to this question in the context of Kant's discussion of whether something like intellectual beauty or sublimity is conceivable. For the time being, I note that by thus acknowledging an aesthetic representation of the morally good, Kant has implicitly opened up the question of a possible relation of the beautiful and the sublime to the moral law. If the moral law allows for an aesthetic representation in which it can be represented as sublime or even as beautiful, the question inevitably arises concerning the commerce of the sublime and the beautiful with the morally good. From the start, however, it must be kept in mind that the possibility of a sublime or beautiful aesthetic representation of the morally good in no way implies that, by nature, or as such, the sublime or the beautiful would necessarily be aesthetic representations of the moral law. In conformity with what has been established throughout the analytics of the beautiful and the sublime, Kant does not renege on the distinctions among the different kinds of pleasure when he returns to this question at the beginning of the "General Remark." They are distinct kinds of satisfactions not to be lumped together. The moral feeling's aesthetic achievement is to be kept neatly separate from other aesthetic accomplishments, especially those of the beautiful and the sublime. Nevertheless, it needs to be remarked that the four kinds of satisfaction listed in the "General Remark" are classified according to the four judgmental moments involved in the judgments upon both the beautiful and the sublime. The pleasant is made intelligible by quantity; the beautiful requires a representation of quality; the sublime consists only in a relation; and the moral feeling is a modality. Undoubtedly, the chief reason for resorting to this classification is to separate the four pleasures as sharply as possible. The absolutely compelling law involved in moral feeling severs that feeling entirely from all the other kinds of satisfactions. But since it is possible to graft onto the moral feeling a modification of the subject that resembles the one found in the sublime and the beautiful, the question becomes whether, in spite of their difference from moral feeling, the beautiful and the sublime do not also in turn allow for the addition of a relation to the morally good? Before exploring this thought, let me stress again that what allows the moral feeling to become an aesthetic representation of the moral law is the formal structure that the moral feeling has in common with the sublime and the beautiful when the feeling is associated with the feeling of hindrances of sensibility and the feeling of superiority at the overcoming of the hindrances. This formal structure is the hinge between the feeling of morality and the other pleasures relevant for judgments of taste. It connects them by way of a process in which moral feeling is added to the other pleasures. But formal likeness gives rise not only to the moral law's aesthetic representation (which the likeness causes to be additive) but to any possible relation of aesthetic feelings such as those of the beautiful and the sublime to the absolutely good. Furthermore, such a relation can have the nature only of an appendage. It follows that for a correct understanding of how the morally good can be linked to pure aesthetic judgments, it is imperative to pinpoint the exact reasons for their formal similarity to each other.

What possible relation, then, can the feelings of the beautiful and the sublime have to the morally good? The definition of the beautiful in the "Analytic of the Aesthetical Judgment," and to some extent the definition of the sublime as well, is far from suggestive in this respect. No wonder that after having put the fourfold distinction of the aesthetically relevant pleasures into place, Kant, while claiming to draw the consequences of what he has established in the "Analytic," proceeds in the "General Remark" to a subtle redefinition of beauty and sublimity: "The *beautiful* is what pleases in the mere judgment (and therefore not by the medium of sensation in accordance with a concept of the understanding). It follows at once from this that it must please apart from all interest. The *sublime* is what pleases immediately through its opposition to the interest of sense" (107). Thus recast, the difference between the beautiful and the sublime rests on the different fates to which they subject the sensible. As we shall see hereafter, this redefinition is necessary for attaching the question of interest to disinterested judgments of taste. In any case, in the beautiful, the sensible is felt to be subjectively purposive for contemplative understanding in general. Since no definite purpose intervenes in such a judgment, the sensible is "reduced" to the mere form that is beneficial for the powers of cognition. It is a disinterested judgment in that the sensible is stripped here of all appeal to the senses (and to the definite concepts of cognition). The sublime, by contrast, is characterized by an all-out resistance to the sensible, and such resistance is felt to be subjectively purposive in terms of practical reason. A judgment upon the sublime is thus an even more disinterested judgment than the one upon the beautiful. Radically turning away from the sensible, it subjectively predisposes the mind to the ideas of reason. Both treatments of sensibility in these judgments, says Kant, "are purposive in reference to the moral feeling. The beautiful prepares us to love disinterestedly something, even nature itself; the sublime prepares us to esteem something highly even in opposition to our own (sensible) interest" (108). Despite the difference between the two pure aesthetic reflective judgments, the way they deal with the sensible opens the space in both for a relation with moral feeling. More precisely, Kant describes them as judgments that prepare the subject for moral feeling. The reason for these aesthetic judgments' anticipatory evocation of moral feeling rests with the status they allot to the sensible. These judgments treat the sensible rather as moral judgments do. In other words, what makes these judgments upon the beautiful and the sublime intimations of moral feeling is nothing less than their disinterestedness. To the extent that judgments upon the beautiful are witness to a disinterested love of a prime object of sensible interest—nature—and to the extent that judgments upon the sublime estimate that the sacrifice of all interest is purposive for higher considerations, they anticipate that other kind of disposition of the mind: the disposition for ideas, or purely intellectual (i.e., moral) judgment. Although entirely distinct from moral feeling, the disinterestedness constitutive of both judgments of taste predisposes them to relate to moral feelings in a mode of relating that Kant calls preparatory. This means that without such disinterestedness they could not assume this preliminary role at all. Furthermore, by giving up on disinterestedness, in other words, by lacking a formal analogy to intellectual judgments, the aesthetic judgment would also fail to provoke any (moral) interest.

Before discussing how reason can take an interest in disinterested judgments of taste, we need to deepen our understanding of how such judgments of taste "prepare" us for moral judgment. Although the beautiful is also said to be purposive in reference to the moral feeling, the feeling of the sublime, and even more narrowly, the sublime in its dynamical aspect, realizes this possibility most properly. In the sublime, Kant recalls, "the unattainability of nature [is] regarded as a presentation of ideas" (108). When faced with an object or a spectacle of nature that we fail to comprehend cognitively even though we "extend our empirical faculty (mathematically or dynamically) . . . reason infallibly intervenes [*so tritt unausbleiblich die Vernunft hinzu*], as the faculty expressing the independence of absolute totality, and generates the unsuccessful effort of the mind to make the representation of the senses adequate to the [ideas]" (108). Undoubtedly, reason's intervention in judgments of the sublime makes these judgments apt for preparing us to experience moral feeling. But how are we to understand this intervention? Does it not at first suggest that reason has been absent from the imagination's attempt to comprehend nature in its totality by extending itself? Furthermore, if reason infallibly supervenes when nature becomes unattainable to the imagination, is it a power very different from the sensible power of the imagination? Coming up to the empirical faculty, reason's intervention consists in adding itself to the imagination. This addition takes place only after the imagination has extended itself yet still has failed to comprehend nature aesthetically. At that moment, the addition becomes infallible. But if reason has not personally been involved, and is a faculty of an entirely different kind, how can it add itself to the imagination in the first place? How are we to think its arrival, and in what way is it present in the sublime?

Kant specifies that at the very moment when the imagination, despite having extended itself, fails to discover an aesthetic fundamental measure for the whole of nature, reason intervenes in the shape of the idea of the supersensible. As the imagination becomes deprived of its aesthetic comprehending powers before a sublime object or spectacle of nature, the *thought* of a supersensible measure or standard forces itself upon this faculty. Although even nature in its totality could not serve to present this idea objectively, Kant holds that the aesthetically unattainable nature can be construed as the presentation of the idea of the supersensible. If reason infallibly joins the empirical faculty in its quandary, it does not add itself from the outside, as it were, to the imagination's doings. Instead the imagination itself is led to do something out of the ordinary, namely to conceive of a supersensible idea, something that can only be thought, and thereby becomes aware of its own supersensible determination or destination. It is thus not the heterogeneous faculty of reason itself that intervenes in the imagination's perplexed situation but, rather, reason in the form of the imagination's realization (and actualization) of the thought of a destination, or determination, different from the sort of epistemological destination the imagination realizes in its usual employment. Clearly, the imagination itself sets out to conceive of the supersensible idea and hence of its own supersensible potential. The imagination alone arrives at the realization that there is a higher standard for comprehending infinitely unbounded nature, without knowing exactly what this standard consists in, and it alone realizes the existence of such a standard in its failure to comprehend nature. Indeed, the very judgment that the incomprehensible phenomenon of nature is subjectively purposive—hence, sublime—does not come about without a sense of a higher destination of the mind. Kant writes:

> But this idea of the supersensible, which we can no further determine—so that we cannot *know* but only *think* nature as its presentation—is awakened in us by means of an object whose aesthetical appreciation strains the imagination to its utmost bounds, whether of extension (mathematical) or of its might over the mind (dynamical). And this judgment is based upon a feeling of the mind's destination, which entirely surpasses the realm of the former (i.e. upon the moral feeling), in respect of which the representation of the object is judged as subjectively purposive.

In fact, a feeling of the sublime in nature cannot well be thought without combining therewith a mental disposition which is akin to the moral. (108–9)

Yet even though judgment upon the sublime is not possible without the feeling of a destination of the mind that is different from its involvement with nature, this is not yet the supersensible destination of which the moral feeling is the expression. If the mental disposition present in aesthetic judgments upon the sublime resembles (*ähnlich*) the moral feeling, it does so to the extent of having all the formal characteristics of moral feeling, but without itself being properly one. The prime characteristics of this feeling immanent to aesthetic judgment—a feeling that forms the basis for judging the representation of nature that unseats the imagination as subjectively purposive—are spelled out in the following passage:

And although the immediate pleasure in the beautiful of nature likewise presupposes and cultivates a certain *liberality* in our mental attitude, i.e. a satisfaction independent of mere sensible enjoyment, yet freedom is thus represented as in *play* rather than in that law-directed *occupation* which is the genuine characteristic of human morality, in which reason must exercise dominion [*Gewalt*] over sensibility. But in aesthetical judgments upon the sublime this dominion is represented as exercised by the imagination, regarded as an instrument of reason. (109)

What makes aesthetic judgments upon either the beautiful or the sublime resemble the moral disposition is that in both a certain freedom with respect to the sensible has been gained. In the judgment upon the sublime, however, the sensible is disowned altogether in the name of a felt higher destination of the mind. As we have seen, this treatment of the sensible constitutes the aesthetic judgment's disinterestedness. Moreover, this negative relation to the sensible (and to existence) opens up within the aesthetic judgment a dimension that is not unlike the one that constitutes moral feeling. It is in the judgment upon the sublime, in particular, that this similarity is the greatest. But in this latter aesthetic judgment, it is not reason itself that resists and rejects sensibility. Rather, the imagination is the agent of this exclusion of the sensible. As a result, Kant can say that the imagination can here be represented as a proxy of reason. From the perspective of morality, the imagination certainly operates in the sublime judgment like an instrument of reason. But since reason is not present as such, that is, present in a determined way, in aesthetic judgment, the imagination does not draw on the faculty in question. It acts alone. Rather than abdicating to reason, the highest sensible faculty, by depriving itself (violently) of what makes it a sensible faculty, even acquires an autonomy of sorts. It contracts a self for itself, and turns itself into a faculty with an identity of its own.[4] Yet although the imagination's self-sacrifice of what characterizes it in its usual, empirical employment bestows upon it "an extension and a might greater than it sacrifices," Kant adds that "the ground of [this extension and might] is concealed from itself" (109). While the imagination *feels* the deprivation, it does not *know* what purpose it serves. But if the negative satisfaction that characterizes the feeling of the sublime is judged to be subjectively purposive in view of an undetermined higher destination and determination of the mind, the sublime feeling is still not yet a moral feeling. Indeed, precisely because it is sublime, this feeling is not moral. The expansion of the imagination, and the might it feels itself to have acquired by the sacrifice of the law that determines its ordinary, empirical employment, is empty. They demonstrate only the mind's ability to discover totality in the absolutely formless. But in fact this extension has carved out within it the space—a depression, of sorts—necessary for receiving moral ideas. In sum, as the example of aesthetic judgment upon the sublime demonstrates in a privileged fashion, the fate incurred by sensibility—in the case of the sublime, this also includes the imagination's own fate as a sensible faculty—causes the aesthetic feeling to have the formal characteristics analogous to those of moral feeling. Given that the imagination deprives itself of its sensible nature in the immanent feeling of a higher destination and determination of the mind without knowing what the latter's ground is, no determined concept operates in the aesthetic judgment in question. Consequently, there is nothing moral in predicating sublimity. Nonetheless, by making room for a higher determination of the mind by surrendering all standards of the senses (though what that determination may be remains undetermined), the aesthetic judgment upon the sublime acquires a formal resemblance to moral judgment. Yet, however formal, the resemblance of aesthetic judgment upon the sublime to moral judgment attracts the attention of reason. The formal nature of the disinterested judgment of taste compels reason to step forward and, in principle, to take an interest in the aesthetic feeling of the sublime. From everything we have seen, this is an interest that arises solely because of what the judgment of taste is capable of achieving when it remains radically disinterested.

But before explicitly broaching the interest reason brings to the sublime, a further remark on the distinct way in which reason bears on aesthetic judgment upon the sublime is certainly appropriate. In a discussion that has the flavor of Kant's precritical and empirical *Observations on the Beautiful and the Sublime*, Kant considers how certain affects, by resisting nature within us, permit one to classify them as sublime.[5] In the course of his remarks, Kant admits that such resistance against everything sensible in the sublime makes it a quite abstract mode of representation. And yet, he writes:

> We need not fear that the feeling of the sublime will lose by so abstract [*eine dergleichen abgezogene*] a mode of presentation—which is quite negative in respect of what is sensible—for the imagination, although it finds nothing beyond the sensible to which it can attach itself, yet feels itself unbounded by this removal of its limitations; and thus that very abstraction [*Absonderung*] is a presentation of the Infinite, which can be nothing but a mere negative presentation, but which yet expands the soul. (115)

As previously seen, the very elimination of all sensible, hence intuitable, presentation in the sublime enables the imagination to enter into a relation of sorts to the purely intellectual. The above passage permits one to grasp with greater accuracy how the imagination's bracketing of the sensible propels reason to join it, what "reason" means in this context, and hence how the relation between the imagination and reason that characterizes the sublime (and that distinguishes it from the beautiful in which the imagination relates to the understanding) is to be thought. Indeed, the imagination's resistance to the sensible (and its interests) is achieved through a separation by means of which it cuts itself off (*Absonderung*) from everything sensible. Having thus severed itself from the sensible, and even from itself as a sensible faculty, the imagination allows reason to add itself to it. But it is not reason in person that steps forward to join the imagination. By isolating itself from the sensible, the imagination has subjected itself to an operation formally similar to the one that reason demands. By cutting all relation to the sensible, the imagination thus opens up a possible relation to reason in judgments upon the sublime. In sum, if the imagination and reason are in a subjectively purposive relation in the sublime, this relation is merely for the self-severing of the imagination from the sensible, by which it becomes unbounded (denaturalized, as it were), and thus, as Kant states, the merely negative presentation of the intellectual power. Schematically speaking, the relation between the imagination and reason in the sublime is one in which a severing of the relation to the sensible has changed the nature of the imagination to the point that it bears a formal similarity to reason. Consequently, reason can be said to have linked onto the imagination's doings, not in the sense that reason itself would have become involved, but in the sense that the imagination's resistance to the sensible is rational.[6] Reason can, therefore, also be seen to take an interest in the imagination's activity in judgments upon the sublime.

The question of interest first emerges in the "General Remark" in the context of another one of Kant's powerful reminders that the Third Critique's transcendental investigation of aesthetic judgments is restricted to the analysis of pure aesthetic reflective judgments, in other words, to aesthetic judgments free of definite concepts. Following a discussion of the strict conditions under which alone the sight of the starry sky, the ocean, or the human figure can give rise to an aesthetic judgment, rather than to a judgment of the senses or a teleological judgment, Kant concludes that if the judgment is determined by sensation or a concept of the understanding, "it may be conformable to law, [but] cannot be the act of a *free* judgment" (111). But a free judgment such as an aesthetic judgment must also be free of intellectual concepts, that is, concepts of reason, or ideas. No determined concept of reason is to serve as its ground. Kant thus objects to the use of notions such as "intellectual beauty or sublimity," the further reason being that the intellectual itself bars all positive commerce with the realm of the aesthetic. He writes:

although both [intellectual beauty and sublimity], as objects of an intellectual (moral) satisfaction, are so far compatible with aesthetical satisfaction, that they *rest* upon no interest, yet they are difficult to unite with it because they are meant to *produce* an interest. This, if its presentation is to harmonize with the satisfaction in the aesthetical judgment, could only arise by means of a sensible interest that we combine with it in the presentation; and thus damage would be done to the intellectual purposiveness, and it would lose its purity. (111)

The morally good is something that pleases in and for itself in that it is purposive in itself. Purely intellectual satisfaction in the good is therefore as disinterested as aesthetic satisfaction with the beautiful or sublime. However, a judgment upon the good always involves some kind of interest, because in a judgment upon the good "there is always involved the concept of a purpose, and consequently the relation of reason to the (at least possible) volition, and thus a satisfaction in the *presence* of an object or an action" (41). Now, by virtue of their intellectual (or moral) quality, intellectual beauty and sublimity are bound to produce interest. As a consequence, such beauty could not be pure. Furthermore, if such beauty were to allow for aesthetic satisfaction, the interest to be produced by the intellectual and moral would necessarily belong to the order of the senses. Under these circumstances, however, the purity of the intellectual or moral would therefore be compromised. The notion of intellectual beauty or sublimity is thus thoroughly self-contradictory. But Kant's refutation of such a notion is not merely negative. Indeed, by implication, the argument that something (such as the morally good) that is bound to produce interest cannot lend itself to a direct aesthetic presentation without contaminating the latter's aesthetic nature already suggests the possibility of an indirect presentation that would harmonize with the satisfaction in aesthetic judgment, in that this satisfaction would combine with a nonsensible interest. Such a configuration would preserve full aesthetic satisfaction. In a nutshell, Kant here advances the view that, aesthetically speaking, the interest produced by the morally good can be a nonsensible interest only if the judgment is to remain an aesthetic judgment. Kant announces here as well that if reason is to take an interest in the beautiful and the sublime, it can also be only an intellectual interest. This is, then, also the point where one begins to understand the full impact of Kant's reformulation, in the "General Remark," however subtle, of beauty and sublimity in terms of the fate incurred by the sensible in their respective representations. This redefinition clears the space for the introduction of an interest that is not sensible and that can be added to aesthetic representation without damaging the latter's constitutive disinterestedness.

As we have previously seen, Kant had admitted moral feeling's aesthetic compatibility. Such compatibility, we recall, arises exclusively from the subject's negative relation to sensibility in the process of the intellectual determination of the will. The feeling associated with the subject's overcoming of hindrances in the order of sensibility enables the modification of the subject's state into an aesthetic representation of the absolute law. Thus, if the morally good is to be judged aesthetically, this can be achieved solely by way of the sacrifice that it demands of sensibility. From the perspective of sensibility, the moral law is adverse to the interest of sensibility. In fact, as Kant contends, the moral law "makes itself aesthetically known to us through sacrifices" (111). The satisfaction in aesthetic judgments about the morally good is also only "negative, i.e. against this interest [of sensibility], but regarded from the intellectual side it is positive and combined with an interest" (112). To judge from everything we have seen, this latter interest derives from nothing less than the deprivation of the interest of the senses. From the viewpoint of morality, intellectual interest stems from the sacrifice of all sensible interest in the aesthetic representation (of the moral law). This is the (only) sense that the expression of an interest in the disinterested can have. Yet the aesthetic presentation of the moral law remains an aesthetic presentation. It consists in the (intuitable) presentation of the (self-)violation of the sensible. But at the same time, the sensible's retreat is also ("positively") a presentation of the moral law, since the interest that the latter cannot but produce is, as a result of the sacrifice of the interest of the senses, inevitably a nonsensible interest rather than a sensible one. No loss of purity occurs here, whether aesthetic or intellectual. The aesthetic presentation remains pure in that it is only the indirect presentation of the law; the interest that combines with that presentation has become intellectual.

A natural consequence of the integrity of the aesthetic and the intellectual is "that the intellectual, in itself purposive, (moral) good, aesthetically judged, must be represented as sublime rather than beautiful" (112). The feeling of the sublime is a feeling in which sensibility is sacrificed, but which is also combined with a certain pleasure, because this sacrifice attests to a higher power in us. Because of the sublime's intransigence with respect to the sensible, it is the preferred mode for aesthetically judging the morally good. But there is another, even more essential reason for this preference. Given that in a sublime representation, a radical evacuation of everything sensible opens up the possible reference to the unconditionally good, the sublime is a judgment that (though still aesthetic) deprives itself almost entirely of anything aesthetic. In sum, within the spectrum of aesthetic reflective judgments, judgment upon the sublime is also a kind of judgment that sacrifices itself even as an *aesthetic* reflective judgment in order to accommodate the moral law. It is barely an aesthetic reflective judgment anymore. Let us not forget, however, that in the sublime the mind discovers merely that it has an additional supersensible destination. In the sublime feeling, no positive reference to reason in any determined sense takes place. But the discovery of the mind's intellectual destination and determination at the expense of the sensible enables the sublime to serve also as an aesthetic representation of the morally good (even though such representation can be aesthetic only on the condition that no definite ideas of the good are involved). In principle, such a judgment can, therefore, also cause interest.

With this reformulation of the sublime, I return to Kant's analysis of the beautiful arts and their potential for being morally relevant. To begin with, let us recall that although the "General Remark" did not categorically preclude the beautiful from having a possible relation (for formal reasons) to the morally good, the sublime was recognized as the privileged representation in which such a relation could be found aesthetically. It is thus within the shadow of what has been established so far about the sublime that the question of an interest in pure judgments upon the beautiful needs to be approached. Granted that the beautiful, too, can cause interest, it is quite significant that Kant, as we will be able to verify, accords the beautiful of nature a privilege in this respect.[7] By contrast, only a rather slim portion of man-made art—the art of genius—is capable of sustaining a moral interest. As is evident from the chapters here under discussion—chapters 41 and 42—the beautiful of nature meets Kant's approval because the judgments about such beauty are disinterested, and thus have the potential of being immediately interesting. The purpose of Kant's elaboration on the arts is precisely to find out whether art, or one kind of art, is compatible with disinterested judgments and as a result disposed to provoking interest.

Kant opens his inquiry into a possible moral interest in the beautiful by arguing that although pure aesthetic judgment excludes all interest as its determining ground, it does not follow "that, after it has been given as a pure aesthetical judgment, no interest can be combined with it" (138–39). How is one to understand such posteriority? What kind of relation can this be if it comes only after disinterested beauty has been judgmentally established, and if, furthermore, the interest that is to be combined with this beauty—an interest in the disinterested—is not to take place at the expense of the constituting disinterestedness? Since a pure judgment of taste in itself is entirely disinterested, any interest must be of the nature of a post hoc addition that does not compromise the purity of a judgment that, as we have previously seen, rests on a certain isolated activity of the faculties involved. The interest to be combined with such a judgment can, therefore, only be "indirect, i.e. taste must first of all be represented as combined with something else, in order that we may unite with the satisfaction of mere reflection upon an object a *pleasure in its existence* (as that wherein all interest consists)" (139). What are these manifestly exterior concerns that could invite one to take an interest in the beautiful? Kant distinguishes two kinds of concerns that can connect with the judgment upon the beautiful. One is empirical, namely, the "inclination proper to human nature" to socialize; the other is "intellectual, [namely] the property of the will of being capable of *a priori* determination by reason." Kant continues, "Both these involve a satisfaction in the presence of an object, and so can lay the foundation for an interest in what has by itself pleased without reference to any interest whatsoever" (139). Given the transcendental sweep of Kant's inquiry into how the disinterested beautiful can become the object of an interest, I will linger only briefly on the empirical concern with the existence of beautiful things. Since feelings are private and singular, the unique ability to communicate a feeling such as the pleasure associated with the beautiful explains the human interest in the beautiful, in that human beings have a natural propensity toward society. In essence, the interest that human beings can connect with taste derives from the latter's furthering of this human inclination. It is an interest, Kant suggests, that arises within society as a *means* to advance communication, and that is thus not only indirect but also mediate and, consequently, empirical. As a transcendental investigation, however, the Third Critique has the task of exploring a possibly more fundamental way in which beauty and interest can combine, in a relation that remains indirect but is also immediate. Of course, there is the interest in the charms that nature bestows upon its beautiful forms. This is an interest that is indeed immediate, but it is also empirical. But in the framework of a transcendental inquiry, only the question of an interest that "may have a reference, although only indirectly, to the judgment of taste *a priori*" (140) will be of importance.

The empirical interest taken in the beautiful is primarily social and serves to further social life. The connoisseur of art who looks at beautiful objects on display not only wishes to share his pleasure with others but also, in regarding these objects as objects of art, judges them with a concept available to all. By contrast, a possible indirect interest in the beautiful that would be immediate and *a priori*—an interest that Kant calls intellectual—would have to arise in solitary contemplation. The solitary spectator and judge of a beautiful wildflower in which he takes interest, unlike the art connoisseur, has no mediate design of communicating his observations to others. Moreover, he looks at this beautiful object with his own eyes alone. Indeed, deprived of all universally shared concepts and reduced to its minimal facultative abilities, the solitary mind is disposed to contemplate, through aesthetic reflective judgments, forms in which it can subsequently take an intellectual interest. I note that this emphasis on solitary contemplation of natural beauty—the only beauty to cause an immediate interest in its existence—as an activity that arouses such an interest (as an addition to what obtains in the disinterested judgment of taste) signals an analogy to solitary contemplation of a sublime "object": both the judgment upon the beautiful and that upon the sublime presuppose a solitary subject. In fact, strict self-isolation, that is, the cutting of all natural ties to human others, can be sublime. In the final part of the "General Remark," after distinguishing several states of mind, especially enthusiasm and apathy, as affects that demonstrate a power to resist sensibility and that consequently can be judged sublime, Kant brings up an even more extreme form of affective resistance to the sensible. He writes: *"Separation [Absonderung] from all society* is regarded as sublime [as well] if it rests upon ideas that overlook all sensible interest. To be sufficient for oneself, and consequently to have no need of society, without flying from it, is something bordering on the sublime, as is any dispensing with wants" (116). With "separation from all society," Kant evokes a sublime affect that not only completes his taxonomy of sublime states of mind but also is interesting for exclusively intellectual reasons. Whereas beautiful and sublime satisfactions (resting on disinterested judgments) provoke an interest because of their general communicability, which interest is therefore empirical, "separation from all society" opens the possibility of a sublime affect that is interesting precisely because it refuses such communicability and in the same breath the empirical interest that comes with communicability. The interest that such a state of mind incites is indeed immediate. Complete isolation from society is a sublime affect because it testifies to intellectual concerns that override even this last residue of the sensible, that is, sociability and communicability. The interest taken in such a sublime has no mediate reasons. It attaches itself to this extreme form of a sublime affect on merely intellectual, or moral, grounds. A case in point is sadness that is exclusively due to moral ideas. It is a sadness of individuals who—for moral reasons alone, and not out of misanthropy or anthrophoby—have renounced the need for society and communication. With this possibility of a state of mind that is so extreme that no empirical interest can attach to it but that the subject finds immediately interesting, the "General Remark" sets the stage for a discussion of a nonempirical interest in the beautiful. Of course, that this possibility is discussed by Kant with reference to the sublime is no accident. The concern with existence, or more precisely with a moral interest, arises primarily in the "presence" of the faculty of reason. It involves an intellectual judgment. Whereas only the imagination and the understanding are in play in pure judgment upon the beautiful, the imagination refers already to reason in judgments upon the sublime.

Before I proceed with the analysis of a possible indirect and immediate interest in the beautiful, let me determine, as precisely as possible, what it is that Kant seeks to figure out. Otherwise, we will not be in a position to assess the stakes of the inquiry as a whole. Kant asks whether there is an *a priori indirect relation*—a relation, consequently, made possible by the very nature of the disinterested judgment—between pure taste and a concern with existence. It is quite a paradoxical question, which inquires into the possibility of appending (*angehängt*) an interest to "taste, taken in its purity," an interest that is not mediate, hence not empirical, but that already inheres in the disinterested judgment itself without jeopardizing its disinterestedness. Such an a priori appendix made possible by pure taste, and on the condition that taste remains pure or entirely disinterested, is to be found in the intellectual interest that can be combined with pure judgments of taste. Kant spells out the stakes of his inquiry: "if an interest should be detected as bound up with this form [that is, indirectly, but in a priori fashion], taste would detect for our faculty of judging a means of passing from sense enjoyment to moral feeling; and so not only would we be better guided in employing taste purposively, but there would be thus presented a link in the chain of human faculties *a priori*, on which all legislation must depend" (140). The demonstration of an indirect but a priori appendable interest in pure beauty and taste would allow one to argue that pure, disinterested beauty plays an intermediary and mediating role between charm and moral feeling, or more generally between nature and freedom. But it is also clear, from what we have established so far, that for a judgment about the beautiful to have moral interest, it must remain fully disinterested and hence entirely distinct from a judgment about the good. Given that all other feelings of pleasure and displeasure are linked to interest, the sole pleasure found in disinterested judgments concerning the mere form of objects reveals that nature (feeling) and reason are capable of agreement. Disinterestedness on the level of the senses—a possibility realized solely in the case of entirely pure judgments of taste—is the provision under which alone a relation between the beautiful and ethics is conceivable. At this point one can no longer overlook the fact that the rigorous sorting out of pure judgments of taste from judgments of the senses and the morally good is the very condition under which aesthetic judgment upon the beautiful can even begin to assume a kind of mediating role and eventually serve as a symbol of morality.

The indirect interest capable of combining with disinterested beauty, sought by Kant to support the idea of an agreement in principle between nature and freedom, cannot be a mediate interest. Beauty is not to be a means for the satisfaction of some need or desire, if it is to have an affinity to the morally good. The interest to be taken in the beautiful must therefore be immediate. Yet, as Kant is quick to remark, the beautiful of art does not meet this requirement. Only the beautiful of nature fulfills this condition. Kant opens his discussion "Of the Intellectual Interest in the Beautiful" by "admit[ting] at once that the interest in the *beautiful of art* (under which I include the artificial use of natural beauties for adornment and so for vanity) furnishes no proof whatever of a disposition attached to the morally good or even inclined thereto" (141). The beautiful of art thus seems to bar all intellectual interest. Undoubtedly, Kant's reasons are at first only empirical, since he takes note only of the fact that those who are connoisseurs in taste are rarely of good moral character. But as we shall see, there are more fundamental reasons, reasons owing to art qua art, that prevent one from taking an intellectual interest in artificial beauty. First, however, the privilege that Kant accords to natural beauty with respect to moral feeling needs to be highlighted. He writes:

If a man who has taste enough to judge the products of beautiful art with the greatest accuracy and refinement willingly leaves a chamber where are to be found those beauties that minister to vanity or to any social joys and turns to the beautiful in nature to find, as it were, delight for his spirit in a train of thought that he can never completely evolve [*den er sich nie völlig entwickeln kann*], we will regard this choice of his with veneration [*Hochachtung*] and attribute to him a beautiful soul, to which no connoisseur or lover [of art] can lay claim on account of the interest he takes in his [artistic] objects. (142)

From the perspective of mere judgment of taste, there is no difference between beautiful objects of nature and of art. What alone counts for such a judgment is whether the object has form. Hence, no consideration of superiority obtains here. But at the very moment interest is taken in the beautiful, the artificiality of art becomes an issue. With the question of how moral ideas can link onto the beautiful, only the forms of nature would seem to guarantee the immediacy of this interest, and thus its intellectual nature. Although the passage just quoted serves only to emphasize the high esteem we bestow upon those who abandon the beautiful social world of the art lovers in order to contemplate solitarily the beauties of nature (thereby revealing a cultivated moral inclination that deserves respect), an analysis of the delight that one's spirit discovers in such contemplation brings to the fore the reasons for the superiority of natural over artificial beauty.

The contemplation (*Beschauung*) of nature in which the good soul takes an immediate interest concerns solely the beauty of nature's forms. Kant tells his reader, "it is to be remembered . . . that I speak here strictly of beautiful *forms* of nature, and I set aside the *charms* that she is wont to combine so abundantly with them, because, though the interest in the latter is indeed immediate, it is only empirical" (141). The intellectual interest in the beautiful of nature is immediate only if it is connected with the forms of nature. Considering Kant's understanding of form, this restriction is not surprising. Natural form alone reveals an aspect of nature that is a priori desirable. Indeed, in disinterested judgments of taste, whenever the mind is capable of sensing in objects of nature forms that the understanding is incapable of recognizing, nature displays its suitability to cognition. The mind attaches an immediate interest to perceived natural form, or the beautiful of nature, because this form indicates nature's adequacy to our faculties of cognition. It is only natural, one might say, that the mind takes an interest in such form and that it thus desires, in an immediate fashion, the presence (existence) of form in nature. One is reminded here of a statement in the "General Remark": "the beautiful prepares us to love disinterestedly something, even nature itself," and from this it follows (on the grounds of the bracketed interest in the sensible) that the beautiful is a feeling "purposive in reference to the moral feeling" (108). But the interest experienced by the mind when faced with beautiful form in nature is not moral interest itself. According to Kant, however, it is at least "favorable to the moral feeling" (141). The feeling, Kant says, is "akin to the moral feeling [*der Verwandschaft nach*]" (143) because what is at stake in it is nature's susceptibility to the precepts of freedom. But Kant adds: "he who takes such an interest in the beauties of nature can do so only in so far as he previously has firmly established his interest in the morally good" (143). In other words, to be able to take an active interest in natural beauty, one must have judged (disinterestedly) the mere forms of the maxims of reason on their own merit and developed an interest in their practical realization and presence—a point similar to that already established in the "General Remark" about our disposition toward the sublime. Apart from pure disinterested judgments concerning the suitability of mere natural forms to cognition in general, a moral formation (*Ausbildung*) not unlike the culture necessary for making judgments on the sublime is required if one is also to manifest a concern with the existence of natural forms. On this condition alone is it possible to develop "without any clear, subtle, and premeditated reflection" "a similar immediate interest in the objects of the former [aesthetic judgment] as in those of the latter [moral judgment]" (143). But, for reasons analogous to those obtaining in the case of the sublime, the need for the moral cultivation in question makes such immediate interest in the beautiful a rare commodity. It is an uncommon, if not extraordinarily rare, mental disposition.

A further condition for the interest in natural beauty to be immediate, Kant observes, is that the thought "that nature has produced it" "must accompany our intuition and reflection on beauty." "On this alone is based the immediate interest that we take in it. Otherwise there remains a mere judgment of taste, either devoid of all interest, or bound up with a mediate interest" (142). Kant brings this point home with his famous examples of the artificial flowers and the mischievous boy who knew how to imitate the song of the nightingale. They are unable to provoke immediate interest because their forms are not perceived as natural. For beautiful forms to arouse such interest, nature must be seen to produce them as signs not only of its passive nonadversity to human cognition but also of its active offering of itself to a disinterested representation (and hence, in the final step, to cognition). Only when nature is seen to be technical and to produce its beautiful forms in accordance with rules beneficial for cognition in general does it incite interest. As Kant remarks, the faculty of the intellectual judgment (reason) takes an interest in the mere forms of practical maxims, which please immediately (as instances of the good) without this judgment's being based on any interest. In addition, intellectual judgment involves an interest in the realization of rational ideas. Intellectual judgment wishes

> that the ideas (for which in moral feeling it [reason] arouses an immediate interest) should have objective reality, i.e. that nature should at least show a trace or give an indication [*eine Spur zeige, oder einen Wink gebe*] that it contains in itself a ground for assuming a regular agreement [*gesetzmäßige Übereinstimmung*] of its products with our entirely disinterested satisfaction (which we recognize *a priori* as a law for everyone, without being able to base it upon proofs). Hence reason must take an interest in every expression on the part of nature of an agreement of this kind. Consequently, the mind cannot ponder upon the beauty of nature without finding itself at the same time interested therein. (143)

Such immediate interest in the forms of nature arises only if they are perceived as active hints by nature of its pliability to reason. Nature's beautiful forms must present themselves as expressions of its suitability to reason, as nature's way of speaking to us, and for us to attach an interest in them, an interest in what in itself pleases in a disinterested fashion. As Kant observes, the beautiful forms of nature are "that cipher [*Chiffreschrift*] through which nature speaks to us figuratively" (143). Reason has a stake in the existence of the mere natural forms that we judge purposive in disinterested pleasure, and beneficial to cognition in general (and hence beautiful), only if these forms are also perceived as the characters or ciphers through which nature announces to us that its products are intended for us. For, indeed, the existence of these forms is proof of the objective realization in nature of what is so different from it: the ideas, the exigencies, the precepts of reason.

At this point, it is certainly appropriate to confront a quite common misunderstanding in Kant criticism. The interest taken in natural beauty is easily misunderstood as resulting from the moral ideas themselves that are associated with such beauty, or that are supposed to inhere in the latter. But if this were the case, judgment upon natural beauty would no longer be a judgment of taste. Further, the interest in the beautiful would be merely mediate (as would be the case if something like intellectual beauty were conceivable). I recall that the question Kant addresses in chapters 41 and 42 of the *Critique of Judgment* concerns an interest in disinterested judgments of taste. If natural beauty is superior to artificial beauty, it is because natural beauty pleases in and by itself, rather than "by means of its purpose" as does artificial beauty (144). The interest provoked by natural beauty is not caused by the moral idea itself that can be found associated with it. Although the beauty of an object of nature interests us insofar as it is attached to a moral idea, it is not this idea itself that is decisive. Kant amply clarifies that what makes natural beauty immediately interesting is not the fact that a moral idea is associated with it but instead "the character [of this beauty] as such in virtue of which it is qualified for such an association, and which therefore intrinsically belongs to it [*sondern die Beschaffenheit derselben an sich selbst, dass sie sich zu einer solchen Beigesellung qualifiziert, die ihr also innerlich zukommt, interessiert unmittelbar*]" (144, trans. modified). Natural beauty attracts only our interest because internally, in and by itself, natural beauty qualifies for the appendage in question. Interest in the beauty of nature arises merely by virtue of natural beauty's capacity for the indirect and a priori moral appendix, and in no way by virtue of the moral ideas themselves. Even though the beautiful pleases without any consideration of existence whatever, and does so by way of its form alone, it incites an interest because it manifests an a priori disposition (a structural potential) of nonadversity, or rather, of a susceptibility to an indirect moral addendum. This potential for an a priori appendix renders natural beauty superior to the beautiful of art. Kant concludes:

It is easy to explain why the satisfaction in the pure aesthetical judgment in the case of beautiful art is not combined with an immediate interest, as it is in the case of beautiful nature. For the former is either such an imitation of the latter that it reaches the point of deception and then produces the same effect as natural beauty (for which it is taken), or it is an art obviously directed designedly to our satisfaction. In the latter case the satisfaction in the product would, it is true, be brought about immediately by taste, but it would be only a mediate interest in the cause lying at its root, viz. an art that can only interest by means of its purpose and never in itself. (144)

The beauty of nature alone deserves our interest because only such beauty permits the attachment of an indirect and immediate moral appendage. If certain products of the beautiful arts happen to incite our interest, it is because they deceive us by taking on the appearance of nature. This, then, is the context within which Kant will briefly discuss the arts in the Third Critique. This context shows that art is not the prime focus of Kant's aesthetics and that the basic propositions of his aesthetics are not derived from the study of the arts. Natural beauty is the paradigm for what Kant calls form and for the judgment of taste thereupon. Natural beauty is privileged as well when the question arises concerning beauty's relation to the morally good. This ascendancy of nature over art in Kant's aesthetics is clear evidence of this aesthetics' para-epistemic concerns. Kant's analysis of the arts in chapters 43 through 53 is an appendix of sorts to the beautiful of nature: all the more so in that its aim is to carve out within the realm of what Kant calls "only [*nur*] art" (145)—that is, the art that only imitates nature and to the beauties of which no immediate interest lets itself be attached—one rather meager domain of art, namely the art of genius. The products of the art of genius achieve without deception the look of products of nature and therefore can also legitimately command our interest.

7

The Arts, in the Nude

As Kant elaborates it throughout the Third Critique, form is not an objective attribute of certain things. It is not a construct of lines that objectively draws the contours of a thing, or the delineation (*Zeichnung*) that interlaces its characteristics into the definite shape of a figure. Form names a subjective condition concerning the representability of certain things, that is, their fitness for being judged. If "formal" is synonymous with "merely subjective,"[1] the form of an object designates its agreement with and adequacy to the powers of cognition. The perception of such form, in the face of things for which the understanding does not provide concepts, elicits pleasure and causes the mind to call these things beautiful; such pleasure arises in the mere judgment of taste, regardless of whether the things are of nature or of art. More precisely, since beautiful form can be predicated of art objects only if they are not viewed as works of art, the concept of form in the *Critique of Judgment* presupposes the methodological privileging of natural over artificial beauty. Given the epistemic, or rather para-epistemic, thrust of this aesthetic concept of form, this bias should not come as a surprise. The judgment that something is beautiful because of its form alone merely establishes its cognizability in the absence of all determinate concepts. For Kant, nature is the totality of what is cognizable. To judge a thing to be beautiful is to hold it to have natural form, the form of an object of nature, and such a judgment concerns things of nature just as it does things of art.

Kant's aesthetics is not primarily concerned with the fine arts; indeed, it is frankly not about art at all. In judgments about natural beauty, "I need not have beforehand a concept of what sort of thing the object is to be, i.e. I need not know its material purposiveness (the purpose), but its mere form pleases by itself in the act of judging it without any knowledge of the purpose" (154). By contrast, judgments concerning the beauty of artificial objects are not aesthetic reflexive judgments.

If the object is given as a product of art and as such is to be declared beautiful, then, because art always supposes a purpose in the cause (and its causality), there must be at bottom in the first instance a concept of what the thing is to be. And as the agreement of the manifold in a thing with its inner destination, its purpose, constitutes the perfection of the thing, it follows that in judging of artificial beauty the perfection of the thing must be taken into account. (154)

Art requires a determined concept, or purpose, of the product, and thus when art is judged as such—through judgments that take its work character explicitly into consideration—it cannot, by definition, lend itself to a pure judgment of taste. The attested beauty of objects of art does not concern their (mere) form but instead stems exclusively from the perfection with which the originary concept or purpose guiding its production has been realized in the product. Such a judgment, therefore, is a determining judgment, as distinct from a reflective aesthetic judgment. But toward the end of the "Deduction of Pure Aesthetical Judgments," having established the tenets of his aesthetics—*ex abrupto*, it would seem—Kant nonetheless proceeds to a discussion of the arts, even though the section is limited to barely ten chapters. Notwithstanding the fact that art cannot be thought without a concept of its intended objects, is it possible that art (or perhaps some art) allows for pure judgments of taste, and more precisely, for judgments concerning their beauty, even in the full awareness that the artistic objects are man-made. Indeed, this possibility is explored by Kant throughout chapters 41 through 53. Given the constitutive importance of the concept or the purpose in art, the question that such a possibility faces concerns primarily the status and fate of the concept in the arts. Thus we must inquire into what the nature of the concept must be if works of art are to warrant aesthetic reflective judgments, and into the precise conditions under which an object of art, despite being the effect of a concept, can still lay claim to beauty.

Artificial beauty does not hold any aesthetic privilege in Kant's aesthetics, and nor does it enjoy any special privilege with respect to morality. The two chapters preceding Kant's discussion of the arts (chapters 41 and

42) demonstrate that the beautiful of nature alone is capable of producing an immediate interest (from a moral perspective). Yet if under certain conditions the arts, or rather a certain art, can be shown to become beautiful, and hence to become the object of a pure disinterested aesthetic judgment, there is the possibility that even artificial beauty could become an object of intellectual interest. Since Kant's analysis of man-made beauty is framed by his discussion of the interest in the arts, the question of how concept-sponsored objects can be judged beautiful will overlap with the investigation of the precise conditions under which artificial beauty can, like the beautiful of nature, trigger an immediate moral interest.

Before embarking on the analysis of the beautiful arts, Kant proceeds to a threefold demarcation of art in general, in order to distinguish it from nature, science, and handicraft. All three differences are of consequence, but the difference from nature is the broadest and most decisive, and it requires our special attention. Kant explains: "Art is distinguished from nature as doing (*facere*) is distinguished from acting or working generally (*agere*), and as the product or result of the former is distinguished as work (*opus*) from the working (*effectus*) of the latter" (145). Nature, in the context of this demarcation, is defined as "working generally [*Handeln oder Wirken*]." As compared to the "doing" of art (in general), "acting" or "working" is a more extensive concept. Since "by right we ought only to describe as art, production through freedom, i.e. through a will that places reason at the basis of its actions" (145), the "doing" of art, which results in works, is an "acting" or "working" that is subject to a purpose or end. The doing of art is a "doing," rather than an "acting" or "working," because it is subject to a finality. One must assume that any work of art—unlike the "working" of nature, whose effects (*Wirkung, effectus*) do not exhibit rational deliberation and are consequently without finality—is such that "a representation of it in its cause must have preceded its actual existence" (146). Art in general is the doing of human agents, and differs from the acting or working of nature in that it presupposes a concept, in accordance with and in view of which its works are produced, and to which these works owe their form. By contrast, the effect of the acting or working of nature comes about without a will or a determinable purpose. In a word, the activity of art in general is fully determined (because it yields to a concept), whereas the working and acting of nature lack any determining end and are entirely undetermined. Unlike the concept-driven *facere* of art, the *agere* of nature is an undetermined activity; and unlike the effects of works of art, those of nature do not evidence any conceptual blueprint. This is the crucial difference between art and nature in general, and it provides the backdrop against which Kant will subsequently define art in terms of skill rather than of science, and as characterized by play (though not without a mechanism) rather than by compulsory work (as is the case in handicraft). The distinction between *facere* and *agere* also subtends the further distinction of the fine, or beautiful, arts from the arts in general, and most important, the distinction of the beautiful arts from the arts of genius. On this distinction between *facere* and *agere* also hinges the possibility of securing a status for the beautiful of the arts of genius that would compare favorably with the beautiful of nature, to which Kant has given his undivided attention until this point.[2]

The admission that art can be beautiful implies that art is initially divided into beautiful and nonbeautiful art. But Kant proposes an even more complex division:

> If art which is adequate to the *cognition* of a possible object performs the actions requisite therefore merely in order to make it actual, it is *mechanical* art; but if it has for its immediate design the feeling of pleasure, it is called *aesthetical* art. This is again *pleasant* or *beautiful*. It is the first if its purpose is that the pleasure should accompany the representations [of the object] regarded as mere *sensations*; it is the second if they are regarded as *modes of cognition*. (148)

The counterpart of mechanical art is aesthetic art, which in turn separates into pleasant and beautiful art. Just as *agere* is the broader concept in the distinction between *agere* and *facere*, mechanical art is the more embracing category in the division of mechanical from aesthetic arts. Kant has already emphasized that even the free arts are not without mechanism, and aesthetic art describes a limited domain within the mechanical arts. The mechanical arts render actual the pregiven concepts of desirable things, with the result that the produced objects are fully adequate to their concept. These arts presuppose the artist's or artisan's knowledge of the thing that is to be realized with relative skill. From this conception of the mechanical arts, it follows that any judgment concerning their products is determining, and not aesthetic, since such judgments proceed from the pregiven concept and evaluate the product's adequacy (or its perfection) according to this concept. By contrast, if the goal of the products of the arts is not so much to be recognizable (in terms of their concepts) as to cause the immediate feeling of pleasure, the arts in question are aesthetic. But if the pleasure caused by the representations of the products of these latter arts is a pleasure of the senses, we are dealing with pleasant arts. By contrast, the beautiful, or fine, arts are those whose objects give rise to representations in which the powers of cognition are in play, and which are felt pleasurable because these powers have come to stand in a relation that is beneficial to cognition generally. In distinction from the pleasant arts, such as the "charming arts that can gratify a company at table" (148), the beautiful arts bring about representations that are not of the order of the senses but must be regarded, as Kant puts it, "as modes of cognition." More specifically, the pleasure that arises immediately from the representations of beautiful objects of art concerns their form, and consequently relates to their capacity to yield a representation that is beneficial for the cognitive accomplishments of the faculties.

Contrary to both the mechanical arts and the pleasant arts, the beautiful arts have representations that are purposive in themselves. They further cognition generally; that is, they are purposive without a (definite) purpose or concept. But does this not imply that, strictly speaking, the beautiful arts are not arts at all? In the beautiful arts, action or working does not become determined by a concept, and hence is not transmuted into a doing. But obviously, beautiful art still falls within the domain of the arts; it is not nature, and qua art, it presupposes not only skill but a concept that is to be rendered actual. These two seemingly exclusive exigencies—free doing *and* a concept or purpose, or more generally, nature and *téchnē*—must somehow combine in the production of the beautiful arts. The task that Kant faces is to think these two exigencies together. In other words, as *arts*, the beautiful arts are subject to determining or cognitive judgments, but as *beautiful* arts they invite aesthetic reflective judgments, whose determining ground is the immediate pleasure provided by the representations (of form) that further the powers of cognition. We need to ask under what conditions a product of the arts can lend itself to a pure, disinterested judgment about its form alone. Simply put, what conditions must obtain for one to be able judge an artwork as beautiful?

Before sketching out an answer to this implicitly contradictory demand, Kant formulates the paradox in chapter 45, entitled "Beautiful Art Is an Art in so far as It Seems Like Nature." He writes: "In a product of beautiful art, we must become conscious that it is art and not nature; but yet the purposiveness in its form must be seen to be as free from all constraint of arbitrary rules [*willkürliche Regeln*] as if it were a product of mere nature" (149). Products of beautiful art must be judged as such: that is, as the result of works originating in a doing, in an activity guided by concepts that become actualized in these products. They must be judged in the full awareness that their form is a function of concepts and is realized in conformity with what Kant calls a mechanism, which is to say, compulsory rules. At the same time, the purposive form of the product of such doing must seem to be free from any concept and from any (man-made) rules to which its producer would have firmly adhered in order to create the object. The object's form must appear to be the effect of a general acting or working, which is to say, of an activity of nature. If the product reveals rules deriving from a determined concept that has acted as its model, the product in question will not impart a representation to the powers of cognition that puts them into harmonious swing. The product of beautiful art must be free of all determining constraints, and Kant specifies: "On this feeling of freedom in the play of our cognitive faculties, which must at the same time be purposive, rests that pleasure which alone is universally communicable, without being based on concepts. Nature is beautiful because it looks like art, and art can only be called beautiful if we are conscious of it as art while yet it looks like nature" (149). In sum, then, art is beautiful when the purposiveness of its form lacks the purpose or concept that characterizes the products of art as such. Art is beautiful if, in addition to being the product of a determined design (and hence, guided by a concept), it is at the same time a product for which no determining concept has stood as a model.

As Kant recalls, in judging the beauty of a thing (regardless of whether it is an object of nature or of art), one is concerned only with its form,

> which pleases in the mere act of judging it (not in the sensation of it or by means of a concept). Now art has always a definite [*bestimmte*] design of producing something. But if this something were bare sensation (something merely subjective), which is to be accompanied with pleasure, the product would please in the act of judgment only by mediation of sensible feeling. And again if the design were directed toward the production of a definite [*bestimmten*] object, then, if this were attained by art, the object would only please by means of concepts. But in both cases the art would not please *in the mere act of judging*, i.e. it would not please as beautiful but as mechanical. (149)

Two interrelated questions arise at this juncture. First, if all art qua art, including beautiful art, inevitably presupposes a design, what must happen to the definite concept behind the design of the beautiful arts if their products are to be judged beautiful, that is, if they are not to please as mechanical? Second, if only determining judgments are appropriate for judging the arts as arts, what justifies the bracketing or suspending of determining judgment in the case of beautiful products of art? What permits one to judge the beautiful arts as products of a design without inevitably having to resort to cognitive judgment? There is only one possible solution to this dilemma: the concept in question, without which the beautiful arts could not be arts, cannot be a definite concept but must instead be undetermined. Only if the requisite presiding concept is rendered indefinite, and its determinateness blurred, does art become beautiful art. This is the sole condition under which the determining judgment required by art qua art can be stripped of its determining power and be "reduced" to *"the mere act of judging"* which asserts the beauty of the product. Pure aesthetic judgments upon the beautiful are possible only in the absence of all determinate concepts, and this condition is met when the concept in man-made art is rendered indeterminate. But whereas an absence of concepts for certain objects of nature is passively experienced by the mind that judges the objects beautiful, such an absence for objects of the beautiful arts must be "actively" engendered in order for them to be judged *beautiful*, and for the judgments to be aesthetically reflective judgments. A double denuding, then,—a double *Entblößung* (the term is mine, not Kant's)—of the arts has to occur for an object of the beautiful arts to come into existence and for the judgment relating to it to be indeterminate. With the divesting of the definite concept behind the design to produce a beautiful object, the mere form of the object becomes exposed, judgment is stripped of its determining character, and *"the mere act of judging"* is laid bare, that is, the sort of judging suited to beautiful objects. Where the concepts guiding their production have undergone such an operation of denudement, or of indetermination, the products of art have the look of objects of nature, that is, of objects of a general acting or working. In a further extrapolation, where it also becomes clear that such denuding of the arts makes up the task of genius, Kant explains: "A product of art appears like nature when, although its agreement with the rules, according to which alone the product can become what it ought to be, is *punctiliously* observed, yet this is not painfully apparent; [the form of the schools does not obtrude itself]—it shows no trace of the rule having been before the eyes of the artist and having fettered his mental powers" (150). The passage deserves attention because it gives us a first hint at how the indetermination of the concept, required for the production of beautiful art, is achieved. Moreover, the passage enables us to straighten out a possible misunderstanding. Although the work of art must agree meticulously with the rules that it presupposes as such, for it to be beautiful no definite rule may show through the work; yet this does not mean that the work is a work of art only if it successfully dissimulates its determining rules, and that artistry thus amounts to the technical skill of producing an illusion of spontaneity. As the reference to the form expounded by the schools demonstrates, no established rule—no known rule whatsoever—may, in the end, have presided over the artist's creative process. Yet if all artistic production requires a rule, rule in the beautiful arts can be only an unknown rule: a rule, more precisely, that has not been known (by anyone, including the artist) before it appears in an individual work of beautiful art. Otherwise, the rule to which the work must conform—in all respects and in totality, for it to have beautiful form—would have been before the eyes of the artist, and his creation would lack the required look of nature. Since the rule that instructs the production of beautiful works of art is an unknown and unpossessed rule—this is one of the senses of this rule's indeterminateness—it could be called a rule *in statu nascendi*, a rule that has not yet been codified as a rule. Thus the rules that are necessary for producing artworks that can be judged beautiful are not identical to those of formalist and aestheticist conceptions of art. The singular rule of a beautiful work of art corresponds to one specific harmonious arrangement of the faculties that is beneficial to cognition in general, as distinct from the rules and from every "form of the schools," though of course the singular rule can be turned into such an academic form once it has taken shape in a singular work. In conformity with this harmonious arrangement, the artwork displays its beautiful form: a form that must be mere form and not a determining or cognitive form. The schools codify the rules governing these forms and turn them into precepts for copying beautiful products of art. The forms are thereby rendered determinate, and hence are incapable of ever again leading to the creation of what Kant terms exemplary beauty.

According to Kant, art that has become beautiful through the requisite indetermination of the concept "must necessarily be considered as art of genius" (150). Indeed, the prime accomplishment of genius, if not the sole one, is to render the concept, or rule, indeterminate. Making the beautiful arts a function of genius means first of all suggesting that their beauty does not originate in aesthetic norms of any sort: in particular those norms concerning the imitation of nature, but also formalist and aestheticist rules. Without exception, as will become clear hereafter, such norms belong to art as craft (*téchnē*) and have no bearing whatsoever on beauty. All such rules determine what the product is to be insofar as it is a product of a will and of rational deliberation. Kant writes:

Every art presupposes rules by means of which in the first instance a product, if it is to be called artistic [*künstlich*, "artificial"], is represented as possible. But the concept of beautiful art does not permit the judgment upon the beauty of a product to be derived from any rule which has a *concept* as its determining ground, and therefore has at its basis a concept of the way in which the product is possible. Therefore beautiful art cannot itself devise the rule according to which it can bring about its product. But since at the same time a product can never be called art without some precedent rule, nature in the subject must (by the harmony of its faculties) give the rule to art; i.e. beautiful art is only possible as a product of genius. (150)

Since the beauty that characterizes the beautiful arts cannot derive from rules originating in art itself, it must arise in nature, in an acting or a working that remains indeterminate. To be precise, it must have its origin in the nature of the subject, in a natural disposition of the faculties that conforms to the law yet is without a definite purpose or concept; in other words, it must originate in the free play of the cognitive faculties. This natural disposition—*ingenium*—is the property of genius, or indeed is genius itself. As Kant explains in chapter 49, genius properly consists in nothing more nor less than "the happy relation" (160) between the faculties of the imagination and the understanding. Thus the sole relevance of genius in Kant's aesthetics is to solve the paradox posed by the beautiful arts: namely, the idea that certain products of art can be conformed to a rule without a definite concept, and hence be beautiful. This definition also attests that Kant, spurning an eighteenth-century tradition of genius, approaches the problematics of genius from an exclusively transcendental (that is, critical) perspective.[3] According to Kant: "*Genius* is the talent (or natural gift) which gives the rule to art. Since talent, as the innate productive faculty of the artist, belongs itself to nature, we may express the matter thus: Genius is the innate mental disposition (*ingenium*) *through which* nature gives the rule to art" (150). As an artist, the genius is involved in an activity, in a doing that is "free" (as opposed to "mercenary" handicraft). But, paradoxically, such freedom comes from nature, in that nature gives the genius the rule guiding what he or she produces.[4] A harmonious innate mental disposition of the faculties is required by all cognition, but here determined concepts are still absent; thus the genius is the paradoxical "entity" in which nature passes into freedom. Indeed, the rule that nature gives to art—a proportioning of the faculties that is beneficial for cognition in general—is an undetermined rule, in that no definite concept limits the play of the faculties to cognition in a rigorous sense. Where this innate natural disposition has bearing as a rule upon art and artistic activity (*agere*), such activity is rendered indeterminate, with the effect that its products become beautiful rather than mechanical. Thus the mental configuration of the genius is one that reveals the possibility of a suspension of necessity in the realm of nature, and this in turn demonstrates nature's susceptibility to the causality of freedom. Although this configuration is not good in the moral sense, its openness to a freedom from determined rules is a further indication of nature's perviousness, and receptiveness, to reason.

While discussing the example (i.e., works by other artists) that the genius needs in order to act upon his or her natural talent, Kant makes a number of observations that, although they concern a phase prior to the creation of beautiful art itself, can help us understand the rule involved in such creation. He asks:

If now it is a natural gift which must prescribe its rule to art (as beautiful art), of what kind is this rule? It cannot be reduced to a formula and serve as a precept, for then the judgment upon the beautiful would be determinable according to concepts; but the rule must be abstracted from the fact, i.e. from the product, on which others may try their own talent by using it as a model, not to be copied but to be *imitated* [*nicht der Nachmachung, sondern der Nachahmung*]. (152)

The rule is not a conscious concept that has guided the genius in the creation of a beautiful work of art, but something intuited (and abstracted) post facto from the products of genius by other talented individuals. Kant notes, "the ideas of the artist excite like ideas in his pupils if nature has endowed them with a like proportion of their mental powers" (152). The example serves as a model against which others may measure their own talent, but is not copied. What is at stake in imitation is not *natura naturata* but *natura naturans*. The work of genius becomes the occasion for another talented individual to imitate the creative process itself by which the exemplary work has been brought to life: by abstracting a rule from it, or in other words, by becoming attuned to the play of the faculties to which the exemplary work owes its existence. To imitate is to create in accordance with the original rule that ("unconsciously") governed the genius's production—the undetermined rule governing the playful cooperation of the faculties for the benefit of cognition in general.

Let us bear in mind that such imitation is not yet the brilliant creation that one expects from people of genius. It is merely an exercise necessary for talented individuals to animate their gift. The rule that they abstract (and which as such involves a cognitive process) cannot yet be the rule that presides over original and unique creation. Let me also suggest that although the abstraction of the rule from exemplary works of art does not make this rule a set of definite concepts, this is the moment at which determined aesthetic conceptions and ideologies can come to light. Indeed, if a budding genius requires a model on which to train his talent, this is because a mechanical moment is necessary to the process of actualizing the genius's gift. In fact, it is a moment that must occur in the creation of beautiful art in general. Despite the fundamental difference between mechanical and beautiful art, there is, Kant contends, "no beautiful art in which there is not a mechanical element that can be comprehended by rules and followed accordingly, and in which therefore there must be something *scholastic* [*schulgerechtes*] as an essential condition" (153). Without a dose of mechanical rules and a conception of a purpose, the *product* of art would not be a product of *art*. It would be, Kant writes, "a mere product of chance." This holds true of beautiful art as well. According to Kant, genius furnishes "rich *material* [*Stoff*] for products of beautiful art"; however, the product's "execution and its *form* require talent cultivated in the schools, in order to make such a use of this material as will stand examination by the judgment" (153). Kant's recourse here to the form/matter distinction is quite unusual within the whole of the Third Critique. Throughout the *Critique of Judgment*, the mere form of an object is typically contrasted not with matter but with the object's determining cognition. Even in the present context the traditional form/matter distinction is considerably complicated by the rich material that Kant evokes, since this material, as we will see later, is that of the aesthetic ideas and thus of something rather different from matter in the classical sense. It remains, however, that form in this context refers to the determined aesthetic rules and codified conceptions of art that certain aesthetic schools have abstracted from great works of art, and according to which the rich material of genius must be shaped if it is to be judged as conforming to taste.[5]

Form, then, is a significant element in beautiful artworks, when it is understood in the sense of a set of determined aesthetic rules abstracted from great works of art and codified by schools—a sense that is entirely distinct from the prevailing concept of form in the Third Critique. It is an important element in art precisely to the extent that art is art and not nature. However, in chapter 47 Kant elaborates on the fact that the beautiful arts can be handed down to posterity only by means of their exemplary role in the genius's training of his talents, and certain of Kant's remarks in this context reveal the true significance of "form" in this sense. As he explains, the handing down of the arts "cannot be done by mere descriptions [of the exemplary works of fine art]"; and as for these descriptions themselves, "only those which have been preserved in the old dead languages, and which are now reduced to the learned languages, can become classical" (152, trans. modified). The reputed classicism of these descriptions is thus a function of their having been cast in dead languages, languages that, by definition, are learned only in the schools. These descriptions are insufficient, as Kant suggests, to secure the bequeathing of the models, although they play their part in the process. The real vehicle of transmission consists in the geniuses' study of the great classical works themselves, in order to *imitate* the rules that have presided (without the artists' awareness) over their production. Only through such imitation do the dead works of the past become alive again, and by studying the mechanism of these dead works, the genius brings them alive and hands them down as models. One gathers from this that the mechanism, the rules, and the forms of past works of genius are dead, and remain dead as long as they are simply being learned (and applied). In that it processes the rich material intrinsic to the classical models, form is indeed a kind of dead element of them, and remains dead as long as it remains describable, hence determinable and teachable. Although no beautiful art comes into being without reference to such a dead substratum, copying it as such will not give rise to beautiful art. But when the form of dead works is imitated by talented individuals and brought to life in what (as we will see) amounts to a process of indetermination, the classical models are effectively handed down as models that have stood behind the creation of new beautiful works of art.

While analyzing the relation of genius to taste, Kant meticulously circumscribes the part that the dead element in question occupies in the beautiful arts. Taste is required to give form to the rich material furnished by the genius: as Kant observes, "to give this form to the product of beautiful art, mere taste [*bloss Geschmack*] is requisite." He stresses that "this form is not, as it were, a thing of inspiration or the result of a free swing of the mental powers, but of a slow and even painful process of improvement, by which [the genius] seeks to render it adequate to his thought, without detriment to the freedom of the play of his powers" (156). Kant thereby dispels the misconception that taste amounts to nothing more than a mechanical application of the rules provided by the aesthetic schools. Undoubtedly, the artist must be aware of these schools and of their conceptions of what is beautiful; he must, as we noted above, have tried his talent according to the rules abstracted from the art of genius. But if "by taste the artist estimates his work after he has exercised and corrected it by manifold examples from art or nature, and after many, often toilsome, attempts to content himself he finds that form which satisfies him" (155), the mere taste required to form this beautiful work of art is too unusual to reflect a school concept of form. Furthermore, the inordinate amount of work that goes into such form-giving intimates that form-giving consists in a toilsome "reduction" of the taste sanctioned by the schools to mere taste; that is, it reduces the taste of the schools to the taste that judges, not how well a work meets the standards of taste set by these schools, but only whether the object produced has the form of mere form.

Kant goes even a step further, and suggests that form as it is understood by the various aesthetic schools has no bearing on beautiful art. After noting that "taste is merely a judging and not a productive faculty," he continues: "What is appropriate to it is therefore not a work of beautiful art. It can be a product belonging to useful and mechanical art or even to science, produced according to definite rules that can be learned and must be exactly followed" (156). The reference to these "definite rules," according to which taste judges man-made objects, indicates that at this point Kant has in mind not the pure judgment of taste (whose appropriate object is mere form, preferably that of objects of nature) but rather the products of art in general. The taste shaped by the schools is directed toward the evaluation of artistic products, and applies primarily if not exclusively to products that are of the order of the useful and mechanical arts. The examples provided by Kant of the objects of such judgments of taste include such things as "table appointments." Taste, in this context, judges the "pleasant form" of these useful or mechanical products, or as he also puts it, their form for having "the form of beautiful art [*Form der schönen Kunst*]" (156).

As we saw in the preceding chapter, Kant has qualified the beautiful arts as imitations, going so far as to say they deceptively simulate natural beauty. Since the beautiful arts therefore presuppose a concept of their object and a determined rule for rendering it, they are not to be confused with the arts of genius, whose whole effort aims to render any given rule indeterminate. After distinguishing the art of genius from the arts that endow works of craft with a pleasing form, Kant undertakes a final narrowing down of the only art that merits the qualification of an art of genius, and distinguishes it further from art that merely emulates the beautiful art of genius.

The distinction concerns mechanical products that please not only because they are tastefully shaped or designed but because they have the look of beautiful art; however, it is precisely because this imitative art form vies with the beauty of the fine arts that it must be kept separate from them. One might regard this distinction as scholastic, not least because Kant gives no examples of an art that only emulates great art. Nonetheless one could think of some such examples: copies of great artworks, works in the style of great masters, and works produced according to the rules of the schools. The distinction may be tenuous, but it is, I believe, one that needs to be made: first, because of the difference between what pleases through the tasteful shape of its form and what pleases because it imitates beautiful form; and second, because, as we will see, there is indeed a beautiful art, an art distinct from the mechanical arts per se, that is spiritless, and hence not beautiful like the art of genius. In any case, the form given to useful and mechanical artifacts to make them look pleasant or even to make them reflect the form of beautiful art is, according to Kant, "only the vehicle of communication and a mode, as it were, of presenting" these artifacts. Form in this sense comprises such things as pleasant arrangement, composition, and delineation—in short, everything associated with a formalist and aestheticist conception of form. In other words, the form that is judged here corresponds to what we would call today a product's (architectural, artistic, or industrial) design. Form, especially in a formalist and aestheticist understanding, is thus essentially an attribute of the arts in general and the object of determining, or cognitive, judgments rather than reflective aesthetic judgments.[6] The form that correlates artifacts with the form of beautiful art is not the same form that they would have were they products of genius. As Kant remarks, certain products "of which we expect that they should at least in part appear as beautiful art," and in which "we find nothing to blame . . . on the score of taste" in that they are "neat and elegant," "exact and well arranged," "solid and at the same time elaborate," are nevertheless spiritless (156). That is, when taste evaluates the form of a beautiful work of art according to established rules of what is considered beautiful, it is not truly dealing with beautiful art. It mistakes the beautiful for the mechanical when it judges a work according to formalist or aestheticist criteria. Yet, as we have seen, taste is a necessary element in the productions of genius. If this is the case, taste must be something other than a power that evaluates the extent to which an artifact observes the rules set forth by schools and dominant tastes.

Beautiful art is distinct from natural beauty; as an art of genius, and to the extent that it is art, it presupposes a concept. But if it is to be distinguished from the arts in general, including arts that take on the form of the beautiful arts, this concept cannot be a determinate concept. Before exploring how "concept" is to be understood here, we must return to Kant's differentiation between natural and artificial beauty. In chapter 48, Kant proceeds to the following terse distinction: "A natural beauty is a *beautiful thing*; artificial beauty is a *beautiful representation* of a thing" (154). This distinction, which is easy to misunderstand as being based on the difference between the original and its copy, by opposing "thing" and "representation of a thing," stresses the artificiality of the representation. Although the distinction seems to oppose a material, natural thing to a representation (of a thing) that has been given material reality, this is not to be taken to imply the independence of representation in artificial beauty. As will become clear in a moment, the distinction does not suggest that in the beautiful arts representation occurs for its own sake. A natural thing is judged beautiful if its form allows for the representation of it as a thing; by contrast, an artificial thing is judged beautiful primarily if its form allows it to be the representation of a thing. Such judgments concern not whether the representation is an excellent copy of a beautiful thing, but whether the representation succeeds in representing a thing at all. When it is found to succeed in having the form of a thing (whatever it may be), the representation is judged beautiful. In short, artificial beauty exclusively concerns the representation as a product, and thus involves the form itself of the representation—that is, its form *as* a representation. Kant provides a further hint at how the beautiful representation of an object, as it characterizes artificial beauty, is to be understood: he writes that it "is properly only the form of the presentation of a concept, by means of which this latter is communicated universally" (155). In the beautiful representation of a thing, no reproduction takes place; no matter how important the represented object is, the beauty of its representation derives neither from this object nor from the skill involved in its depiction. Rather, Kant suggests in this highly condensed statement, the beauty of such a representation is due to the form that serves to present a concept and hence to render a concept intuitable. The representation is judged beautiful not because it is representation for its own sake but because it accomplishes the presentation of a concept. By giving form to the concept, that is, by presenting it in a thing, the representation renders the concept itself (rather than the thing) universally communicable. Thus the concept in question is not (simply) the concept of the thing; instead the thing serves only as the occasion of presentation of the concept in question. In what sense, then, is "concept" to be understood here? The question is all the more urgent since the beautiful *representation* of a thing is not the same as the represented thing. Indeed, as a presentation of the concept—its sensibly intuitable form—the beautiful representation of a thing is not at all the same as the representation of a known thing (one that has already been subsumed under its concept) in the beautiful arts. Otherwise it would be strictly impossible, for instance, to beautifully depict what is naturally ugly.[7] The concept that is presented in the representation of a thing in beautiful art cannot be the determining concept of that thing, the concept by which the thing is known. Bearing this in mind, we can attempt to better grasp the kind of concept involved in the beautiful arts, which are, after all, arts. Only in this way will we be able to understand how artificial beauty can provoke pure reflective judgments of taste, despite the fact that, if they are to take the work character of the beautiful arts into account, such judgments also have to take stock of their inner destination, their purpose, their concept as products of art.

I would recall here that for a product to be beautiful, it is not enough for it to have a form that pleases taste. In fact, if taste is understood as a power for evaluating the pleasing shape of artifacts (especially useful ones), taste and form cannot do justice to beautiful artworks. According to Kant, the criterion that distinguishes works of genius from pleasing artifacts is that the former have spirit (*Geist*). In the section entitled "Of the Faculties of the Mind That Constitute Genius," spirit is identified as the distinguishing trait of the arts of genius. Works of truly beautiful art, as opposed to the beautiful arts that only imitate the form of beautiful art, animate the powers of the mind, putting them purposively into swing. To this end, spirit has recourse to aesthetic ideas—ideas that are the material (*Stoff*) to which spirit gives sensible shape.[8] Spirit presents aesthetic ideas, and thus invigorates the mind by bringing its powers into a relation that benefits representation and cognition in general. Kant defines the aesthetic idea as "that representation of the imagination which occasions much thought, without however any definite thought, i.e. any *concept*, being capable of being adequate to it" (157); the aesthetic idea is, consequently, the "concept" that is presented in the arts of genius. But we must pause here to consider in what sense it can be called a "concept." Kant writes:

If now we place under a concept a representation of the imagination belonging to its presentation, but which occasions in itself more thought than can ever be comprehended in a definite concept and which consequently aesthetically enlarges the concept itself in an unbounded fashion, the imagination is here creative, and it brings the faculty of intellectual ideas (the reason) into movement; i.e. by a representation more thought (which indeed belongs to the concept of the object) is occasioned than can in it be grasped or made clear. (158)

The presentation of a definite concept (of a thing) by way of a representation that belongs to such presentation, but that also exceeds its presenting function if it contains more characteristics and implications than this concept could comprehend, enlarges the definite concept in an unbounded fashion. By placing under a determined concept a representation that causes more thought than the specific occasion requires, the productive imagination transcends thereby the bounds of the concept, and compels the mind to contemplate the possibility of a higher order of comprehension. For this reason such presentation "brings the faculty of intellectual ideas (the reason) into movement." As our earlier discussion has shown, aesthetic ideas are representations produced by the imagination, which resemble rational ideas (rational ideas by definition cannot be sensibly presented) given that it is impossible to discursively exhaust them or conceptually pin them down. As representations of the (productive) imagination, aesthetic ideas are neither concepts (of the understanding) nor rational ideas. They resemble concepts because they are presented by way of sensible things; they bear a likeness to ideas insofar as they give more to think about than any concept can comprehend. Aesthetic ideas are, as it were, enlarged concepts: because they resist any discursive fixity, they are concepts that are not determinate and that therefore resemble ideas. They are also the concepts in view of which genius creates beautiful art; they are, in short, the concepts whose presentation and expression make up works of genius.

Concepts are rendered unbound, or indeterminate, by presentations whose representations contain certain additional or secondary representations beyond those that are essential to the presentation of the concepts. Such partial representations are added on to the forms that are necessary to render a concept intuitable; they overrun the determining power of the concept precisely because, as implications or consequences associated with it, they belong to its presentation. Kant explains: "Those forms which do not constitute the presentation of a given concept itself but only, as approximate representations [*Nebenvorstellungen*] of the imagination, express the consequences bound up with it and its relationship to other concepts, are called (aesthetical) *attributes* of an object whose concept as a rational idea cannot be adequately presented" (158). These aesthetic attributes are loaded onto the form that presents the concept in question, and give much more to think about than what the concept can grasp. As *aesthetic ideas*, these enriched forms of representation intimate that, in addition to the demand of discursive language, another exigency bears on the mind: the exigency of thinking, that is, of reason and its ideas. Kant provides the following summary of his elaborations on aesthetic ideas:

> In a word, the aesthetical idea is a representation of the imagination associated with a given concept [*einem gegebenen Begriffe beigesellte Vorstellung*], which is bound up with such a multiplicity of partial representations [*Teilvorstellungen*] in its free employment that for it no expression marking a definite concept can be found; and such a representation, therefore, adds to a concept much ineffable thought [*viel Unnennbares hinzu denken lässt*], the feeling of which quickens the cognitive faculties, and with language, which is the mere letter, binds up spirit also. (160)

The partial representations add much ineffable thought to a given concept. More precisely, they render the concept indeterminate because they denote attributes for which discursive or conceptual language has no (determinate, and determining) words or concepts. They consist of "an abundance of undeveloped material for the understanding, to which the understanding paid no regard in its concept" (160). Thus spirit, in the aesthetic sense, is bound up with the letter of cognition, and gestures toward thinking (reason) and its exigencies. This is why beautiful works of art have spirit; and this realization brings to light the exact accomplishment of the arts of genius, as arts that express aesthetic ideas. Free from the yoke of the understanding, the imagination, in its productive employment, produces such a multiplicity of additional representations in the presentation of a concept of the understanding that the conceptually inexhaustible meaning of the resulting artwork animates the mind, by putting the power of thinking (reason) into movement. The impossibility of conceptually determining and totalizing the aesthetic ideas expressed in the art of genius is the same as the impossibility of converting the meaning of such works into determining (cognitive) language. The feeling that this induces in us is conducive to the exercise of the faculty of reason. Of course, the feeling of spirit is certainly not reason itself; but on the level of feeling, it is an analogon of reason, as it were. Or rather, it is a feeling that has the potential to vivify a mental capacity of a completely different order: the capacity to think.

If a man of genius is rich in the material of aesthetic ideas, he must also give form to them, express them, and make them universally communicable in beautiful works of art. In fact, Kant remarks, genius is not only the "happy relation [between the faculties] . . . by which ideas are found for given concepts" but also the ability to find "the expression by means of which the subjective state of mind brought about by [these ideas], as an accompaniment of the concept, can be communicated to others" (160). The different arts, and above all, the verbal arts, are the media through which, or as which, such expression takes place.[9] Before addressing the question of the expression of aesthetic ideas and the giving of form that such expression seems to imply, a word of caution is certainly in order. Since the whole problematic of genius exclusively concerns "a happy relation" of the faculties, it has, in Kant's text, a primarily transcendental thrust. The expression of aesthetic ideas by way of a beautifying form must therefore not be understood in terms of anthropology, psychology, sociology, or the history of the arts. Even though Kant occasionally seems to encourage an empirical interpretation of artistic expression, such expression (and the concept of form that comes with it) should be read from a critical perspective.

At first, in discussing expression (*Ausdruck*), Kant seems to be carrying on the legacy of the form/matter distinction. But if form is a contributing factor in expression, is it to be understood here as the orderly configuration of the matter to be expressed? One complication arises from the fact that the form through which the expression is communicated does not shape the material of aesthetic ideas. Instead the expression seeks to communicate the subjective state of mind that accompanies these ideas. But the forms through which the expression is achieved do not format this state of mind either. Kant evokes the talent of expressing the feeling that accompanies aesthetic ideas, and continues:

The latter talent is, properly speaking, what is called spirit; for to express the ineffable element [*das Unnennbare*] in the state of mind implied by a certain representation and to make it universally communicable—whether the expression be in speech or painting or statuary—this requires a faculty of seizing the quickly passing play of imagination and of unifying it in a concept (which is even on that account original and discloses a new rule that could not have been inferred from any preceding principles or examples) that can be communicated without any constraint [of rules]. (160–61)

The representations of concepts loaded with secondary representations brings about a state of mind that induces in us the feeling of a higher power than the power of understanding: that is, the power of thinking. This state of mind cannot be conceptually fixed; and the aim of expression is to make it universally communicable. Since the concept or form through which such expression is to take place does not rest on prior principles or examples, and is communicated without any constraint of rule (and hence is immediate), the concept or form in question must be indeterminate. This concept or form cannot be discursively circumscribed, either. Indeed, everything that has been said so far about taste, and especially the point that the art of genius presupposes a reduction of taste to mere taste, is also valid for expression. Expression does not serve to make aesthetic ideas determinate but instead gives them a form that permits them to put reason into movement—something that can be achieved only by a form that has been rendered indeterminate. Thus the form through which aesthetic ideas are made communicable is in no way already in place in the arts, or already sanctified by some aesthetic doctrine (formalistic or otherwise). In its uniqueness and originality, and in the new rule that it discloses, the concept or form by which the expression is to be brought about emerges as an entirely different order from that of the forms that prevail in art in general. This includes those arts that imitate the beautiful of art, and the forms that have already been realized in the beautiful arts.

According to Kant, artificial beauty is a *beautiful representation* of a thing, as distinct from the *beautiful thing* of natural beauty. As we have seen, the subjective state of mind that accompanies aesthetic ideas is a state that indicates the power of thinking. This feeling that accompanies the undetermined concept of that power must adopt representational form when it is expressed. By being expressed as a *beautiful representation* of a thing, it is not shaped in the way that matter is by form; rather, the feeling of this power takes on the form of form, that is to say, the form that permits this power's representation. Since the feeling in question is only an indication of a power higher than the understanding, it remains indeterminate. When faced with aesthetic ideas, spirit unifies the quickly passing play of the imagination with a concept or form that must therefore also remain indeterminate. Consequently, the representation achieved by the indefinite concept is a beautiful representation. The feat of genius, then, consists in giving the product that expresses aesthetic ideas a form, and more precisely, the form of a thing. Given that what is to be expressed is unnameable, and that aesthetic ideas are bound up with a multiplicity of unnameable representations, this form-giving is indeed a feat. Yet this unnameable lets itself be communicated by way of the form of a thing. It is a beautiful representation of a thing, because this representation exceeds the constraints and the directness of the concept;

but it is, after all, the representation of a thing, at a point where one would have expected a complete failure of the representational powers. A beautiful product of genius causes pleasure because it has form. The universal communicability of the feeling that accompanies aesthetic ideas is at the heart of this pleasure, and puts the power of thinking into movement.

The beautiful arts rest on a double denudement, an indetermination that concerns both form and content; and as arts of genius, they can give rise to pure aesthetic judgments. Unlike the products of all the other arts, which presuppose given concepts, the products of genius produce unheard-of concepts; moreover, these concepts are indefinite. The genius's accomplishment consists in creating intelligibility for something that remains unnameable, where no representation or form seemed possible. He or she does this by producing an indeterminate form and thereby securing the minimum requirement for representation, or a minimal representation. This form arouses disinterested pleasure, but it also hints at a power superior to the understanding and sets into motion the power of thinking, or reason. In a manner similar to the beautiful of nature, the disinterested beauty of the art of genius can cause interest, and this is to say that moral ideas may be linked to it. This interest in the existence of beautiful art arises not because such art contains ideas of reason but because it contains aesthetic ideas that are beneficial to the exercise of the power of thinking.

Let me conclude with a final reflection on the place of the beautiful arts within Kant's aesthetics. If we set aside the beautiful arts' capacity to beautifully render things that are naturally ugly, natural beauty has appeared to be far superior to artificial beauty, in that it conveys hints of a natural susceptibility (sensibility) to the ideas of reason, and hence causes interest. Indeed, Kant insinuates that the beautiful arts' power to evoke moral ideas is rather tenuous. Yet it also transpires from Kant's text that the beautiful arts are necessarily bound up in a relation to the idea of the good. But moral ideas seem to emerge primarily as supplements without which the beautiful arts would inexorably descend into the distasteful, a situation that underscores the fragile status of the beautiful arts. Kant broaches the possibility of a beautiful presentation of the sublime, in order to show that such presentation would not further the fine arts, since it only contributes to making them look more artificial (*künstlicher*). He recalls that

> in all beautiful art the essential thing is the form, which is purposive as regards our observation and judgment, where the pleasure is at the same time cultivation and disposes the spirit to ideas, and consequently makes it susceptible of still more of

such pleasure and entertainment. The essential element is not the matter of sensation (charm or emotion), which has only to do with enjoyment; this leaves behind nothing in the idea, and it makes the spirit dull, the object gradually distasteful [*anekelnd*], and the mind, on account of its consciousness of a disposition that conflicts with purpose in the judgment of reason, discontented with itself and peevish. (170)

Kant reminds us here that form, not artifice, is the essence of the beautiful arts, and by extension, that form is at the heart of a universally communicable pleasure that attunes the mind to the ideas of reason. Kant also mentions again that charm is the opposite of form. Why does he provide these reminders?[10] Since the repeated pleasure taken in the "matter of sensation" does nothing to animate the higher faculties and little by little causes the object to become distasteful (if not abject), there is a danger of losing everything that has been wrested from nature. It is a threat of relapsing into the distasteful, that is, into what absolutely defies all presentation, direct or indirect. Artificial beauty is prone to being enjoyed for its charms and for the emotions it provokes, as we recall from several passages in the Third Critique—in particular chapter 14, where the difference between form and charm is elucidated by means of examples, and chapter 42, which argues the superiority of natural beauty over artificial beauty, because the former alone gives rise to an immediate interest, while the latter ministers to vanity and social joys. The beautiful arts are internally threatened by a possible reversion into something disgusting. Natural beauty, if it is understood as signaling nature's susceptibility to the ideas of reason, triggers an immediate interest; but artificial beauty needs the moral ideas as a supplement to prevent it from relapsing into the distasteful. Kant writes: "If the beautiful arts are not brought into more or less close combination with moral ideas, which alone bring with them a self-sufficing satisfaction, this latter fate must ultimately be theirs [*ihr endliches Schicksal*]. They then serve only as a distraction. . . . The beauties of nature are generally of most benefit in this point of view, if we are early accustomed to observe, appreciate, and admire them" (170). Compared to the "beauties of nature," whose pure forms vivify the faculties of the mind, the beautiful arts are inherently liable to becoming perverted; they may be used merely for entertainment, since they do not have the indirect (yet a priori) disposition that allows an immediate interest to be appended to their beauty.[11] Only an enforced relation to moral ideas can protect them from what is their finite, final, and inexorable fate. But in order for such a correction to be possible, beautiful art must yield to the addendum: it must make such an addendum possible, and lend itself to a correction without which it runs the risk of reverting to what evokes only disgust. But for almost all the beautiful arts, such a correction is exterior, or mediate. It is imposed on them, as it were, from the outside. The arts that fall within the province of genius, however, are immediately beautiful, because they express aesthetic ideas by way of a tasteful form that is entirely original; hence they inscribe within themselves the indirect and a priori relation that permits their linkage with moral ideas. Because they express aesthetic ideas, works of beautiful art animate the faculty of reason and thereby permit an immediate interest in their beauty. Of all the beautiful arts, therefore, the arts of genius alone are shielded from the relapse in question. But, paradoxically, these are also the arts in which nature gives the rule to art, and it is only on this account that they merit inclusion in an aesthetic whose prime paradigm is the beauty of natural forms.

8

Hypotyposis

Kant's invectives against rhetoric in *Critique of Judgment* not only seem to continue philosophy's classical condemnation of that art but at times even seem to share the Enlightenment's open hostility toward it, particularly when they insist that the art of the orator is "worthy of no *respect.*" Indeed, the "treacherous art" of speech seeks "to move men in important matters like machines to a judgment that must lose all weight for them on quiet reflection," Kant notes. Moreover, it is said to be a decadent art that flourishes when states are hastening to their ruin and "true patriotic sentiment has disappeared."[1] Yet Kant's treatment of rhetoric may well reveal greater complexity when scrutinized. Some scholars have already argued that Kant's position on this issue differs from the traditional evaluation of the art of speech in important ways, foremost among them that he would attempt "to assign history the function that classically is accorded rhetoric."[2] What I will suggest in this chapter is that although Kant in the Third Critique fiercely condemns the art of the orator, he does not substitute for it another notion against which the same philosophical objections could be made; instead he argues for a certain philosophical appropriation of rhetoric that transforms its essence. Thus, it is not simply a question of showing that, like all philosophers, Kant too would have recourse to figural inference as a mode of philosophical argumentation. Rather, what I intend to show is that the very scope and thrust of the *Critique of Judgment* depends on an elemental and constructive takeover not of what Kant dismisses as *ars oratoria* but of rhetoric proper, which he conceives of as an integral part of beautiful art.

It is important to remark that the discussion of both the art of the orator and the art of rhetoric proper, that is, of readiness and accuracy in speaking (*Beredsamkeit*), occurs in the *Critique of Judgment* at the moment when Kant, in chapter 51, proceeds to what he terms a tentative classification of the arts on the basis of their ability to *express* aesthetic ideas. If art is conceived of by *analogy* "with the mode of expression of which men avail themselves in speech, in order to communicate to one another as perfectly as possible not merely their concepts but also their sensations," then those kinds of art that achieve such communication through words, or through articulation (rather than through linguistic gesticulation and modulation), are necessarily the superior arts (164). Of the arts of speech, Kant distinguishes two—rhetoric and poetry—but it is the latter that ranks first. The reason for poetry's excellence is that it is freer than rhetoric and therefore in a better position to realize the essence of beautiful art. Poetry, Kant says, "owes its origin almost entirely to genius" and is "least guided by precept or example." Poetry is thus autonomous, up to a certain point at least (170). But it is free as well because it is not subject to any purpose, material or spiritual, theoretical or moral. Poetry, indeed, does not seek payment of any sort. In addition, it promises little and, therefore, escapes deception. In Kant's own words: "In poetry, everything proceeds with honesty and candor" (172). But this freedom from all purpose, that is, this mere "entertaining play with ideas," or "entertaining play of the imagination" (165), nonetheless lets itself "be purposively used by the understanding" (171). Kant writes, "The poet promises an entertaining play with ideas, and yet it has the same effect upon the understanding as if he had only intended to carry on its business" (165). Indeed, because poetry promises very little, it achieves "something which is worth occupying ourselves with [*was eines Geschäftes würdig ist*]" (165). In its play with illusion and its pretense to be little more than mere play, one may ask, what precisely is this business that poetry performs for the understanding?

Poetry's achievement is to provide, "in this play, food for the understanding and, by the aid of imagination, to give life to [its] concepts" (165–66). It combines and harmonizes both cognitive faculties—sensibility and understanding—thus actualizing, as Kant clearly demonstrates in the case of the beautiful, the minimal conditions for theoretical cognition in general, as well as for the pleasure associated with them. Yet, rather than further embroidering on these conditions of cognition in general, Kant seems at this point of his development to emphasize the invigoration of the mind created by the play of poetry. Such invigoration is achieved not by stealing upon and ensnaring the understanding with the aid of sensible presentation but by expanding (*erweitern*) the mind by allowing the imagination to bring form and the laws of the understanding together harmoniously. Instead of leading to an intuitive presentation of a determinate concept, the free play of imagination produces only presentation as such, that is, not determinate intuitive fulfillment of concepts but their fullness, their vivid, lively filling out in general. This indeterminate, intuitive fullness of the concepts that occurs in the play of the imagination in poetry livens up the mind. It conveys life to the mind, a life yet indeterminate, but purposive to the extent that it brings about the minimal arrangement of the faculties necessary for cognition in general.

But poetry also involves reason in its mere play with illusion. Kant writes that poetry

> expands the mind by setting imagination at liberty and by offering, within the limits of a given concept, amid the unbounded variety of possible forms accordant therewith, that which unites the presentment of this concept with a wealth of thought to which no verbal expression is completely adequate, and so rising aesthetically to ideas. It strengthens the mind by making it feel its faculty—free, spontaneous, and independent of natural determination—of considering and judging nature as a phenomenon in accordance with aspects which it does not present in experience either for sense or understanding, and therefore of using it on behalf of, and as a sort of schema for, the supersensible. (171)

By setting the imagination free to conceive of nature as a schema for the supersensible in general, poetry also provides food for reason and gives life to its ideas. Although the ideas of reason cannot, of course, be represented in any determinate manner, the mere fact that nature can be shown to be intelligible to us suggests that it is designed for and adapted to our contemplative faculties. Thus the supersensible can be said to be expressed by nature, not in any determinate manner but in a merely schematic fashion, or rather, since there cannot be a direct presentation of reason, in a merely symbolic fashion. What poetry achieves in this manner is the production of an indeterminate intuition of the supersensible, an intuition without which the supersensible would have no reality in general. Such an intuition, Kant says, *strengthens* the mind, makes it *feel* its spontaneity and autonomy, thus livening up the mind by an arrangement of the faculties in a play that can be said to enact the minimal condition for morality in general.

Whereas poetry is "the art of conducting a free play of the imagination as if it were a serious business of the understanding" and of reason, rhetoric as elegance of speech—eloquence and style—is said to be "the art of carrying on a serious business of the understanding as if it were a free play of the imagination" (165). Rhetoric, which belongs to the beautiful arts along with poetry, is not as free as poetry. Rhetoric lets itself be guided by precepts and examples, which one can assume it borrows from poetry. As eloquence and style, rhetoric has in its power "a wealth of pure speech." It proceeds "without any offense against the rules of euphony of speech or propriety of expression." Where such skills are combined with a clear insight into things human and "a lively sympathy with what is truly good," rhetoric puts the imagination fruitfully into the service of a "lively presentation" through examples of "ideas of reason (which collectively constitute eloquence)," as Kant writes (171–72). Without art (the art of deception), rhetoric, rather than accomplishing a fundamental arousing (*Erweckung*) of the mind—its animating predisposition for cognition and morality in general, a predisposition also found in the free beauty of poetry—creates a lively impression on the mind through vivid examples of subjectively unspoiled actions taken for the sake of what is right. Such vivification of specific ideas of reason is the highest achievement of the orator without art, or in Cicero's terms, of the *vir bonus dicendi peritus*.

But Cicero, Kant insists, may not always have remained true to this ideal. Indeed, even as mere elegance of speech, rhetoric has something dishonest about it. It pretends, says Kant, to be engaged in serious business, but in truth gives something that it did not promise, namely, an entertaining play of the imagination. Rhetoric proper has a touch of deception about it. If the orator who promises a serious business conducts it as if it were a mere play with ideas, it is because he is not free of purposes. He wishes to entertain his audience. This is why rhetoric as elegance of speech, as the lively presentation in examples of concrete ideas of reason, can easily turn into the art of the orator (*ars oratoria*). Such art is one of persuasion. Kant characterizes it as a dialectic, that is, in the aftermath of Aristotle's definition of dialectic as probable reasoning, as a "logic of illusion." This art, which deceives by a beautiful show, "borrows from poetry only so much as is needful to win minds to the side of the orator before they have formed a judgment and to deprive them of their freedom" (171). For this art, Kant has no good word. What amounts in poetry to an arousing of the mind to its independence from nature through a presentation of the supersensible, and amounts in rhetoric to a vivid exemplification of ideas of reason, becomes a mere illusion in the service of the orator's attempt to deprive people of their autonomy. Rather than enhancing the life of the mind by enlarging its ability to judge, the "machinery of persuasion" treacherously saps the audience's spiritual life by ensnaring "the understanding by the aid of sensible presentation" (172).

This classification of poetry and rhetoric, as well as Kant's vituperation against the art of the orator, presupposes that the beautiful arts are the expression of aesthetic ideas. An aesthetic idea, we should recall here, "is that representation of the imagination which occasions much thought, without however any definite thought, i.e., any *concept*, being capable of being adequate to it." Because these ideas "strive after something which lies beyond the bounds of experience," but "especially because no concept can be fully adequate to them as internal intuitions," they "approximate to a presentation of concepts of reason (intellectual ideas)" (157). The presentation of concepts of reason through aesthetic ideas "puts the mental powers purposively into swing, i.e., into such a play as maintains itself and strengthens the mental powers in their exercise," Kant remarks (156). The sensible presentation of the supersensible through aesthetic ideas animates the mind through a purposive combination of its powers, a combination that, as Kant puts it, maintains itself, and that therefore guarantees its autonomy and freedom. Now, it is "properly speaking the art of the poet, in which the faculty of aesthetical ideas can manifest itself in its entire strength" (158). Poetry, then, is the art that produces the animating presentation through which the mental powers are purposively put into swing. Poetry is the art that secures the life of the mind in the first place, the mind's life in general. It would seem from what we have shown up to now that rhetoric derives from poetry and is, thus, secondary. In what follows I do not intend to question this hierarchy. Undoubtedly, what Kant referred to as the "schematization through aesthetic presentation of the suprasensible" is more fundamental, in that it is more animating, than the exemplification of the truly good and right in rhetoric, not to mention the treacherous sensible presentations of the art of the orator.

Yet is it not striking that Kant's attempt to thematize presentation itself, that is, the very principle of the mind's life, resorts to a notion whose origin is most evidently the rhetorical tradition? In chapter 59, entitled "Of Beauty as the Symbol of Morality," he speaks of *Darstellung* (presentation) as sensible illustration, by referring to the Greek concept of *hypotyposis*. This word, from *hypo*, under, below, beneath, and *typosis*, a figure made by molding or modeling, means originally "sketch," "outline." Sextus Empiricus used *hypotyposes* in this sense as the name of his work on the Pyrrhonic philosophy (*Outlines of Pyrrhonism*). A philosophical use of the verbal form *hypotypoun* is to be found in Aristotle's *Metaphysics* and *Nichomachean Ethics*. Although traditionally translated and interpreted as "presenting tentatively, in a rough, schematic outline," Aristotle's use of *hypotypoun* corresponds, as Rudolf Boehm has demonstrated, to a very specific philosophical thought. Rather than meaning an unclear and undetermined sketch or scheme (as opposed to a well-articulated concept), *hypotypoun*, particularly in the discussion of essence in *Metaphysics* (1028 b 31–32), refers to what "forms," shapes, or molds essence itself. The shapedness of essence (*das Wesensgepräge des Wesens selbst*) is, by right, something very different from what essence means in any particular case.[3] Nevertheless, Kant's invocation of hypotyposis does not refer to this technical and philosophical meaning of the term. As his parenthetical explanation of hypotyposis clearly shows, it must be taken as a rhetorical term. Indeed, Kant chooses to define hypotyposis as *subjectio sub adspectum*, that is, "visual presentation," or more precisely, "throwing under the eyes" or "exhibiting under its appearance or aspect." This is the definition of hypotyposis that Cicero gives in *De oratore* when he explains that "dwelling on a single point" and "clear explanation and almost visual presentation of events as if practically going on" are very effective devices in stating a case or amplifying a statement.[4] Quintilian's account of the figure in *De institutione oratoria* further emphasizes this vivid illustration's specificity when he characterizes it as an "appeal to the eye rather than the ear."[5] Hypotyposis thus does much more than explain or provide clarity. Whereas "the latter [the clarity of the narrative] merely lets itself be seen . . . the former [vivid presentation] thrusts itself upon our notice [*se quodam modo ostendit*]," Quintilian writes.[6] In short, as a rhetorical notion, hypotyposis means an illustration in which the vividly represented is endowed with such detail that it seems to be present, and to present *itself* in person and completely by itself. Some of the figure's synonyms, such as *enargeia*, *evidentia*, *illustratio*, and *demonstratio*, further stress the ability of hypotyposis to present a subject matter as if it were actually beheld by the eye.

As a result of the figure's emphasis on vivid sensible and visual presentation, hypotyposis has all the qualifications of pictorial representation. Du Marsais translates "hypotyposis" as "image" or "painting" (*tableau*),[7] and Fontanier speaks of it as a mode of painting that is so vivid and energetic that it puts things, as it were, before the eye. Hypotyposis, he concludes, turns a narration or description into an image, a *tableau*, or even a living scene.[8] With this, another important feature of the rhetorical notion of hypotyposis comes into view; for what is a *tableau* if not the gathering and grouping of a manifold into a unique ensemble? Indeed, hypotyposis is traditionally tied to subjects that have all the characteristics of a whole. According to Henri Morier, hypotyposes vividly depict, as if in paint, collective civil activities, events of war, natural catastrophes such as tempests, shipwrecks, and earthquakes, public ceremonies and festivities, plagues, and so on. The hypotypotic description of these subjects, Morier continues, serves to underline the exemplarity, the moral grandeur, of the *tableaux* in question—human activity and solidarity in work, the cruelty and fatality of natural forces, the tragedy of fate, courage and sacrifice—as well as the sheer pleasure of the eye.[9] These are the major features that characterize hypotyposis as a rhetorical figure of style, and it is to them that Kant refers when he introduces the question of presentation or exhibition. Consequently, in spite of Kant's relegation of rhetoric to a second-rank type of beautiful art, rhetoric, or at least one of its figures, becomes revalorized at the moment when Kant needs to address the philosophical problem of presentation in general. To evaluate this gesture by Kant, we must first recall, at least briefly, at what point in the development of the *Critique of Judgment* Kant has recourse to the rhetorical notion in question.

If the deduction of pure aesthetic judgments is to prove the legitimacy of the claim they lay to necessity, it is not enough to seek confirmation for that necessity in the social pressures on us to have taste and to communicate our feelings. Empirical justification of this sort cannot constitute a ground for the claim to universal validity of judgments of taste and hence for our demand that others share our judgment. Only an a priori principle can secure aesthetic judgments' universal validity. Hence the aesthetic judgment needs to be grounded on a concept that, as Kant shows in "Dialectic of the Aesthetical Judgment," must be, in the last instance, a concept of reason, that is, the concept of the supersensible substrate. Yet, as is well known, the supersensible can be beheld only in the sphere of morality. Hence, in order to complete the deduction of aesthetic judgment, Kant must demonstrate a connection between purely aesthetic enjoyment of sensible representations of objects on the one hand and moral feeling on the other. According to Donald W. Crawford, if the beautiful in both nature and art is "able to be seen by any moral being as such a symbol (of morality), then there is a basis for implying that others ought to agree with our judgments of taste, because they ought to be morally sensitive."[10] Kant offers proof for a connection between the beautiful and the moral in chapter 59, "Beauty as the Symbol of Morality." But did not the whole "Analytic of the Beautiful" emphasize time and again the separation of the beautiful from the moral? Obviously this distinction is not to be repealed. Kant, then, must attempt to show in chapter 59 that in spite of the distinction, or perhaps because of it, there exists some sort of relation between the beautiful and the good. To determine this relation, Kant broaches the problem of presentation, or hypotyposis. But what is presentation (*Darstellung*)? Unlike *Vorstellung*, or representation, which Kant uses very broadly to designate the mode in which something is given to a subject, *Darstellung*, or presentation, has a technically very concise and limited meaning—notwithstanding Kant's notoriously lax use of terminology. Presentation is intuitive, sensible showing forth of pure concepts. Without such "reality of our concepts" (196) through intuitions, that is, ultimately, through pure intuitions of space and time, there would be no cognition whatsoever. It is this reality-producing function that Kant addresses in his discussion of presentation in general. Although one may perhaps wish to conclude that if Kant chooses, at this point of his argumentation, to speak of hypotyposis rather than of presentation, it is because of the tour de force that the context calls for—the demonstration of a relation of sorts between two heterogeneous spheres, the beautiful and the moral—the choice of the term "hypotyposis" is motivated primarily by the need to elaborate on the reality-producing function of presentation. Hypotyposis, a figure characterized by the force of its illustrations, its synoptic qualities, its sublime connotations, offers precisely the resources required to thematize the function in question. Hypotyposis, indeed, is a mode of presentation that pictures things so vividly that they appear to present themselves. Hypotyposis also presents in entirety, and the moral grandeur or aesthetic spectacle that it provides is constitutive of a subjective reflection. Hence, what is presented in hypotyposis is endowed with reality, it is alive and self-conscious. But does this recourse to a rhetorical figure to conceptualize the elemental relation between intuition and concept—and hence the reality, life, and self-affection of the mind—leave that figure unchanged, or is it modified in the process? In other words, is what Kant names "hypotyposis" the same rhetorical figure that has been handed down through the tradition? To answer this question, we must determine the exact modalities of Kant's appropriation of this rhetorical figure.

Jean Beaufret has argued that the footnote on demonstration appended to chapter 59 makes it possible to distinguish four modalities of presentation—example, symbol, construction, and scheme. But the beginning of the chapter seems only to demarcate clearly the intuitions that correspond to pure concepts of understanding and rational concepts from the intuitive presentation of empirical concepts through examples.[11] Kant writes:

> All *hypotyposis* (presentation, *subjectio sub adspectum*), or sensible illustration, is twofold. It is either *schematical*, when to a concept comprehended by the understanding the corresponding intuition is given, or it is *symbolical*. In the latter case, to a concept only thinkable by reason, to which no sensible intuition can be adequate, an intuition is supplied with which accords a procedure of the judgment analogous to what it observes in schematism, i.e. merely analogous to the rule of this procedure, not to the intuition itself, consequently to the form of reflection merely and not to its contents. (197)

Exemplification, undoubtedly, is not a mode of presentation dignified enough to merit being called hypotyposis. Examples are only empirical intuitions for concepts, and not a priori or pure intuitions as are schematic and, as I will argue, symbolic presentation. Presentation by construction is more tangled, since it represents an a priori addition of an intuition to a concept or form of judgment. It would thus not be altogether excluded from hypotyposis, but would be only a part of schematic hypotyposis. It is understood that Kant limits construction to the sole concept of magnitude, in short, to mathematical concepts alone, for which it provides a figure in space. Therefore, schematization in fact differs from construction in that schematization applies to all pure concepts—the one of magnitude included —by providing them with figures in time.[12] Yet, since Kant calls schematic presentation *demonstrative* (197), demonstrative implying construction, one can surmise that in the *Critique of Judgment* at least, construction is only one mode of schematism. Hypotyposis, then, applies exclusively to the presentation of pure concepts of the understanding and reason through a priori intuitions. It is this very limited but also extremely essential type of presentation, one without which our pure concepts would remain *lifeless*, that Kant refers to as hypotyposis, as sensible presentation, or vivid illustration. In contrast to the rhetorical use of the term "hypotyposis," whose restricted application to the lively painting of a variety of scenes of aesthetic or moral interest is still quite broad, Kant's very new and original use of the term narrows hypotyposis down to the production of the reality of our concepts, and with it the life of the mind and its powers. Hypotyposis is thus best called a transcendental presentation. Its function is to relate the powers of the mind in such a way that they come into swing and become capable of cognition and moral praxis. If this way of relating sensibility, understanding, and reason is called hypotyposis by Kant, this is because its presentation is that of the tableau, the *scène d'ensemble*, of the life of the mind. The rhetorical figure is here "essentialized" to designate the minimal interrelatedness of the faculties, their minimal orchestration into a whole, without which they would remain unanimated. But this overall *tableau* of the mind, a spectacle based on the harmony or strife of the faculties, not only animates the mind but also affects the mind thus animated. Coming into life through a presentation that takes the faculties together, the mind becomes affected by its own spectacle. It experiences, and feels itself as, a unity, and hence either as beautiful and consequently capable of cognition, or as sublime and consequently capable of moral action. No better word than the rhetorical term "hypotyposis," with its connotations of liveliness, tableau, and moral grandeur, could be found to designate this elementary presentational interconnecting of concepts and intuitions that accounts for both the mind's life and its self-affection. But the nature of this figure from the rhetorical tradition is essentially modified, not only by such use, which restricts the figure's function to the elemental presentation outlined above, but also by the very way in which the figure brings this presentation about.

As we have seen, Kant distinguishes two types of hypotyposes: first, those provided through schematism, which are, as Kant puts it, direct or demonstrative presentations of concepts comprehended by the understanding by means of a priori corresponding intuitions—the schemata—and second, those provided through indirect presentations of concepts of reason (whose objective reality cannot be demonstrated). The latter type of hypotyposis operates not by means of a priori corresponding intuitions but by means of symbols in which the intuition itself does not count but which nonetheless have been produced according to the rules observed in schematism. Because only the procedure observed in schematism and not the content of the intuition produced corresponds in an a priori fashion to the concepts of reason in question, symbolic presentation is indirect, or analogous.[13] The difference, therefore, between the two types of presentation is the difference between, on the one hand, schemata, or "pure images" as Kant calls them in the *Critique of Pure Reason*, in which concepts of understanding are presented through the pure intuitions of space and, especially, time, and on the other hand, symbols, in which concepts of reason are presented not by the content of a corresponding intuition but only by the form of reflection that applies to it. To better understand this latter type of presentation, which

Kant terms indirect or analogous, let me inquire briefly into what Kant understands by analogy.

An extensive definition of analogy appears in the "Analytic of Principles" in the First Critique, where Kant writes:

> In philosophy analogies signify something very different from what they represent in mathematics. In the latter they are formulas which express the equality of two relations, and are always *constitutive*; so that if three members of the proportion are given, the fourth is likewise given, that is, can be constructed. But in philosophy the analogy is not the equality of two *quantitative* but of two *qualitative* relations; and from three given members we can obtain *a priori* knowledge only of the relation to a fourth, not of the fourth member itself. The relation yields, however, a rule for seeking the fourth member in experience, and a mark whereby it can be detected. An analogy of experience is, therefore, only a rule according to which a unity of experience may arise from perception. It does not tell us how mere perception or empirical intuition in general comes about. It is not a principle constitutive of the objects, that is, of the appearances, but only regulative.[14]

Knowledge by analogy, Kant further explains in the *Prolegomena*, "means not, as the word is commonly taken, an imperfect similarity of two things, but a perfect similarity of two relations between quite dissimilar things."[15] This definition, supported by examples that Kant gives of analogy in the *Critique of Judgment*, a definition that neither abolishes the heterogeneity of the things to be related nor affirms their complete separation, shows these dissimilar things to be similar merely in the way they themselves relate or depend on certain other things. To take Kant's own example: a hand mill can be shown to represent a despotic state in spite of the absence of any similarity between the two "items," because both function only if manipulated by an individual absolute will. Thus, analogical presentation does two things, as Kant notes. First, it applies the concept (here the despotic state) to the object of a sensible intuition (the hand mill), and then it applies "the mere rule of the reflection made upon that intuition [on the type of causality it implies] to a quite different object of which the first is only the symbol" (198). The analogical presentation of a concept does not produce a proper schema for it. Analogical presentation does, however, observe the rule of this procedure by applying a sensible intuition to a concept, which, rather than being an intuition for the concept, instead produces a "symbol for the reflection" that allows reflection to perceive a similarity between the intuition and the concept: namely, the exact similarity of the relations that the two have to what depends on them or to what they make possible. In short, in this sort of presentation, in which the intuition does not directly correspond to the concept, cognition nonetheless takes place to the extent that concept and intuition become comparable for reflection. By transposing the rule of reflection about the intuition to the concept, that concept loses its emptiness and acquires a specific figurality. In analogy, concepts can be presented by things dissimilar in nature to them, if rather than pure forms of intuition, pure forms of judgment can be shown to formally apply to them. Indeed, analogical presentation is not only formally similar to schematic presentation because it attaches an intuition to a concept, but also formally different from schematization insofar as the application "of the mere rule of reflection made upon that intuition to a quite different object" mobilizes judgmental functions (relation and its different modes) rather than the form of inner sense.

Indirect or analogous presentation of concepts proceeds, as seen, by means of symbols. As Kant explains in chapter 59, a symbol is not a (arbitrary) sign, that is, a "*mere characterization*," that would, without an intrinsic link to a concept, serve as an expression for the concept (197). In conformity with the tradition, Kant uses the concept of symbol as implying an intrinsic common ground between the symbol and the symbolized. If Kant, in the *Critique of Judgment* and the *Anthropology* as well, shows symbolic presentation to partake (together with schematism) in intuitive presentation, and therefore to be opposed to intellectual or discursive cognition, it is because of this assumed common nature between the symbol and what it presents. Symbols as defined by the *Anthropology* are "forms of objects (as perceived), as far as they serve only as means of perception through notions [*Gestalten der Dinge (Anschauungen), so fern sie nur zu Mittel der Vorstellung durch Begriffe dienen*]." These mere instruments of the understanding, Kant continues, "are only indirect instruments by analogy to certain perceptions [*Anschauungen*] to which the notion of the symbol can be applied, so that the notion [*Begriff*] can be provided with meaning through the presentation of an object." What is important in this definition is that the symbol that serves to provide meaning (and nothing but meaning) to concepts is defined as the form of an object resulting from the application of concepts of understanding to it, without, however, producing any intellectual cognition (through concepts). Cognition through symbols, Kant writes in the *Anthropology* is "*figürlich*," figurative (*speciosa*).[16] Symbols must consequently be understood as figures of concepts as well, which, unlike the spatial and temporal figuration of pure concepts of understanding in schematism, result from a merely formal transposition of forms of judgment to concepts of reason without producing definite cognition. Kant writes in the *Critique of Judgment*, "this matter [*Geschäft*, i.e., a business or an undertaking of the faculties of the mind] has not been sufficiently analyzed hitherto, for it deserves a deeper investigation" (198). Yet Kant decides not to linger over it. By pointing out that language, especially German philosophical language, is full of such indirect presentations, Kant gives only empirical evidence of the commonness of symbolic hypotyposis and thus of this enigmatic process of securing the meaningfulness of concepts. The symbol, to conclude, is a figure that presents *de iure* nonintuitable concepts by calling upon understanding to apply its reflection upon a given object to that concept, thereby making the concept meaningful without making it intelligible. Symbolic hypotyposis presents, indirectly, not by casting a pure concept of the understanding onto the pure forms of space and time but by transposing forms of determinate reflection, that is, judgmental forms, to a pure rational concept, thus endowing it with an air of cognition that makes it meaningful without being discursive.

At this point let us summarize what happens in schematic and symbolic hypotyposes. Schemata are direct presentations, according to (pure) forms of space and time, of the categories of understanding, pure images, as it were, that make the mediation of sense perceptions (images) and concepts possible. Symbols are indirect presentations—indirect because the content does not matter—of concepts of reason, figures or forms (*Gestalten*) that result from the transposition of the form of reflection from an intuition to a concept that thereby loses it emptiness and becomes meaningful. *Schema*, which also means "form," "shape," "figure," is frequently found not only in the rhetorical writings of Cicero and Quintilian, but in later writers such as Du Marsais as well. Here, it designates figures of speech and rhetorical figures in general. Kantian transcendental schemata as the intuition in (space and) time of the categories, that is, of the rules according to which objects in general become determined, are not particular concrete schemes. Although there should be in principle an array of twelve identifiable schemata, corresponding to the twelve judgmental functions, these pure transcendental images are merely the intuitive, that is, temporal articulations of rules regarding the determination of objects in general. When Kant, in the *Critique of Pure Reason*, says that schemata are what make images possible, it becomes clear that, even though they can be numbered and identified, they are not empirical figures but modifications of the transcendental possibility of figures. The same must be ascertained of the symbols. Although their content may be empirical, it is the rule of reflection transposed to a concept that makes them present this concept. The rule of reflection especially, however, in that its form alone becomes presentative of the concept, shows the symbol to be a properly transcendental figure. It is a transcendental operator in the becoming meaningful of nonintuitable and noncognizable concepts of reason. There are perhaps several types of symbols, distinguishable according to the various forms of the rules that are transposed to concepts, but again, as in the case of schemata, symbols are merely figures or forms (*Gestalten*) before all concretization.

With this we may circle back to the question concerning hypotyposis. Hypotyposis brings into appearance—throws before the eye, as it were —in essentially two distinct ways, each of which corresponds to the two different realms of the understanding and reason. In schematic presentation, hypotyposis achieves a transcendental synthesis of the pure forms of intuition and the pure concepts of the understanding. In symbolic presentation, hypotyposis serves to make concepts of reason meaningful by projecting the mere form of the rules of reflection applicable to specific empirical intuitions onto these concepts.[17] Both types of presentation result in figural, formal syntheses that are precognitive in both a theoretical and a practical sense, and that actualize an operation of the power of judgment without which no theoretical or practical cognition would be possible. Hypotyposis is thus a mode of presentation that is transcendental and that proceeds by creating the elemental and transcendental figures, schemata, and forms required for there to be particular, that is, determined figures on the one hand, and concrete examples of a rule of reason on the other. From this we may advance another reason for Kant's choice of the term "hypotyposis." Indeed, as a term, "hypotyposis" perfectly describes the presentation of these precognitive figures as "types" (*typoi*), that is, as impressions (in a seal), hollow molds, or engravings that provide the general outline, the prescribed form, the model for any particular (cognitive and practical) realization. "Hypotyposis" names the being-shaped of all particular and determined presentation, the presentedness of presentations. Yet if Kant initially chose the rhetorical notion of hypotyposis because of its connotations of lively presentation, synoptic breadth, and the qualities of moral grandeur, it now becomes obvious that the dominant motif for the choice of the term is not rhetorical but philosophical. Since the whole thrust of the elaboration of the modes of presentation concerns the transcendental schemata and symbols that provide the figural molds for all coming into determinate appearance, hypotyposis serves to conceptualize the elemental philosophical distinction of the shapedness of shapes, of the formedness of forms, and so on, in a way similar to what Aristotle intended with the verbal form of *hypotypoun*. But the passage through the rhetorical register of hypotyposis was of course not accidental, for the attributes of liveliness, synopsis, and grandeur traditionally not associated with the philosophical usage of hypotyposis serve to fundamentally transform the philosophical notion of the moldedness of what presents itself or is presented. What Kant is able to demonstrate, by making use of the specifically rhetorical properties of hypotyposis, is that the transcendental figures of the schemata and symbols are the figures that endow the mind with life, secure it as a whole, and provide the means by which it affects and feels itself. It is through the schemata and symbols that the powers of the mind come into swing, powers without which the mind would remain unanimated. It thus appears that Kant totally recasts the philosophical notion of hypotyposis by endowing it with qualities that originate with this notion's rhetorical usage. Yet the latter's attributes—vividness, synopsis, moral grandeur—become fundamentally transformed as well because, by exclusively concerning the mediating figures of the faculties, they pertain to the life of the spirit alone, to its totality and to its self-affection through the moral grandeur of its own spectacle.

Kant's recourse to the rhetorical concept of hypotyposis to conceptualize and elaborate presentation in general, presentation from a transcendental point of view, is, as we have seen, grounded in the vividness, liveliness, and forcefulness associated with this notion and, indeed, with rhetoric in the first place. The art of persuasion, defined, in *Gorgias*, for instance, as "the semblance of a part of politics" (463 d) is a routine—and thus, as Socrates holds, not an art, especially not a reputable one—whose aim is to use the might of the word to ensure the individual's survival in the nonphilosophical city. Rhetoric as the art of persuasion is an entirely profane and nonphilosophical practice cultivated to help one "liv[e] as long as possible" (511 b–c) and to enhance natural life through flattery, make-believe, and especially force of speech. From it, Socrates distinguishes the art of dialogue, or dialectic (448 d–e, 471 d–e), as a good rhetoric whose goal is the pursuit of righteousness and truth even at the expense of life. Yet it is important to note that in spite of his radical negative position on the art of persuasion, Socrates in *Gorgias* does not entirely exclude high-pressure persuasion from good rhetoric if its aim is to improve men (517 b–c).[18] With this, however, the worldly, natural qualities of vividness and forcefulness, as well as an emotive element, are shown to have a bearing, however limited, on rational discourse.[19] These profane qualities become even more insistently privileged in Kant's attempt to thematize the presentation of pure concepts of the understanding and reason. The mere word "hypotyposis," and with it, rhetoric as excellence of style (thus not as the art of the orator), stands for this powerful surge in importance of the attributes of life and of life itself in the philosophical attempt to understand the harmonious working together of the mental faculties.

Vivid presentation, which on the transcendental level of the schemata and the symbols brings the faculties together in a harmonious living whole, is an achievement of imagination (*Einbildungskraft*), as is well known. Imagination as productive, or as Kant also puts it in the *Anthropology*, as poetical imagination, is "a faculty of the original representation" preceding experience (*exhibitio originaria*).[20] No longer merely reproductive or mimetic, as it was in the history of philosophy from the Greeks to Descartes, imagination is assigned an essential role in synthesizing the disparate mental realms of sensibility, understanding, and reason. It is important to recall here, as Beaufret has pointed out, that the meaning of Kantian imagination draws not on the semantics of the Latin *imago*, which according to Thomas Aquinas is believed to originate in the verb *imitari*, but instead on the German meaning of *Bild* in *Einbildungskraft*. Beaufret notes that *Bild* is closer in meaning to painting, *tableau*, or scene than to image. It is in this sense that imagination in Kant synthesizes the manifold of intuition into a tableaulike unity.[21] But by producing the temporal schemata by means of which concepts become figuratively intuitable, imagination's synthesizing activity goes far beyond these empirical syntheses of apprehension. Yet the properly transcendental activity of imagination, when analyzed on the level of presentation in general, also reveals, in what Rudolf Makkreel has called a "regress of imagination," "certain transcendental conditions of the mind."[22] The imagination causes the faculties to gather, to form a whole, a formal whole, the figure of a whole that represents the minimal condition of the mind's life. It shapes, molds, or fashions the disparate powers of the mind into the vivid figure of its unity whose (sublime) spectacle provides the animating swing for the mind to assess its own life in difference from nature. By following Kant's terminology in the *Anthropology*, we learn that such shaping of the formative power (*Bildung*) of *Einbildungskraft* of the mental faculties is *Dichtung*, that is, poetry or fiction, not in the sense of deception but rather in the sense of forming, fashioning, or shaping according to the etymology of *fingere*. Such *Dichtung* of the imagination is composition, or discovery (*Erfindung*).[23]

To conclude, I wish to formulate a question. Considering the philosophically innovative use of imagination in Kant, the question arises as to whether Kant's development of this notion is not indebted to a tradition other than the explicitly philosophical one, namely, to the rhetorical tradition. The aesthetic theory developed by Alexander Gottlieb Baumgarten in the eighteenth century has been linked to a revival of rhetoric. As Alfred Baeumler has pointed out, the century of "taste" was very much in love with Cicero and Quintilian.[24] Indeed, aesthetic theory—and this is still true of Kant—is primarily a poetics, one that is to a large extent a rhetoric. Imagination is a familiar concept in the rhetorical tradition as well. Discovery or invention, the finding of the available means of persuasion, inventive wit, the facility of making connections between separate and seemingly unrelated things, ingenuity, and so on, are rooted in the animating faculty of the imagination. It is the imagination that secures the liveliness of style and the surprising and invigorating connections that make the communication of arguments persuasive. It would thus seem that Kant's recasting, especially in the *Critique of Judgment*, of imagination as a faculty of synthesis, which on a transcendental level invents through shaping the animating form of the mind, may well have drawn on the resources of rhetoric. The worldly attributes of life, force, and vividness associated with the imagination as the poetical faculty that fashions the faculties of the mind into a living unity, cast an aura of rhetoric about this central concept of Kant's doctrine. But as is the case with the rhetorical notion of hypotyposis that Kant reappropriates for philosophical thought, his whole theory of the imagination may also be the result of an attempt to put the rhetorical concept of the imagination to work for the philosophical understanding of the life of the mind.

REFERENCE MATTER

Notes

INTRODUCTION

1. In *Aesthetic Theory*, Theodor W. Adorno remarks: "Since Schelling, whose aesthetics is entitled the *Philosophy of Art*, aesthetic interest has centered on artworks. Natural beauty, which was still the occasion of the most penetrating insights in the *Critique of Judgment*, is now scarcely even a topic of theory. . . . Natural beauty vanished from aesthetics as a result of the burgeoning domination of the concept of freedom and human dignity, which was inaugurated by Kant and then rigorously transplanted into aesthetics by Schiller and Hegel; in accord with this concept nothing in the world is worthy of attention except that for which the autonomous subject has itself to thank" (trans. R. Hullot-Kentor, Minneapolis: University of Minnesota Press, 1997, pp. 61–62). Among the few exceptions to this repression of natural beauty in contemporary aesthetics is the recent publication by Martin Seel, *Eine Ästhetik der Natur*, Frankfurt/Main: Suhrkamp, 1996.

2. Immanuel Kant, *Critique of Pure Reason*, trans. N. K. Smith, New York: St. Martin's Press, 1965, p. 66.

3. Ernst Cassirer, *Kant's Life and Thought*, trans. J. Haden, New Haven, Conn.: Yale University Press, 1981, p. 304.

4. On a theoretical level, this refinement of the concept of the a priori is a function of the problem of nature's logical conformity to the faculties of cognition. The extension of what is a priori cognizable is therefore linked to the issue of teleology, and the a priori foundation of Kant's aesthetics is to be viewed as a part of the system of a general teleology (see Cassirer, *Kant's Life and Thought*, p. 305). This systematic dimension of Kant's thought is essential to understanding the basic tenets of his aesthetics. Though aesthetic judgment is thoroughly distinct from teleological judgment, it is not by accident that the part in the Third Critique that deals with the former is followed by one on the latter.

5. I follow here a distinction made by Robert B. Pippin in "The Significance of Taste: Kant, Aesthetic and Reflective Judgment," *Journal of the History of Philosophy*, 34, no. 4, 1996, pp. 550–51. For his part, Pippin advocates a middle position. The interpretation of Kant's aesthetic that I hope to offer does not mediate between those one-sided interpretations or seek to reconcile them. Still, I would maintain that morality, and more precisely reason, holds a distinct role in the formation of

pure judgments of taste, and in particular those judgments that concern the form of an object.

6. On this score see Carsten Zelle, *Die doppelte Ästhetik der Moderne. Revisionen des Schönen von Boileau bis Nietzsche*, Stuttgart: Metzler, 1995.

7. For a fine discussion of Kant's overall theory of formality in the First Critique, see Robert B. Pippin, *Kant's Theory of Form: An Essay on the "Critique of Pure Reason,"* New Haven, Conn.: Yale University Press, 1982. In this exacting investigation into the limitations of Kant's foundational notion of formality, Pippin stresses the status of the Kantian notion of form as a subjective rule for our knowledge of objective reality, a knowledge that, moreover, is judgmental in essence. Kant's notion of form, and by extension the whole question of formality, is shown to be intimately tied to the transcendental enterprise, that is, to Kant's attempt to spell out the *necessary* requirements for human experience in general. Pippin also notes that Kant's transcendental enterprise is inseparable from his theory of empirical knowledge, and that "until we understand it thoroughly, we will not have understood his notion of form" (p. 223). Even though aesthetic judgment is not cognitive, the following analysis of the form that is found beautiful, or altogether missing, will further evidence this intrinsic connection between the empirical and the transcendental in the Third Critique.

8. Jean-François Lyotard's reflections on the relevance of the sublime for an understanding of avant-garde art must certainly be mentioned in this context. His book-length study of the Kantian sublime—*Lessons on the Analytic of the Sublime* (trans. E. Rottenberg, Stanford, Calif.: Stanford University Press, 1994)—is still framed by the thesis that the sublime interrupts the aesthetics of form and that consequently the sublime can help to account for contemporary art. Nevertheless, this admirable study, significantly enough, does not offer any substantial reasons why the problematic of the sublime would be more important than that of the beautiful. Olivier Chédin's work *Sur l'esthétique de Kant et la théorie critique de la représentation* (Paris: Vrin, 1982) is a fine example of a recent study that shows to what extent Kant's concept of beauty can serve to illuminate modern art.

9. In fact, a non-aestheticist aesthetics of the beautiful and the sublime—one that brings into relief the para-epistemic accomplishments of the judgments of taste, whether on the beautiful or the sublime—may have the potential to overcome the duality that has been constitutive of this discipline since the *Querelle des Anciens et des Modernes*; for it seems to me that neither the category of the beautiful nor that of the sublime can as such truly make sense of what takes place in contemporary art.

10. Giorgio Tonelli, "La formazione del testo della *Kritik der Urteilskraft*," *Revue Internationale de Philosophie*, 30, no. 8, 1954, pp. 423–48.

11. Kant, *Critique of Pure Reason*, pp. 276–81.

CHAPTER 1

1. Immanuel Kant, *First Introduction to the "Critique of Judgment,"* trans. J. Haden, Indianapolis: Bobbs-Merrill, 1965, p. 46.

2. Ibid., pp. 50, 9.
3. Ibid., pp. 8–9.
4. Ibid., p. 16.
5. Immanuel Kant, *Critique of Judgement*, trans. J. H. Bernard, New York: Hafner, 1951, p. 15. All page references in the text are to this edition. Note that this edition's title uses the spelling *Judgement*, while its text uses the spelling "judgment." To achieve consistent spelling in the present study, I refer to Kant's work as the *Critique of Judgment* in my text and discussion notes, reverting to the spelling *Judgement* only in source citations of the Bernard edition.
6. As Donald W. Crawford has argued, "pleasure and sharing pleasure are the only ends hypothesized for our judgments of beauty." Whereas the pleasure we take in the sublime "is quasi-cognitive or propositional in character" in that it is subjectively purposive for our rational faculty, nothing other than "the sharing of pleasure," that is, no quasi-cognitive end, "is suggested as the end of aesthetical activity" ("The Sublime in Kant's Aesthetic Theory," in *The Philosophy of Immanuel Kant*, ed. R. Kennington, Washington, D.C.: Catholic University of America Press, 1985, p. 181).
7. It is interesting to note that, in the transcendental doctrine concerning the determining power of judgment, the question of how to apply the synthesis of pure concepts to possible experience leads Kant to introduce the distinction between the mathematical and the dynamical. This distinction then resurfaces in the discussion of the merely reflective—that is, not determining—judgment of the sublime. See Immanuel Kant, *Critique of Pure Reason*, trans. N. K. Smith, New York: St. Martin's Press, 1965, pp. 195–96.
8. "Reflection" is not explicitly thematized in the First Critique, but this does not prevent it from being at work everywhere, most notably in the Second Division. For a nuanced discussion of the role of "reflection" in the First Critique, see Jean-François Lyotard, *Lessons on the Analytic of the Sublime*, trans. E. Rottenberg, Stanford, Calif.: Stanford University Press, 1994, pp. 26–43.
9. Kant, *First Introduction*, p. 17.
10. Kant, *Critique of Pure Reason*, p. 276.
11. Kant, *First Introduction*, p. 16.
12. Olivier Chédin, *Sur l'esthétique de Kant et la théorie critique de la représentation*, Paris: Vrin, 1982, p. 37.
13. The same point is made by Béatrice Longuenesse when she discusses "the unity of the *Critique of Pure Reason* and the *Critique of Judgment*," in *Kant and the Capacity to Judge: Sensibility and Discursivity in the Transcendental Analytic of the "Critique of Pure Reason,"* trans. Charles T. Wolfe, Princeton, N.J.: Princeton University Press, 1998, pp. 163–64.
14. Kant, *First Introduction*, p. 16.
15. Louis Guillermit is one of the few critics to have signaled the overwhelming use Kant makes of *bloss* in the "Critique of the Aesthetical Judgment." See Louis Guillermit, *L'élucidation critique du jugement de goût selon Kant*, Paris: Editions du CNRS, 1986, p. 98.

16. Here is just one example among many where Kant uses "mere" three times in a single sentence (in the original): "There is always a great difference between [considering] representations so far as they, related *merely* to the object and the unity of [our] consciousness of it, belong to knowledge, and referring them to the faculty of desire through that objective relation in which they are regarded as the cause of the reality of the object. This latter case is further distinct from considering representations *merely* in relation to the subject, in which case they afford their own grounds for *merely* maintaining their existence in the subject and are regarded in relation to the feeling of pleasure" (*First Introduction*, p. 13, trans. modified, emphasis mine).

17. In the First Critique, Kant explains: "Any knowledge is entitled pure, if it be not mixed with anything extraneous. But knowledge is more particularly to be called absolutely pure, if no experience or sensation whatsoever be mingled with it, and if it be therefore possible completely *a priori*" (*Critique of Pure Reason*, p. 58).

18. In chapter 14 of the *Critique of Judgment*, in a discussion of color and tone, Kant characterizes purity as a determination of form. He writes: "'pure' in a simple mode of sensation means that its uniformity is troubled and interrupted by no foreign sensation, and it belongs merely to the form [*gehört bloss zur Form*]" (p. 60). But what about the relation of the pure to the "mere form" that is, as we will see in Chapter 3 of this book, the singular object of reflective aesthetic judgments upon the beautiful? Mere form is certainly not pure form, although the entire "Analytic of the Beautiful" is involved in isolating it, in its purity, from any foreign ingredient.

19. G. W. F. Hegel, *Aesthetics: Lectures on Fine Art*, trans. T. M. Knox, Oxford: Clarendon, 1975, pp. 96–97, trans. modified.

20. Edmund Husserl, *The Crisis of European Sciences and Transcendental Phenomenology*, trans. D. Carr, Evanston, Ill.: Northwestern University Press, 1970, pp. 125–26.

21. At this point, some readers may perhaps object that to clarify the meaning of *bloss*, one need only consult Kant's *Religion Within the Limits of Reason Alone* (*Die Religion innerhalb der Grenzen der blossen Vernunft*), in which *bloss* appears conspicuously in the very title. Unfortunately, in this work, *bloss* serves only to distinguish a religion based on a morality in accord with the principles of reason from revealed religion, and thus does nothing to clarify the complex use of this restrictive in the Third Critique.

22. Although he does not explicitly take up the question of *bloss*, in "Parergon," Jacques Derrida claims that all aesthetics "makes of art in general an object in which one claims to distinguish an inner meaning, the invariant, and a multiplicity of external variations *through* which as through so many veils, one would try to see or restore the true, full, originary meaning: one, naked" (*The Truth in Painting*, trans. G. Bennington and I. McLeod, Chicago: University of Chicago Press, 1987, pp. 21–22). This thesis is exemplified by a reading of Kant's *Critique of Judgment*, and seems to refer to this meaning of *bloss*, and also to suggest that the limiting function (or stricture) of the restrictive *bloss* is to lay bare the internal unifying element of art.

23. Johann Christoph Adelung, *Grammatisch-kritisches Wörterbuch der hochdeutschen Mundart*, Leipzig, 1793; reprint, Hildesheim: Olms, 1970, pp. 1083–84.

24. Jacob Grimm and Wilhelm Grimm, *Deutsches Wörterbuch*, Leipzig: S. Hirzel, 1936, pp. 144–50.

25. Such a shift from "pure" to "scanty" or "poor" can be observed in "The Origin of the Work of Art," as Heidegger attempts to pin down the thing-character of the work of art. Having reached "the narrow precinct of mere things," which, as is traditionally assumed, permits access to what a thing (as such) is, Heidegger writes: "'Mere' here means, first, the pure thing, which is simply a thing and nothing more; but then, at the same time, it means that which is only a thing, in an almost pejorative sense. It is mere things, excluding even use-objects, that count as things in the strict sense" (Martin Heidegger, *Poetry, Language, Thought*, trans. A. Hofstadter, New York: Harper and Row, 1971, pp. 21–22).

26. Kant, *First Introduction*, p. 52.   27. Ibid., p. 30.

28. Ibid., p. 37.   29. Ibid., p. 27.

30. Ibid., p. 33.

31. As Lyotard has convincingly argued, "subjective," in the Third Critique, refers not to the subject in a substantive sense but only to what thinking feels when it thinks. See Lyotard, *Lessons*, pp. 12–15.

32. Kant, *First Introduction*, p. 16.   33. Ibid., p. 47.

34. Ibid., p. 18.   35. Ibid., p. 15.

36. Ibid., p. 15.

37. Taking his lead from Kant's essay "What Is Orientation in Thinking," Rudolf A. Makkreel has shown that the reflective principle of purposiveness serves "to orient reflective judgment concerning a possible order in nature's immense variety" ("The Role of Reflection in Kant's Transcendental Philosophy," in *Transcendental Philosophy and Everyday Experience*, ed. T. Rockmore and V. Zeman, Atlantic Highlands, N.J.: Humanities Press, 1997, p. 92).

38. Kant, *First Introduction*, pp. 16–17.

39. Ibid., p. 13.

40. Ibid., pp. 18–19.

41. For a discussion of the meaning of the term "purposiveness," see Giorgio Tonelli, "Von den verschiedenen Bedeutungen des Wortes Zweckmässigkeit in der Kritik der Urteilskraft," *Kant-Studien*, 49, no. 2, 1957–58, pp. 154–66.

42. Cassirer writes that the standpoint of reflection

> arises neither from the mere awareness of the given, nor from its arrangement in causal connections, but the interpretation which we attach to it is a special and independent one. It can in a certain sense, of course, be quite generally asserted, from the standpoint of the critical view of the world, that it is the form of knowledge which determines the form of objectivity. Here, however, this proposition is valid in a more restricted and specific sense, for it is a second-stage formation [*eine Formung zweiten Grades*], as it were, that we have before us here. A whole, which as such is contained directly under the

pure intuitions of space and time, as well as under the pure concepts of the understanding, and experiences its objectification through them, now embodies a new meaning, in that the interrelations and mutual dependence of its parts are subjected to a new principle of contemplation. (Ernst Cassirer, *Kant's Life and Thought*, trans. J. Haden, New Haven, Conn.: Yale University Press, 1981, p. 296, trans. modified)

Manfred Riedel also conceives of reflective judgment as interpretive (*deutend*). See his *Urteilskraft und Vernunft. Kants ursprüngliche Fragestellung*, Frankfurt/Main: Suhrkamp, 1989, p. 56.

43. Considering the similarity of the para-epistemic achievements of teleological and aesthetic judgments, the following exacting description by Jay M. Bernstein of what happens in aesthetic judgments is certainly appropriate here: "I can think of no more apt way of expressing what is happening on such occasions than to say that in aesthetic judgments we are non-discursively cognizing what is there, and that in such non-discursive cognitions we become aware of a meaningfulness without meaning—lawfulness without law, in Kant's jargon" ("Judging Life: From Beauty to Experience, From Kant to Chaim Soutine," *Constellations: An International Journal of Critical and Democratic Theory*, 7, no. 2, June 2000, p. 165).

44. There is no understanding here of anything for which there is no concept. Teleological reflective judgment, like aesthetic reflective judgment, brings about a kind of intelligibility prior to any understanding. If one can speak of hermeneutics at all in this context, it is only in terms of the *feeling* that the unexplained phenomena are in agreement with the powers of cognition and are thus capable of being observed and explored. The interpretation (*Deutung*) of the "language by which nature speaks to us," which Kant evokes while he discusses natural beauty, is a function of the interest taken in what is naturally beautiful (*Critique of Judgement*, pp. 144–45). It follows from this that the mere judgment of taste regarding natural beauty is still prehermeneutical. For a discussion of the antecedence of the judgment on natural beauty to the interest taken in it, see Chapter 6 of this book.

45. Once such concrete conformity to law is witnessed by merely reflective judgment, cognition can investigate those natural forms that at first escaped all cognitive approach.

46. Kant, *First Introduction*, p. 11. 47. Ibid., p. 16.
48. Ibid., p. 11. 49. Ibid., p. 10, trans. modified.
50. Ibid., p. 8.

51. "We perceive finality in our judgment insofar as it merely reflects on a given thing, perhaps on the empirical intuition of it, to bring it under some (as yet undetermined) concept; or on the concept of experience itself, to bring the laws it contains under common principles. Thus it is the faculty of *judgment* that is essentially technical" (ibid., p. 24).

52. Ibid., p. 18, trans. modified. See also p. 52, where Kant writes that determining judgment "proceeds only *schematically*, under laws of another faculty (the understanding); the latter [reflective judgment], however, proceeds purely [*allein*] techni-

cally under its own laws. Fundamental to this activity is a principle of the technic of nature, hence the concept of a purposiveness necessarily presupposed a priori in it."

53. Ibid., p. 53, emphasis mine.

54. It is true that at one point Kant specifies that the beauty of nature "is ascribed to objects only in reference to reflection upon their *external* aspect [*über die äussere Anschauung derselben*], and consequently only on account of the form of their external surface" (*Critique of Judgement*, pp. 221–22). But this does not at all suggest that the beauty of an object resides in an objectively discernible harmonious composition of forms and colors, or in the symmetry of the delineating lines of its outer surface. Rather, a reflective consideration of the exterior aspect of the object concerns the possibility of its being intuited in the first place.

55. Undoubtedly, this second-order nature—empirical nature that is unified by higher empirical laws—is distinct from "the other nature" (*Critique of Judgement*, p. 147) produced by the imagination in the creation of aesthetic ideas. The question remains, however, whether this other nature is not also involved in the merely reflective judgment that predicates the formal purposiveness of its objects. See Chapter 4 of the present study, entitled "Presenting the Maximum."

56. Kant, *First Introduction*, p. 25.

57. Ibid., p. 37.

58. Ibid., p. 39.

59. Needless to say, Kant's talk of "obscurity" is not supposed to suggest imprecision, uncertainty, or even murkiness. From the *Metaphysics of Morals* we know that the opposite of "obscurity" is "popularity," that is, the explication, or communication, that appeals to the senses. Now, it is impossible to make a critique of faculty of reason popular, since a certain "obscurity" is inevitable in such an undertaking, and this is so precisely because such a system, and everything that can be established only by means of it, "has to do with the distinction of the sensible in our knowledge from that which is supersensible but yet belongs to reason. This can never become popular—no formal metaphysics can—although its results can be made quite illuminating for the healthy reason (of an unwitting metaphysician). Popularity (common language) is out of the question here" (Immanuel Kant, *The Metaphysics of Morals*, trans. M. Gregor, Cambridge, Eng.: Cambridge University Press, 1991, p. 36).

CHAPTER 2

1. Andreas Heinrich Trebels, *Einbildungskraft und Spiel. Untersuchungen zur Kantischen Aesthetik*, Bonn: Bouvier, 1967, pp. 133, 172.

2. Immanuel Kant, *Critique of Judgement*, trans. J. H. Bernard, New York: Hafner, 1951, pp. 32–33. All page references in the text are to this edition.

3. Trebels, *Einbildungskraft und Spiel*, p. 59.

4. Rudolf A. Makkreel, *Imagination and Interpretation in Kant: The Hermeneutical Import of the "Critique of Judgment,"* Chicago: University of Chicago Press, 1990, pp. 88, 106.

5. Dieter Henrich has argued that Kant does not sufficiently expound on the structure of the play of the faculties, and that the text of the *Critique of Judgment* "accomplishes very little, almost nothing in this regard" (*Aesthetic Judgment and the Moral Image of the World: Studies in Kant*, Stanford, Calif.: Stanford University Press, 1992, p. 40). However, by taking Kant's references to the life of the mind and, in particular, the whole question of *Stimmung* (mood, or state of mind) into consideration, this concept of the play of the faculties can, as I hope to show, be given much greater substance.

6. Makkreel, *Imagination and Interpretation in Kant*, p. 62.

7. Ibid., p. 66.

8. Trebels, *Einbildungskraft und Spiel*, p. 50.

9. Ibid., p. 134.

10. This seems to be contradicted by the following statement from the *First Introduction*: "if reflection on a given representation precedes the feeling of pleasure (as the determining ground of the judgment), the subjective finality is *thought* before its effect is *felt* [*empfunden*], and in that case an aesthetic judgment belongs by reason to the faculty of judgment under whose subjective yet universal conditions the representation of the object is subsumed" (Immanuel Kant, *First Introduction to the "Critique of Judgment,"* trans. J. Haden, Indianapolis: Bobbs-Merrill, 1965, p. 29). Reflection and judgment are here understood entirely in terms of thought as opposed to feeling. But since the kind of judgment that takes place in reflective aesthetic judgments presupposes the pleasurable harmony of the faculties, thinking in this case must be intimately tied in with the feeling of the life of the mind, a state that subsequently will be felt as pleasurable as well.

11. Robert B. Pippin's careful discussion of chapter 9 in "The Significance of Taste: Kant, Aesthetic and Reflective Judgment" (*Journal of the History of Philosophy*, 34, no. 4, 1996, pp. 549–69) needs mentioning here. One of the merits of this discussion is that it highlights the moment of reflection in the judgment upon the beautiful as necessary for the judgment's being to be followed by pleasure.

12. Kant also characterizes the animation of the faculties in free play as giving rise "to indeterminate but yet . . . harmonious activity, viz. that which belongs to cognition in general" (*Critique of Judgement*, pp. 53–54). "Harmonious" translates the German *einhellig*. Kant adds that this "harmony [*Einhelligkeit*] in the play of the mental powers . . . can be felt [only] in sensation" (p. 65). This harmonious relating of the faculties is the ground on which the universal claims of judgments of taste can be made, claims whose validity are distinct from "the agreement [*Einhelligkeit*], as far as is possible, of all times and peoples," regarding certain beautiful objects (p. 68). The experience of "a complete agreement [*Einhelligkeit*] of judgments as to the beauty of a certain object" being impossible (p. 74), "the agreement [*Einhelligkeit*] of different judging persons" must rest on a subjectively universal principle (p. 76). For our purposes it is not uninteresting to note that the word *einhellig*, of which Kant makes repeated use in *Critique of Judgment* and which is to be translated as "unanimous," "in agreement," derives from a verb that is no longer extant, *hellen*, or

hellan, "to ring," "to sound," "to resound." The proper meaning of *einhellig* is thus "to sound together [*zusammenklingen*]," "to agree [*übereinstimmen*]." *Einhelligkeit* denotes a harmony of voices that resound unanimously, sounding as one voice.

13. Gilles Deleuze, *Kant's Critical Philosophy: The Doctrine of the Faculties*, trans. H. Tomlinson and B. Habberjam, Minneapolis: University of Minnesota Press, 1984, p. 50.

14. Ibid., pp. 60–61. Note also this comment: "Thus the first two Critiques set out a relationship between the faculties which is determined by one of them; the last Critique uncovers a deeper free and indeterminate accord of the faculties as the condition of the possibility of every determinate relationship" (p. 68).

15. Kant does not provide any criteria for a possible discordance (*Mißhelligkeit*) (*Critique of Judgement*, p. 128) in the play of the faculties that would inhibit the cognitive process. When a natural object is ugly, the displeasure felt would seem to indicate that the faculties do not enter the harmonious and purposeful relation beneficial for cognition in general. But such disfunctioning of the faculties cannot mean that an ugly object of nature could not be known. It is not insignificant here that things that "may be in nature ugly and displeasing" can be described as beautiful by beautiful art (pp. 154–55). Yet as Kant's discussion of the "only one kind of ugliness which cannot be represented in accordance with nature," namely disgust (*Ekel*), demonstrates, there is a limit to what art can represent at all. This may also indicate an absolute limit of knowledge, a limit that arises where either sensibility abandons its object-constituting role or imagination is prevented from comprehending a manifold of sense, or understanding simply refuses to understand. Indeed, with the discovery, in the Third Critique, of the transcendental property of the play of the faculties, Kant comes up against not only the thought of a possible disfunctioning of the cognitive faculties but also the thought of a "realm" of "something" that (in the same way as the nouminal, but differently from it) remains unknowable. Let us recall here that Kant calls "nature" the totality of what can be known. Objects of nature are beautiful, as are those artworks that look like nature. The "realm" in question might thus be one of an "unnaturalness," of an *Un-Natur* only to be met with in disgust.

As Winfried Menninghaus has shown, the theme of disgust is one that Kant shares with many other eighteenth-century thinkers (see his *Ekel. Theorie und Geschichte einer starken Empfindung*, Frankfurt/Main: Suhrkamp, 1999). Notwithstanding the fact that references to this theme in the Third Critique are very few, it plays a systematic role in this work. Indeed, if the *Critique of Judgment* is to prove reason adequate to nature even on those occasions when no concepts are available to comprehend its phenomena, nature must be construed as the foil against which nature itself becomes susceptible to reason. Nature's pliancy to concepts of the understanding and of reason must be wrenched from a nature that neither yields to any formal representation nor incites in us the feeling of the power of reason because it (nature) is absolutely formless (the disgusting is not the sublime). The part of nature that is disgusting is the part that does not conform to any power of cognition, including the power of judgment in its merely reflective employment. As I have tried to show elsewhere, according to Kant, all accomplishments of the mind are wrested from this disgusting dimension of nature and are constantly threatened by a possible relapse. (See my "Über das Wegsehen. Aufmerksamkeit und Abstraction bei Kant," trans. A. Budzinski and J. Luftig, in *Liechtensteiner Exkurse III: Aufmerksamkeit*, Eggingen: Edition Isele, 1998, pp. 129–59.)

16. Immanuel Kant, *Critique of Pure Reason*, trans. N. K. Smith, New York: St. Martin's Press, 1965, p. 59.

17. Ibid., p. 97.

18. Ibid., p. 100. Needless to say, this account of the meaning of the transcendental according to the First Critique would have to be completed through a consideration of the *Critique of Practical Reason* and its analysis of the transcendental conditions under which objects of reason (the good) can be practically made real. It remains, however, that within the framework of the Second Critique, no isolated employment of these principles is conceivable either.

CHAPTER 3

1. Immanuel Kant, *Critique of Judgement*, trans. J. H. Bernard, New York: Hafner, 1951, p. 59. All page references in the text are to this edition.

2. Jacques Derrida, in "Parergon," discards from the outset the preconception according to which Kantian aesthetics is a formalist aesthetics, adding that "we could show, from another point of view, that it is the contrary." Nonetheless, he also starts out from chapter 14, in an attempt to demonstrate that the formality presupposed by the formal (as opposed to material) judgments that alone are judgments about the beautiful is "formality as the space of aesthetics in general, of a 'formalism' which . . . merges with the history of art and with aesthetics itself," and hence is not limited to Kant's aesthetics but lies at the heart of aesthetics as such (*The Truth in Painting*, trans. G. Bennington and I. McLeod, Chicago: University of Chicago Press, 1987, p. 67). Rather than indicating a formalist aesthetics, Kant's "requirement of formality," as Derrida terms it (p. 73)—in other words, Kant's demand that judgments about the beautiful be rigorously distinguishable from material judgments and be capable of purity, and that the beautiful thing be free of all attraction and all seductive power—only spells out the demand for a clear-cut separation of the beautiful from all material and exterior ingredients. If it is true, as Derrida states, that it is "the pureness which gives us the sense of beauty in general" (p. 100), the very possibility of an aesthetics hinges on the possibility of drawing a line. Hence Derrida's interest in Kant's examples in chapter 14. But as Derrida also argues, such formality "is always tied to the possibility of a framing system that is both imposed and erased" (p. 67), and "Parergon" is mainly concerned with demonstrating how, in the text of the Third Critique, this frame, by logic (the logic of the parergon), constantly undoes what it also make possible.

3. Theodor Edward Uehling, for one, has based his account of form in *The Notion of Form in Kant's "Critique of Aesthetic Judgment"* (The Hague: Mouton,

1971) largely on chapter 14, and on Kant's comments on Euler's theories about color and tone; but so does Walter Biemel in his Heideggerian interpretation of form in the Third Critique, *Die Bedeutung von Kants Begründung der Aesthetik für die Philosophie der Kunst* (Cologne: Kölner Universitätsverlag, 1959).

4. If in the third edition of the *Critique of Judgment* Kant changes his opinion about the nature of color, this change of mind, as Eckart Förster has convincingly shown, is the result of Kant's commitment by 1796 "to the assumption of a dynamical ether, on the basis of his own theory of matter," a notion Kant elaborated on in the *Opus Postumum* ("Kant's Third Critique and the Opus Postumum," *Graduate Faculty Philosophy Journal*, 16, no. 2, 1993, p. 356).

5. "The regularity which leads to the concept of an object is indeed the indispensable condition . . . for grasping the object in a single representation and determining the manifold of its form." Kant adds: "Regularity consisting in symmetry must express the unity of the intuition that accompanies the concept of purpose, and this regularity belongs to cognition" (*Critique of Judgement*, p. 79).

6. As Winfried Menninghaus has argued, "not the Romantics, but Kant was the first to turn the grotesque from being an exception and a laboriously legitimated special freedom, into a paradigmatical character of the aesthetical in general" (*Lob des Unsinns. Über Kant, Tieck und Blaubart*, Frankfurt/Main: Suhrkamp, 1995, p. 35).

7. As Derrida recalls in *The Truth in Painting*, Saussure—an author whom Kant qualifies as brilliant and thorough, and whose account of his Alpine travels Kant quotes several times—writes: "I found, in the woods above the hermitage, the wild tulip, which I had never seen before" (quoted in *Truth in Painting*, p. 85). Kant does not cite this passage, but he obviously knew it.

8. Kant's valorization of the interlaced features of form in wild nature contrasts starkly with what Hegel, in his aesthetics, writes about the jungles (*Verschlingungen*), and what he considers a self-centered way, that is, a very low way, of relating, in which the merely sensuously concrete relates to itself. Hegel writes: "The variegated richly coloured plumage of birds shines even when unseen, their song dies away unheard; the torch-thistle, which blooms for only one night, withers in the wilds of the southern forests without having been admired, and these forests, jungles themselves of the most beautiful and luxuriant vegetation, with the most sweet-smelling and aromatic perfumes, rot and decay equally unenjoyed" (G. W. F. Hegel, *Aesthetics: Lectures on Fine Art*, trans. T. M. Knox, Oxford: Clarendon, 1975, p. 71). Distinct from this naive self-centeredness of nature and its beauties is the work of art and its form, which for Hegel alone deserves inclusion in a philosophy of art. I will return to Hegel's treatment of the relation of intertwining on another occasion.

9. Biemel, *Die Bedeutung von Kants Begründung der Aesthetik*, p. 54.

10. Immanuel Kant, *First Introduction to the "Critique of Judgment,"* trans. J. Haden, Indianapolis: Bobbs-Merrill, 1965, p. 36, trans. modified.

11. Discussing Kant's characterization of form as constituted by delineation, and the interpretation of figure as outline, Samuel Weber remarks: "In the course

of the Analytic of the Beautiful, it becomes increasingly apparent that what he calls *form* is incessantly in the process of *deforming* and *transforming* itself into something quite different from what the term traditionally implies.... Charged with the task of circumscribing and demarcating form as figure [*Gestalt*], the outline unravels into a 'scrawl'" (*Mass Mediauras: Form, Technics, Media*, ed. A. Cholodenko, Sydney: Power Publications, 1996, pp. 19–21).

12. Louis Guillermit, *L'élucidation critique du jugement de goût selon Kant*, Paris: Editions du CNRS, 1986, p. 96.

13. Immanuel Kant, *Logic*, trans. R. S. Hartman and W. Schwarz, Indianapolis: Bobbs-Merrill, 1974, p. 110.

14. Immanuel Kant, *Critique of Pure Reason*, trans. N. K. Smith, New York: St. Martin's Press, 1965, p. 108.

15. Guillermit, *L'élucidation critique*, pp. 24ff.; Claudio La Rocca, "Forme et signe dans l'esthétique de Kant," in *Kants Ästhetik/Kant's Aesthetics/L'esthéthique de Kant*, ed. H. Parret, Berlin: de Gruyter, 1998, pp. 532–36. For a discussion of Kant's notes on the beautiful in the *Nachlass*, particularly in the *Dissertation*, see Mary J. Gregor, "Aesthetic Form and Sensory Content in the *Critique of Judgment*: Can Kant's 'Critique of Aesthetic Judgment' Provide a Philosophical Basis for Modern Formalism?" in *The Philosophy of Immanuel Kant*, ed. R. Kennington, Washington, D.C.: Catholic University of America Press, 1985, pp. 187–94.

16. La Rocca, "Forme et signe dans l'esthétique de Kant," pp. 536–37.

17. Kant, *First Introduction*, p. 10.

18. Ibid., p. 9. One could thus say that the judgment upon the beautiful is the limiting case of the empirical employment of the understanding.

19. See, for instance, Kant, *Critique of Judgement*, p. 16.

20. Dieter Henrich, in *Aesthetic Judgment and the Moral Image of the World: Studies in Kant* (Stanford, Calif.: Stanford University Press, 1992), makes a powerful case for the distinction in question.

21. Guillermit is one of the few to have paid attention to the overwhelming use Kant makes of the restrictive adverb *bloss* throughout the whole of the "Critique of the Aesthetical Judgement." See Guillermit, *L'élucidation critique*, p. 98.

22. It seems to me that only Paul de Man has paid attention to this particular glance, but he has given quite an idiosyncratic interpretation of it. See my *Wild Card of Reading: On Paul de Man*, Cambridge, Mass.: Harvard University Press, 1997.

23. Kant, *First Introduction*, p. 27.

24. Kant, *Critique of Pure Reason*, pp. 65–66.

25. Kant, *First Introduction*, pp. 27–28.

26. Ibid., p. 24.

27. Ibid., p. 19.

28. Considering that aesthetic reflective judgments are called upon by empirical manifolds for which the understanding has no concept, and that, further, these judgments proceed on the assumption of a subjective purposiveness of these manifolds, the question arises as to whether the whole problematic of the Third Cri-

tique is not the unfolding of a subjective facet of the Kantian concept of a formal nature—which is distinct from material nature and which, according to the *Critique of Pure Reason* and the *Prolegomena*, names the conformity to law of all still-undetermined yet existing objects of experience. As Jacques Rivelaygue has shown, this concept of formal nature finds its systematic place on "an intermediary level between that of determined objects and that of the pure syntheses of the understanding"; consequently its rules "must come after the schemata that provide the concepts with a sensible meaning" (*Leçons de métaphysique allemande*, 2 vols., Paris: Grasset, 1992, 1: 240). This question will be followed out on another occasion.

29. Kant, *First Introduction*, p. 9.

30. Though it is by and large absent from the "Analytic of the Beautiful," the issue of the formal purposiveness of nature in its entirety reemerges in the "Analytic of the Sublime." It does so primarily in the negative guise of the formlessness of the sublime, which, at least as far as the natural sublime is concerned, is triggered not by objects but by spectacles and vistas that show nature as a whole in upheaval. Within the main body of the *Critique of Judgment*, the first explicit reference to the formal purposiveness of nature in fact occurs in the first chapter of the "Analytic of the Sublime." This introduction of such formal purposiveness refers to the empirical manifold of its forms that no concept of understanding can totalize; as when Kant writes, "independent natural beauty discovers to us a technique of nature which represents it as a system in accordance with laws, the principle of which we do not find in the whole of our faculty of understanding" (p. 84).

31. Kant, *First Introduction*, p. 55.

32. Ibid., p. 55. As we will see below in Chapter 7, in order to save the beautiful arts from the fate of being judged like any artifact, Kant will argue that the role of genius consists in rendering indeterminate the concept that they presuppose qua art. Such rendering is the process by which the beautiful arts take on the look of nature.

33. Kant, *First Introduction*, p. 24.
34. Ibid., p. 24.
35. Ibid., p. 10.
36. Ibid., p. 10.
37. Ibid., p. 11.
38. Ibid., pp. 16–17.
39. Ibid., p. 18.
40. Ibid., p. 18.
41. Ibid., p. 25.
42. Ibid., p. 25.
43. Henrich, *Aesthetic Judgment*, pp. 29, 34.

44. In this context it is not insignificant to mention the status of sculpture in the *Critique of Judgment*. The products of sculpture, that is, a species of the beauty of art, are "almost interchangeable with nature," Kant notes (p. 155). Sculpture, he writes, "presents corporeally concepts of things [*Begriffe von Dingen*], *as they might have existed in nature*" (p. 166). In other words, rather than a beautiful thing, sculpture is thus a plastic *representation* of the concept of a possible thing.

45. These passages will be discussed in much greater detail below in Chapter 7.

46. To define form in this sense does not at all imply that just anything could therefore be judged beautiful. It must be noted that judgments upon the beautiful

occur only where concepts for an intuited manifold are lacking. Yet given the absence of determinate concepts, it is always possible that the power of judgment might not find the manifold in question to have the form of an object, and hence to be formally purposive. After all, the determining ground of an aesthetic judgment is either pleasure or displeasure. Displeasure occurs where the power of judgment is unable to shape a formless manifold of intuition into the form of a (still undetermined) thing. The object is subsequently judged ugly. As Kant has noted, the ugly allows for an aesthetic representation; consequently, it is not altogether formless—it can be given a form of sorts! The ugly must therefore be distinguished from what is disgusting, which refuses not only form but also totalization.

47. Kant, *First Introduction*, p. 28.
48. Ibid., p. 36, trans. modified.
49. Ibid.
50. La Rocca, "Forme et signe dans l'esthétique de Kant," p. 531.
51. Kant, *First Introduction*, pp. 53–54.

CHAPTER 4

1. "To *construct* a concept means to exhibit *a priori* the intuition which corresponds to the concept" (Immanuel Kant, *Critique of Pure Reason*, trans. N. K. Smith, New York: St. Martin's Press, 1965, p. 577).
2. Immanuel Kant, *Critique of Judgement*, trans. J. H. Bernard, New York: Hafner, 1951, p. 30. All page references in the text are to this edition.
3. I will therefore postpone elaborating on chapter 59—which is devoted, as a whole, to the notion of presentation—until the final chapter of this book.
4. For an excellent overview of the history of the concept of presentation, see the entry by Dieter Schlenstedt, "Darstellung," in *Aesthetische Grundbegriffe*, ed. K. Barck et al., Stuttgart: Metzler Verlag, 2000, 1: 831–75. A detailed discussion of the notion of presentation before Kant, and its philosophical filiation, is to be found in Inka Mülder-Bach, *Im Zeichen Pygmalions. Das Modell der Statue und die Entdeckung der "Darstellung" im 18. Jahrhundert*, Munich: Fink Verlag, 1998. Concerning the various post-Kantian elaborations of the term, and in particular its romantic appropriation, see Martha B. Helfer, *The Retreat of Representation: The Concept of Darstellung in German Critical Discourse*, Albany: State University of New York Press, 1996, pp. 22–50.
5. Immanuel Kant, *First Introduction to the "Critique of Judgment,"* trans. J. Haden, Indianapolis: Bobbs-Merrill, 1965, p. 5.
6. Dieter Henrich, *Aesthetic Judgment and the Moral Image of the World: Studies in Kant*, Stanford, Calif.: Stanford University Press, 1992, p. 47.
7. In the final chapter of this book, I discuss Kant's philosophical emancipation of presentation from its rhetorical origins. In chapter 59 of *Critique of Judgment*, Kant refers to presentation as *hypotyposis*, that is, the rhetorical figure of a vivid illustration used to put something before the eyes. This suggests that Kant's appropriation of *Darstellung* for the discourse of critical philosophy is based on a

transformation and foregrounding of the basic features of the rhetorical notion of presentation. For a discussion of how, in hypotyposis, presentation as actualization is linked to a putting before the eyes, see also Rüdiger Campe, "Vor Augen stellen: Über den Rahmen rhetorischer Bildgebung," in *Poststrukturalismus. Herausforderung an die Literaturwissenschaft*, ed. G. Neumann, Stuttgart: Metzler, 1997, pp. 208–25.

8. Henrich, *Aesthetic Judgment*, p. 48.
9. Kant, *First Introduction*, p. 28.
10. Ibid., p. 37.
11. Ibid., p. 24.
12. Javier Ibanez-Noé, "Urteilskraft und Darstellung," in *Akten des siebenten internationalen Kant-Kongresses*, ed. G. Funke, Bonn: Bouvier, 1991, p. 123.
13. I will discuss this statement in greater detail below in Chapter 7.
14. Kant, *Critique of Pure Reason*, p. 193.
15. In the case of the sublime, the imagination must perform an even greater feat, given that the boundless sublime "object" lacks all form. Here presentation is deprived of directness and must become negative presentation.
16. For a detailed discussion of Kant's attempt to overcome the subsumption of thinking under intuition by the ancients, see Manfred Riedel, *Urteilskraft und Vernunft. Kants ursprüngliche Fragestellung*, Frankfurt/Main: Suhrkamp 1989, pp. 35–40.
17. The distinction between idea and ideal is made with great clarity in *Critique of Pure Reason*. In the chapter entitled "The Ideal of Pure Reason," Kant writes: "By the ideal I understand the idea, not merely *in concreto*, but *in individuo*, that is as an individual thing, determinable or even determined by the idea alone." For what follows, it is also important to remember that "as the idea gives the *rule*, so the ideal in such case serves as the *archetype* for the complete determination of the copy . . . [the ideals] supply reason with a standard which is indispensable to it, providing it, as they do, with a concept of that which is entirely complete in its kind, and thereby enabling it to estimate and to measure the degree and defects of the incomplete" (*Critique of Pure Reason*, pp. 485–86). For the distinction between idea and ideal, see also Jean-François Lyotard, *L'enthousiasme. La critique kantienne de l'histoire*, Paris: Galilée, 1986, p. 20.
18. Indeed, the point to be made here is this: ultimately, the purposiveness without a purpose (characteristic of beautiful form) is grounded in the practical notion of a final purpose; and this notion, according to the section on the teleological judgment, is proper solely to the human being.
19. In *Critique of Pure Reason*, a distinction similar to the one between rational idea and normal idea is made. It is the one between the ideal of reason and those products of the imagination that Kant calls *monograms*. A monogram is defined as "a mere set of particular qualities, determined by no assignable rule, and forming a rather blurred sketch drawn from diverse experiences [*eine im Mittel verschiedener Erfahrungen gleichsam schwebende Zeichnung*] than a determinate image" (p. 487).
20. But Kant also acknowledges shortly after chapter 49 that natural beauty can

express aesthetic ideas. He writes in chapter 51: "We may describe beauty in general (whether natural or artificial) as the expression of aesthetical ideas; only that in beautiful art this idea must be occasioned by a concept of the object, while in beautiful nature the mere reflection upon a given intuition, without any concept of what the object is to be, is sufficient for awakening and communicating the idea of which that object is regarded as the expression" (*Critique of Judgement*, p. 164). The passage is remarkable in several respects. Given that the problematic of aesthetic ideas is brought up exclusively in the context of a discussion of artificial beauty, it is surprising to see that such ideas can also be expressed by natural beauty. But "expression" had not been an issue in this analytic, which is predominantly interested in clarifying the structure of judgments of taste. Yet although Kant contends that beauty in general may be called an expression of aesthetic ideas, an important distinction must be made concerning such expression in either artificial or natural beauty. In the beautiful arts, art qua art rests upon the concept of the object; and as we will see below in Chapter 7, this concept is rendered indeterminate in the beautiful arts, which fact occasions aesthetic ideas. When we are faced with an object of nature for which we have no concept, the mere reflection on the intuitive manifold by which this object is given (that is, its mere or undetermined form, and its suitableness for cognition in general) awakens aesthetic ideas in us. When an object of nature is found to have the undetermined form of an object, the indeterminateness of its form causes the aesthetic ideas; it can thus be said to be the expression of these ideas, even though no production is involved. I add that the acknowledged fact that natural beauty can also express aesthetic ideas is, as will become clear later in this book, only one more reason why aesthetic ideas can prompt Kant, in his analysis of artificial beauty, to elaborate on the ideal of the beautiful arts in the first place.

21. Donald W. Crawford, *Kant's Aesthetic Theory*, Madison: University of Wisconsin Press, 1974, p. 119.

22. Some commentators have taken offense at Kant's talk of *Zucht* in this context. Undoubtedly, the term means "discipline," but it refers to discipline in the context of education and cultivation. The term *Erziehung* derives from *Zucht*, which is rooted in the verb *ziehen*, "drawing" or "pulling."

23. Jens Kulenkampff, *Kants Logik des ästhetischen Urteils*, Frankfurt/Main: Klostermann, 1978, p. 154.

24. One of the achievements of Olivier Chédin's study *Sur l'esthétique de Kant et la théorie critique de la représentation* (Paris: Vrin, 1982) is to have shown the extent to which the regulative principles of reason, exhibited in the First Critique, also operate in the imagination's comprehension of an intuitive manifold into the form of an aesthetic object.

25. Kant's definition of aesthetic ideas as representations that occasion much thought echoes Longinus's claim that true sublimity either touches the spirit of an intelligent and well-read man "with a sense of grandeur or leave[s] more food for reflection in his mind than the mere words can convey" (Longinus, "On the Sublime," in Aristotle, Horace, and Longinus, *Classical Literary Criticism*, trans. T. S. Dorsch,

London: Penguin Books, 1965, p. 107). Is there a relation between the beautiful arts of genius and the sublime of nature? I will not take up this issue explicitly in this book, but in the chapter devoted to the sublime (Chapter 5), I will provide a few hints in the direction of such an investigation.

26. Jacques Derrida, *The Truth in Painting*, trans. G. Bennington and I. McLeod, Chicago: University of Chicago Press, 1987, pp. 92–93. See also, in this context, Derrida's analyses of the examples of a purposiveness without purpose given in chapter 42 of the Third Critique. It is certainly no accident that these include "the beautiful figure of a wild flower" (*Truth in Painting*, pp. 85, 91).

27. In his discussion of the examples of free beauty in the Third Critique (most of which are borrowed from the decorative and ornamental arts), Olivier Chédin has forcefully argued that Kant had no other choice but to resort to these examples, since he had no knowledge of any of the creations of informal and abstract art. As Chédin remarks, Kant's theory of taste is an aesthetic theory that arrived too early. Only the "decorative arts," as abstract art *avant la lettre*, could therefore illustrate Kant's theory. Chédin writes: "Kant's aesthetics came too early. No doubt, this prematurity explains the mediocrity of his examples. Yet the weakest of these examples—the foliage for borders, gardens, tatoos, fire, and waterfalls, all of which provide spectacles of purely decorative ambiance—are those, nonetheless, that serve best to elucidate the aesthetic phenomenon" (*Sur l'esthétique de Kant*, p. 243).

28. In my discussion of the sublime (Chapter 5), we will see that judgments of the sublime also imply this double presentation. It reemerges here in a different shape: for example, in the mathematical sublime (which is closest to theoretical reason), the dual relation is between, on the one hand, a measure for an aesthetically produced sense of magnitude as such, and on the other hand, an absolute standard for this sense.

CHAPTER 5

1. Carsten Zelle has pointed out that since the end of the seventeenth century, that is, since the *Querelle des Anciens et des Modernes*, all aesthetics has been double. It is made up of two aesthetic experiences that oppose each other. He writes: "In the medium of aesthetics the Enlightenment of the Enlightenment takes place as a critique of the beautiful by the sublime. Aesthetics in modernity has therefore always been a double aesthetics" (*Die doppelte Ästhetik der Moderne. Revisionen des Schönen von Boileau bis Nietzsche*, Stuttgart: Metzler, 1995, p. 3). Zelle devotes only a few pages of his work to Kant, and these mainly present Zelle's convincing refutation of the belief (held by Paul de Man, for instance) that Friedrich Schiller is responsible for the romantic distortion of the Kantian aesthetics of division (*Entzweiung*). In any event, with respect to Kant, Zelle holds (following Jean-François Lyotard) that "with the aesthetics of the sublime everything that had been repressed in the poetics of the beautiful makes a return" (p. 154). Undoubtedly, Kant's aesthetics is a double aesthetics, but, as I hope to show in the present chapter, the relation between the beautiful and the sublime in Kant cannot easily be made to fit

the mold characteristic of modern aesthetics. Rather than a relation of opposition, exclusion, and criticism, it is a relation marked by a certain appendancy. Ultimately, Kant's aesthetics, however double, escapes the doubleness of modern aesthetics because of the specific nature of what Kant understands by mere form and the absolutely great.

2. Giorgio Tonelli, "La formazione del testo della *Kritik der Urteilskraft*," *Revue Internationale de Philosophie*, 30, no. 8, 1954, pp. 423–48. For a critique of Tonelli's position, see, for instance, Louis Guillermit, *L'élucidation critique du jugement de goût selon Kant*, Paris: Editions du CNRS, 1986, p. 106.

3. Ernst Cassirer, *Kant's Life and Thought*, trans. J. Haden, New Haven, Conn.: Yale University Press, 1981, pp. 326–27.

4. Jean-François Lyotard, *Lessons on the Analytic of the Sublime*, trans. E. Rottenberg, Stanford, Calif.: Stanford University Press, 1994, p. 78.

5. Immanuel Kant, *Critique of Judgement*, trans. J. H. Bernard, New York: Hafner, 1951, p. 82. All page references in the text are to this edition.

6. Immanuel Kant, *First Introduction to the "Critique of Judgment,"* trans. J. Haden, Indianapolis: Bobbs-Merrill, 1965, pp. 53–54, trans. modified.

7. The distinction between inner and relative purposiveness forms the basis for the distinction, within reflective aesthetic judgment, between the beautiful and the sublime; furthermore, it divides the analytic of teleological judgment concerned with objective purposiveness. In the First Introduction, Kant writes: "Objective finality is based either on the inner possibility of the object or on the relative possibility of its outward consequences. In the first case, teleological judgment regards the *perfection* of a thing according to an end that lies in itself (since the manifold in it is interrelated reciprocally as end and as means); in the second case, teleological judgment extends only to the *utility* [*Nützlichkeit*] of a natural object, namely, its agreement with a purpose lying in other things" (*First Introduction*, p. 54). Given the systematic parallelism between, on the one hand, reflective aesthetic judgment upon the sublime and, on the other, reflective teleological judgment upon relative objective purposiveness, a comparison between the two would seem warranted, in order to fully evaluate the status of sublime itself. Kant's often biting criticism of judgments concerning relative objective purposiveness may well retrospectively affect the way one has to look at the "Analytic of the Sublime."

8. The claim that a judgment upon the beautiful is universal needs some justification, and for this reason the exposition of the beautiful has to be followed by a deduction. In the case of the sublime, by contrast, the defining characteristic is "quantity," which is universal from the outset; thus exposition and justification go hand in hand.

9. The emotion that characterizes the sublime might be related to the classical problematic of the soul as the source of movement, and the whole problematic of the sublime could then be discussed in the context of what Plato refers to, in the *Phaedo*, as the care or tendance of the soul (*tes psyches epimeleisthai*). An analysis of the Kantian sublime from this perspective would help displace the seemingly sym-

metrical relation between the beautiful and the sublime. See Jan Patočka, *Plato and Europe*, trans. Petr Lom, Stanford, Calif.: Stanford University Press, 2002, pp. 124, 126–27, 187, 197–98.

10. The reason for likening this feeling to that of respect is that, faced with a sublime object, the subject discovers that it has the power to elevate itself above the province of the senses and to submit the realm of the senses to a demand that is incommensurable with them: namely, the supersensible demand for totality that originates in reason. For a detailed refutation of the belief that the feeling associated with the sublime is identical to the moral feeling of respect, see Guillermit, *L'élucidation critique*, pp. 105ff., and especially Lyotard, *Lessons*, pp. 116–18, 182–86, 227–39.

11. Yet as I have tried to show in Chapter 4 of this book, Kant's hint, in chapter 17, at a standard of beauty is a clear indication that intellectual ideas have a bearing on cognizability in general.

12. Kant's inattention to these judgments is rather surprising, especially given that they are pure reflective aesthetic judgments. Why do they not deserve greater consideration? Why is mere size less important than mere form? The question is all the more urgent (it would seem) because, as we will see, judgments that something is simply great (or small) extend to just about everything. Obviously, absolute size, or size that is beyond comparison, is at the heart of the sublime. The fact that judgments upon mere size are the originary templates for the possibility of judgments upon the sublime, and are limit cases of these judgments, compels me to ask another question. Is judgment upon beauty equally rooted in a type of judgment upon form in general, of which it would be an extreme case? Why is there no allusion whatsoever, in the Third Critique, to the existence of such a type of judgment, which would be anterior to judgments upon beauty?

13. According to the "Analytic of Principles," magnitude (*quantum*) is an attribute of all appearances, or phenomena, and is rooted in the latter's continuity, or homogeneity. Quantum refers to the ability of a thing to be "one and the same with several others, that is, a magnitude" (Immanuel Kant, *Critique of Pure Reason*, trans. N. K. Smith, New York: St. Martin's Press, 1965, p. 253, trans. modified; see also pp. 201–8).

14. Having used these architectural artifacts (the pyramids and St. Peter's) to illustrate comprehension's failure to apprehend the manifold of magnitude in one whole and to form an aesthetical intuition, Kant quickly discards them as examples of sublimity. There are several reasons for this: First, if objects of nature cannot be sublime in themselves, neither can artifacts. The pyramids are just as little sublime as is the stormy ocean. Furthermore, Kant says that the sublime in art is derived from the sublime in nature. But the main reason for excluding man-made artifacts from the elaboration of the concept of the sublime is that a pure judgment upon the sublime cannot have the "purpose of the object as its determining ground if it is to be aesthetical and not mixed up with any judgment of understanding or reason." Such determination is inevitable in the case of products of art. In fact, the sublime is lacking not only "in products of art (e.g. buildings, pillars, etc.) where

human purpose determines the form as well as the size, nor yet in things of nature *the concepts of which bring with them a definite purpose* (e.g. animals with a known natural destination), but in rude nature (and in this only in so far as it does not bring with it any charm or emotion produced by actual danger) merely as containing magnitude" (*Critique of Judgement*, p. 91).

Just as the feeling of the beautiful, in the "Analytic of the Beautiful," is stirred essentially by natural form, so the feeling of the sublime is aroused by natural magnitude. Yet whereas Kant examines artificial beauty to determine under what strict criteria it could lay claim to pure judgments of form, he does not proceed to a similar analysis concerning the sublime. Nor does he implement a distinction equivalent to the one he makes between arts in general and the beautiful arts. The examples of the pyramids and of St. Peter's are illustrations of arts in general. They are distinguishable from the domain of sublime art, with respect to which pure aesthetic judgments would be conceivable. In contrast to Hegel, Kant is concerned only with not radically excluding the possibility of an artificial sublime. On this last point, see Guillermit, *L'élucidation critique*, p. 123.

15. Kant is quick to remark the following: if conceiving of the mathematical infinite as a totality indicates a power of the mind that surpasses all theoretical or cognitive standards, nothing is thereby added to the theoretical realm. Cognition is not made greater by bringing the purely intellectual standard of reason to bear upon sensible and mathematical infinites. Yet this standard of reason expands the mind. It expands it in a direction that transgresses the boundaries of sensibility; indeed, while such transgression would not even be possible in the realm of the theoretical, it is not only possible but mandatory in the realm of sensibility. It is a transgression that furthers practical, or moral, reason.

16. In truth, however, sublimity refers to the subject; this is true to the extent that when the highest faculty of the senses fails, the mind proves capable of a higher mode of comprehension. Kant writes: "The feeling of the sublime in nature is respect for our own destination, which, by a certain subreption, we attribute to an object of nature (conversion of respect for the idea of humanity in our own subject into respect for the object). This makes intuitively evident the superiority of the rational determination of our cognitive faculties to the greatest faculty of our sensibility" (*Critique of Judgement*, p. 96). The mind, capable as it is of reason, can extend the respect that it should show to itself also to objects of nature. This extension of respect is not a fallacious or deceptive suppression of truth, as the notion of subreption might suggest, but rather a transfer that is warranted by reason's need to make the determination of the imagination through reason intuitively discernible. For this reason, the transfer is effectuated by the faculty of presentation. Having failed in its effort to comprehend aesthetically the size of a given object of nature, the highest faculty of the senses demonstrates its own compliance with reason by transposing to nature what properly belongs to the subject: a transposition that implies nature's susceptibility to reason.

17. Lyotard, *Lessons*, pp. 137–38.

18. See the section entitled "System of Cosmological Ideas," in Kant, *Critique of Pure Reason*, pp. 386–93.

19. Since this annihilation of the form of inner sense can also be understood as a consequence of the comprehension necessary to gather into one moment (*Augenblick*) the manifold of what has been successively apprehended, the annihilation of time as succession can be seen to take place at the hands of time as moment. Such a reading is suggested by Gerhard Krüger, "Über Kants Lehre von der Zeit," in his *Philosophie und Moral in der Kantischen Kritik*, 2d ed., Tübingen: J. C. B. Mohr, 1967, pp. 293–94.

20. For a discussion of the imagination's status as a faculty in Kant, see my "Leaps of Imagination," in *The Path of Archaic Thinking: Unfolding the Work of John Sallis*, ed. K. Maly, Albany: State University of New York Press, 1995, pp. 35–47.

21. In what amounts to a critique of Burke's conception of the sublime, Kant underscores that "it is not true conversely that every object which excites fear is regarded in aesthetical judgment as sublime" (*Critique of Judgement*, p. 99).

22. In this context, we see the significance of Kant's remarks about the terror, dread, and holy awe with which the beholder's imagination is struck before "mountain peaks rearing themselves to heaven, deep chasms and streams raging therein, deep-shadowed solitudes that dispose one to melancholy meditations." Indeed, he writes, "In the safety in which we know ourselves to be . . . [this] is not actual fear but only an attempt to feel fear by the aid of the imagination [*nur ein Versuch, uns mit der Einbildungskraft darauf einzulassen*], that we may feel the might of this faculty in combining with the mind's repose the mental movement thereby excited, and being thus superior to internal nature—and therefore to external—so far as this can have any influence on our feeling of well-being" (*Critique of Judgement*, p. 109). A careful analysis of this passage would show that the imagination suffers no coercion in this experience. What happens to it when it is faced with a sublime spectacle is not imposed on it as if it were a passive object. Rather, in the sublime the imagination is actively involved in a *Versuch*, a sort of experiment that it performs on itself, in order to test its own superiority over (internal and external) nature and hence its own supersensible destination.

CHAPTER 6

1. Immanuel Kant, *Critique of Judgement*, trans. J. H. Bernard, New York: Hafner, 1951, p. 138. All page references in the text are to this edition.

2. This motif of disinterestedness, contrary to what many of Kant's commentators seem to believe, is not particular to Kant's aesthetics. Certainly disinterestedness acquires a novel meaning in Kant: narrowed down to designate the lack of concern in pure judgments of taste for the existence of the objects that are seen to be beautiful, disinterestedness not only becomes a concept in its own right but also plays a different role in the Third Critique from the role it played, long before Kant, in the numerous other treatises on aesthetics throughout the eighteenth century. Nonetheless, this refined Kantian meaning is not without relations to the earlier

uses of the term. Introduced into the language of German aesthetics by F. J. Riedel, who himself borrowed it from the British empiricist philosophers involved with aesthetics (Shaftesbury, Hutcheson, Addison, and Burke, for example), disinterestedness is a notion that originated in moral philosophy and theology in the seventeenth and eighteenth centuries, where it referred to a nonegoistic ethics, or represented the principle of a noninstrumentalist theology, in which God is not a means for human needs. When one loves God disinterestedly, one loves him, according to Shaftesbury, simply for his own sake, or for his excellence. For the history of the concept, and in particular its antecedents in theology and moral philosophy, see Werner Strube, "Interesselosigkeit. Zur Geschichte eines Grundbegriffs der Aesthetik," *Archiv für Begriffsgeschichte*, 22, 1979, pp. 148–74. For the role of the term in British empiricist aesthetics, see Jerome Stolnitz, "On the origins of 'Aesthetic Disinterestedness,'" *Journal of Aesthetics and Art Criticism*, 20, 1960–61, pp. 131–43.

3. Louis Guillermit, *L'élucidation critique du jugement de goût selon Kant*, Paris: Editions du CNRS, 1986, p. 151.

4. See my "Leaps of Imagination" (in *The Path of Archaic Thinking: Unfolding the Work of John Sallis*, ed. K. Maly, Albany: State University of New York Press, 1995, pp. 35–47), in which I show that the imagination in Kant is a "faculty" entirely determined by other faculties, hence without self-identity. Only by "depriving itself of its freedom [*der Beraubung der Einbildungskraft durch sich selbst*]," by sacrificing its sensible nature, and by determining itself purposively "according to a different law from that of its empirical employment [by which it] acquires an extension and a might greater than it sacrifices" does the imagination win a self of its own to begin with (Kant, *Critique of Judgement*, p. 109).

5. In the passage in question, Kant discusses certain affects, such as enthusiasm and apathy, that have been privileged by a number of interpreters of Kant (Jean-François Lyotard and Paul de Man, for example) as entrance points into the question of the sublime. But considering the more empirical nature of this discussion, caution is warranted in not overdetermining the significance of these examples for the problematic of the sublime in general.

6. In aesthetic reflective judgment upon the sublime, the relation between the powers in question is thus much more problematic than the relation between the imagination and the understanding in the beautiful. No simple symmetry obtains between the two kinds of judgments. The nature of the relation between the faculties involved is quite different. Even though the understanding is active only as the power of cognition in general in judgments upon the beautiful, the imagination relates to it as to an actual power. In the sublime, the relation to reason is negative. Imagination does not "know" the rule to which it subjects itself. There is only the feeling that resistance to sensibility is subjectively purposive. Reason is only virtually present, as it were.

7. As we have seen, the reason for the beautiful's potential with respect to representing the morally good hinges on the fate of sensibility in judgments concerning the mere form of an object. With the disinterest in charm, and the exclusive

concern with the form of a thing, the judgment of taste about the beautiful reveals a subtle yet decisive "presence" of reason. The ideal of beauty invoked by Kant in chapter 17 anticipates the question of the possible relation of the beautiful to the absolutely good. At no point does Kant turn from a concern with form to so-called more serious questions. Rather, his path is one of continuity.

CHAPTER 7

1. Immanuel Kant, *Critique of Judgement*, trans. J. H. Bernard, New York: Hafner, 1951, p. 30. All page references in the text are to this edition.

2. For a more detailed analysis of the *facere/agere* difference, see Olivier Chédin, *Sur l'esthétique de Kant et la théorie critique de la représentation*, Paris: Vrin, 1982, pp. 201–17.

3. Kant argues in chapter 47, "Elucidation and Confirmation of the Above Explanation of Genius," that "genius is entirely opposed to the *spirit of imitation*" (*Critique of Judgement*, p. 151) and hence excludes all learnedness (*Gelehrigkeit*), all intelligence derived from learning; in this way he sets his own view clearly apart from other eighteenth-century notions of genius. As he explicitly states, between Newton and men of genius there is a difference in species, since Newton made his discoveries and gained his insights by studying and learning. Such a difference, however, does not signify any superiority of men of genius over men like Newton, to whom humanity owes so much. In fact, Kant believes the opposite, and does so for remarkable reasons. He holds that whereas "knowledge and every advantage depending on it" continuously develop thanks to the discoveries made by great men, the exclusive competence of genius is art, which "stands still in a certain way [*irgendwo still steht*]; a boundary is set to it beyond which it cannot be extended further, which presumably has been reached long ago and cannot be extended further" (p. 152, trans. modified). This passage seems to anticipate Hegel's notion of the end of art, yet differs from it in that, for Kant, art has apparently stood still from the beginning. Indeed, the fine arts are merely the expression of the mental disposition of the faculties that is beneficial for cognition in general (a disposition presupposed by the ongoing cognitive operations of the sciences). This disposition of the faculties can be realized in a variety of proportions, which are testimony to a certain contingency and singularity. However, Kant seems to suggest that this play within the play of the faculties has limits. The variety concerns only the production of beautiful forms—forms that things must display to be recognizable and hence cognizable—and the possibilities of achieving such forms may have already been exhausted. Thus art is for Kant, as it will be for Hegel, something passé. Of course, nature continues to offer (infinite) examples of such free form—that is, of beauty—that are constantly new. I consider this statement about the standstill of art further indication that Kant's aesthetics is not primarily an aesthetics of the fine arts. Regarding Kant's critical transformation of the problematics of genius, see also Louis Guillermit, *L'élucidation critique du jugement de goût selon Kant*, Paris: Editions du CNRS, 1986, pp. 178ff.

4. Since genius is nothing but a "happy relation" of faculties, sexual difference has, of course, no bearing on this problematic. By referring to the genius as he or she, one in fact anthropologizes a critical (transcendental) question.

5. Kant may be thinking here only of the aesthetic schools of his time that were primarily concerned with the imitation of nature. Nevertheless, form is also the founding conception of such schools when it is understood, in an aestheticist and formalist sense, as referring to the artful and harmonious composition and arrangement of the parts of the work. Form also denotes a mechanical aspect of the artwork, an aspect without which the creations of genius would not be tasteful, but which does not lead to brilliant art if it is simply copied.

6. In a similar vein, Heidegger has argued that the form/matter distinction is relevant exclusively with respect to equipment (*Zeug*), to artifacts that are produced with a view to their usefulness. Form, in this context, refers to the way in which matter is arranged in accordance with the expected usefulness of the product. It follows that any analogous approach to works of art turns the work of art into a subspecies of equipment. See Martin Heidegger, *Poetry, Language, Thought*, trans. A. Hofstadter, New York: Harper and Row, 1971, pp. 28, 32.

7. As he concludes his discussion of the distinction between natural and artificial beauty, Kant argues for a certain superiority of the beautiful arts. This superiority is owing to the fact that the beautiful arts produce beautiful representations of objects, and are capable of beautifully depicting things that are naturally ugly or displeasing (except for what is disgusting). Yet, as Kant points out, such superiority is possible only because "the artistic representation of the object is . . . distinguished from the nature of the object itself in our sensation" (*Critique of Judgement*, p. 155). But obviously such a distinction holds only if the beautiful representation of the thing is not a copy of the thing, and only if there is no possible confusion (*Verwechselung*) between beautiful representations and things of nature. What counts in art, what gives it its specificity and a certain superiority (in that it seems to supplement nature), is that the representation itself becomes beautiful and is judged in its own right.

8. Kant elaborates on aesthetic ideas only in his discussion of the beautiful arts—a first allusion to them is made in chapter 17—but this does not mean that aesthetic ideas form the defining criterion of such arts. Indeed, as the opening (and unexpected) statement of chapter 51 shows, aesthetic ideas are not the prerogative of the beautiful arts, nor can they serve to establish any superiority of beautiful art over the beauty of nature. Rather, the opposite is the case; as Kant writes: "We may describe beauty in general (whether natural or artificial) as the expression of aesthetical ideas; only that in beautiful art this idea must be occasioned by a concept of the object, while in beautiful nature the mere reflection upon a given intuition, without any concept of what the object is to be, is sufficient for the awakening and communicating of the idea of which that object is regarded as the expression" (*Critique of Judgement*, p. 164). All beauty can be described as the expression of aesthetic ideas; however, such expression takes place differently in

judging natural beauty and in the production of the beautiful arts. In the beautiful arts, a concept gives rise to aesthetic ideas on condition that it is rendered indeterminate (and hence suggestive of ideas) through the supplementary representations that are added to the representation of the thing and that belong to the concept's presentation. But in the case of an object of nature for which we have no concept, the mere reflection upon the intuition (representation) by which this object is given—in short, reflection upon its form—awakens aesthetic ideas (and thus the object in question stands as their expression). How is one to conceive of this? The answer seems to be the following: In the absence of a determining concept, reflection upon the intuitive representation of the object may find that the object has the form of an undetermined object. Such reflection yields an undetermined concept of the object. Once the beautiful object has been judged to have form (that is, to yield to the concept of an object that is indeterminate), it can thus be seen to communicate aesthetic ideas.

9. Kant bases the (admittedly tentative) division of the arts in chapter 51 on the expression of aesthetic ideas, which compares the arts to linguistic articulation and communication, and he thereby suggests that genius-made art is like a language. The question arises therefore as to whether the works of art that express aesthetic ideas are similar to the form-language of nature. Through such form-language, nature announces its susceptibility to ideas of reason. If genius is the talent through which nature gives the law to art, might the expressed aesthetic ideas—which presuppose taste, and hence form—be signs through which nature actively takes on a role comparable to reason?

10. Kant's insistence on form at this particular junction raises the question of whether a presentation of the sublime *in the beautiful arts* would not have to rely primarily on charm. The sublime, claims Kant, is "incompatible with [physical] charm" (*Critique of Judgement*, p. 83), although the beautiful is so compatible. The possibility of a beautiful presentation of the sublime would therefore be completely contrary to the nature of the sublime.

11. Jean-François Lyotard makes a similar point concerning contemporary art: precisely because the fine arts can always revert to mere art as craft, they are intrinsically a limit-phenomenon. See his *The Inhuman: Reflections on Time*, trans. G. Bennington and R. Bowlby, Stanford, Calif.: Stanford University Press, 1991, p. 167.

CHAPTER 8

1. Immanuel Kant, *Critique of Judgement*, trans. J. H. Bernard, New York: Hafner, 1951, p. 172. All page references in the text are to this edition.

2. Robert J. Drostal, "Kant and Rhetoric," *Philosophy and Rhetoric*, 13, no. 4, 1980, p. 223.

3. Rudolf Boehm, *Das Grundlegende und das Wesentliche*, The Hague: Nijhoff, 1965, pp. 57–59.

4. Cicero, *De oratore*, vol. 4, trans. H. Rackham and E. W. Sutton, Cambridge, Mass.: Harvard University Press, 1942, p. 161 (III.53.202).

Quintilian, *The Institutio Oratoria*, trans. H. E. Butler, New York: Putnam, 1922, p. 397 (IX.2.40).

6. Ibid., p. 245 (VIII.3.61).

7. Du Marsais, *Traité des tropes*, Paris: Le Nouveau Commerce, 1977, p. 110.

8. Pierre Fontanier, *Les figures du discours*, Paris: Flammarion, 1968, p. 390.

9. Henri Morier, *Dictionnaire de poétique et de rhétorique*, 3rd ed., Paris: Presses Universitaires de France, 1981, pp. 521–24.

10. Donald W. Crawford, *Kant's Aesthetic Theory*, Madison: University of Wisconsin Press, 1974, p. 149.

11. Jean Beaufret, "Kant et la notion de Darstellung," *Dialogue avec Heidegger*, vol. 2, Paris: Minuit, 1973, pp. 79–81.

12. Ibid., pp. 92–95.

13. Therefore, the nature of the intuitions at the basis of symbolic hypotyposis does not matter. In this case, Kant remarks, one can even avail oneself of empirical intuitions (Kant, *Critique of Judgement*, p. 197).

14. Immanuel Kant, *Critique of Pure Reason*, trans. N. K. Smith, New York: St. Martin's Press, 1965, p. 211.

15. Immanuel Kant, *Prolegomena to Any Future Metaphysics*, trans. P. G. Lucas, Manchester: Manchester University Press, 1959, p. 125.

16. Immanuel Kant, *Anthropology from a Pragmatic Point of View*, trans. V. L. Dowdell, Carbondale: Southern Illinois University Press, 1978, pp. 83–84.

17. Therefore, I cannot agree with Eliane Escoubas's attempt to understand presentation primarily through symbolical hypotyposis in her otherwise excellent study *Imago mundi: Topologie de l'art* (Paris: Galilée, 1986, pp. 346–56). Schematic and symbolic hypotyposis are complementary. Presentation must be understood through what Kant thinks of when he calls it by the Greek name of the rhetorical figure in question.

18. Plato, *The Collected Dialogues*, ed. E. Hamilton and H. Carns, Princeton, N.J.: Princeton University Press, 1980.

19. On this subject of the *pathē*, see also Ernesto Grassi, *Rhetoric as Philosophy: The Humanist Tradition*, University Park: The Pennsylvania State University Press, 1980, pp. 28–32.

20. Kant, *Anthropology*, p. 52.

21. Beaufret, "Kant et la notion de Darstellung," p. 102.

22. Rudolf Makkreel, "Imagination and Temporality in Kant's Theory of the Sublime," *Journal of Aesthetics and Art Criticism*, 42, no. 3, 1984, pp. 303–15.

23. Kant, *Anthropology*, p. 65.

24. Alfred Baeumler, *Das Irrationalitätsproblem in der Aesthetik und Logik des 18. Jahrhunderts bis zur Kritik der Urteilskraft*, Darmstadt: Wissenschaftliche Buchgesellschaft, 1981, p. 168.

Bibliography

Adelung, Johann Christoph, *Grammatisch-kritisches Wörterbuch der hochdeutschen Mundart*, Leipzig, 1793; reprint, Hildesheim: Olms, 1970.
Adorno, Theodor W., *Aesthetic Theory*, trans. R. Hullot-Kentor, Minneapolis: University of Minnesota Press, 1997.
Baeumler, Alfred, *Das Irrationalitätsproblem in der Aesthetik und Logik des 18. Jahrhunderts bis zur Kritik der Urteilskraft*, Darmstadt: Wissenschaftliche Buchgesellschaft, 1981.
Beaufret, Jean, "Kant et la notion de Darstellung," in *Dialogue avec Heidegger*, vol. 2, Paris: Minuit, 1973, pp. 77–109.
Bernstein, Jay M., "Judging Life: From Beauty to Experience, From Kant to Chaim Soutine," *Constellations: An International Journal of Critical and Democratic Theory*, 7, no. 2, June 2000, pp. 157–77.
Biemel, Walter, *Die Bedeutung von Kants Begründung der Aesthetik für die Philosophie der Kunst*, Cologne: Kölner Universitätsverlag, 1959.
Boehm, Rudolf, *Das Grundlegende und das Wesentliche*, The Hague: Nijhoff, 1965.
Campe, Rüdiger, "Vor Augen stellen: Über den Rahmen rhetorischer Bildgebung," in *Poststrukturalismus. Herausforderung an die Literaturwissenschaft*, ed. G. Neumann, Stuttgart: Metzler, 1997, pp. 208–25.
Cassirer, Ernst, *Kant's Life and Thought*, trans. J. Haden, New Haven, Conn.: Yale University Press, 1981.
Chédin, Olivier, *Sur l'esthétique de Kant et la théorie critique de la représentation*, Paris: Vrin, 1982.
Cicero, *De oratore*, vol. 4, trans. H. Rackham and E. W. Sutton, Cambridge, Mass.: Harvard University Press, 1942.
Cohen, Hermann, *Kants Theorie der Erfahrung*, Berlin: Bruno Cassirer, 1918.
Crawford, Donald W., *Kant's Aesthetic Theory*, Madison: University of Wisconsin Press, 1974.
———, "The Sublime in Kant's Aesthetic Theory," in *The Philosophy of Immanuel Kant*, ed. R. Kennington, Washington, D.C.: Catholic University of America Press, 1985, pp. 161–84.

Deleuze, Gilles, *Kant's Critical Philosophy: The Doctrine of the Faculties*, trans. H. Tomlinson and B. Habberjam, Minneapolis: University of Minnesota Press, 1984.
Derrida, Jacques, *The Truth in Painting*, trans. G. Bennington and I. McLeod, Chicago: University of Chicago Press, 1987.
Drostal, Robert J., "Kant and Rhetoric," *Philosophy and Rhetoric*, 13, no. 4, 1980, pp. 223–44.
Du Marsais, *Traité des tropes*, Paris: Le Nouveau Commerce, 1977.
Escoubas, Eliane, *Imago mundi. Topologie de l'art*, Paris: Galilée, 1986.
Fontanier, Pierre, *Les figures du discours*, Paris: Flammarion, 1968.
Förster, Eckart, "Kant's Third Critique and the Opus Postumum," *Graduate Faculty Philosophy Journal*, 16, no. 2, 1993, pp. 345–58.
Gasché, Rodolphe, "Leaps of Imagination," in *The Path of Archaic Thinking: Unfolding the Work of John Sallis*, ed. K. Maly, Albany: State University of New York Press, 1995, pp. 35–47.
———, "Über das Wegsehen. Aufmerksamkeit und Abstraktion bei Kant," trans. A. Budzinski and J. Luftig, in *Liechtensteiner Exkurse III: Aufmerksamkeit*, Eggingen: Edition Isele, 1998, pp. 129–59.
———, *The Wild Card of Reading: On Paul de Man*, Cambridge, Mass.: Harvard University Press, 1997.
Grassi, Ernesto, *Rhetoric as Philosophy: The Humanist Tradition*, University Park: The Pennsylvania State University Press, 1980.
Gregor, Mary J., "Aesthetic Form and Sensory Content in the *Critique of Judgment*: Can Kant's 'Critique of Aesthetic Judgment' Provide a Philosophical Basis for Modern Formalism?" in *The Philosophy of Immanuel Kant*, ed. R. Kennington, Washington, D.C.: Catholic University of America Press, 1985, pp. 185–99.
Grimm, Jacob, and Wilhelm Grimm, *Deutsches Wörterbuch*, Leipzig: S. Hirzel, 1936.
Guillermit, Louis, *L'élucidation critique du jugement de goût selon Kant*, Paris: Editions du CNRS, 1986.
Hegel, Georg Wilhelm Friedrich, *Aesthetics: Lectures on Fine Art*, trans. T. M. Knox, Oxford: Clarendon, 1975.
Heidegger, Martin, *Poetry, Language, Thought*, trans. A. Hofstadter, New York: Harper and Row, 1971.
Helfer, Martha B., *The Retreat of Representation: The Concept of Darstellung in German Critical Discourse*, Albany: State University of New York Press, 1996.
Henrich, Dieter, *Aesthetic Judgment and the Moral Image of the World: Studies in Kant*, Stanford, Calif.: Stanford University Press, 1992.
Husserl, Edmund, *The Crisis of European Sciences and Transcendental Phenomenology*, trans. D. Carr, Evanston, Ill.: Northwestern University Press, 1970.

Ibanez-Noé, Javier, "Urteilskraft und Darstellung," in *Akten des siebenten internationalen Kant-Kongresses*, ed. G. Funke, Bonn: Bouvier, pp. 117–27.
Kant, Immanuel, *Anthropology from a Pragmatic Point of View*, trans. V. L. Dowdell, Carbondale: Southern Illinois University Press, 1978.
———, *Critique of Judgement*, trans. J. H. Bernard, New York: Hafner, 1951.
———, *Critique of Practical Reason*, trans. L. W. Beck, Indianapolis: Bobbs-Merrill, 1956.
———, *Critique of Pure Reason*, trans. N. K. Smith, New York: St. Martin's Press, 1965.
———, *First Introduction to the "Critique of Judgment,"* trans. J. Haden, Indianapolis: Bobbs-Merrill, 1965.
———, *Kants gesammelte Schriften*, 29 vols., Berlin: de Gruyter, 1902–83.
———, *Logic*, trans. R. S. Hartman and W. Schwarz, Indianapolis: Bobbs-Merrill, 1974.
———, *The Metaphysics of Morals*, trans. M. Gregor, Cambridge, Eng.: Cambridge University Press, 1991.
———, *Prolegomena to Any Future Metaphysics*, trans. P. G. Lucas, Manchester: Manchester University Press, 1959.
———, *Werke in sechs Bänden*, ed. W. Weischedel, Darmstadt: Wissenschaftliche Buchgesellschaft, 1966.
Krüger, Gerhard, "Über Kants Lehre von der Zeit," in Gerhard Krüger, *Philosophie und Moral in der Kantischen Kritik*, 2d ed., Tübingen: J. C. B. Mohr, 1967, pp. 269–94.
Kulenkampff, Jens, *Kants Logik des ästhetischen Urteils*, Frankfurt/Main: Klostermann, 1978.
La Rocca, Claudio, "Forme et signe dans l'esthétique de Kant," in *Kants Ästhetik/Kant's Aesthetics/L'esthétique de Kant*, ed. H. Parret, Berlin: de Gruyter, 1998, pp. 530–44.
Longinus, "On the Sublime," in Aristotle, Horace, and Longinus, *Classical Literary Criticism*, trans. T. S. Dorsch, London: Penguin Books, 1965, pp. 99–158.
Longuenesse, Béatrice, *Kant and the Capacity to Judge: Sensibility and Discursivity in the Transcendental Analytic of the "Critique of Pure Reason,"* trans. Charles T. Wolfe, Princeton, N.J.: Princeton University Press, 1998.
Lyotard, Jean-François, *L'enthousiasme. La critique kantienne de l'histoire*, Paris: Galilée, 1986.
———, *The Inhuman: Reflections on Time*, trans. G. Bennington and R. Bowlby, Stanford, Calif.: Stanford University Press, 1991.
———, *Lessons on the Analytic of the Sublime*, trans. E. Rottenberg, Stanford, Calif.: Stanford University Press, 1994.
Makkreel, Rudolf A., *Imagination and Interpretation in Kant: The Hermeneutical*

Import of the "Critique of Judgment," Chicago: University of Chicago Press, 1990.

———, "Imagination and Temporality in Kant's Theory of the Sublime," *Journal of Aesthetics and Art Criticism*, 42, no. 3, 1984, pp. 303–15.

———, "The Role of Reflection in Kant's Transcendental Philosophy," in *Transcendental Philosophy and Everyday Experience*, ed. T. Rockmore and V. Zeman, Atlantic Highlands, N.J.: Humanities Press, 1997, pp. 84–95.

Menninghaus, Winfried, *Ekel. Theorie und Geschichte einer starken Empfindung*, Frankfurt/Main: Suhrkamp, 1999.

———, *Lob des Unsinns. Über Kant, Tieck und Blaubart*, Frankfurt/Main: Suhrkamp, 1995.

Morier, Henri, *Dictionnaire de poétique et de rhétorique*, 3rd ed., Paris: Presses Universitaires de France, 1981.

Mülder-Bach, Inka, *Im Zeichen Pygmalions. Das Modell der Statue und die Entdeckung der "Darstellung" in 18. Jahrhundert*, Munich: Fink Verlag, 1998.

Patočka, Jan, *Plato and Europe*, trans. Petr Lom, Stanford, Calif.: Stanford University Press, 2002.

Pippin, Robert B., *Kant's Theory of Form: An Essay on the "Critique of Pure Reason,"* New Haven, Conn.: Yale University Press, 1982.

———, "The Significance of Taste: Kant, Aesthetic and Reflective Judgment," *Journal of the History of Philosophy*, 34, no. 4, 1996, pp. 549–69.

Plato, *The Collected Dialogues*, ed. E. Hamilton and H. Carns, Princeton, N.J.: Princeton University Press, 1980.

Quintillian, *Institutio Oratoria*, trans. H. E. Butler, New York: Putnam, 1922.

Riedel, Manfred, *Urteilskraft und Vernunft. Kants ursprüngliche Fragestellung*, Frankfurt/Main: Suhrkamp, 1989.

Rivelaygue, Jacques, *Leçons de métaphysique allemande*, 2 vols., Paris: Grasset, 1992.

Schlenstedt, Dieter, "Darstellung," in *Aesthetische Grundbegriffe*, ed. K. Barck et al., Stuttgart: Metzler Verlag, 2000, 1: 831–75.

Seel, Martin, *Eine Ästhetik der Natur*, Frankfurt/Main: Suhrkamp, 1996.

Stolnitz, Jerome, "On the Origins of 'Aesthetic Disinterestedness,'" *Journal of Aesthetics and Art Criticism*, 20, 1960–61, pp. 131–43.

Strube, Werner, "Interesselosigkeit. Zur Geschichte eines Grundbegriffs der Aesthetik," *Archiv für Begriffsgeschichte*, 22, 1979, pp. 148–74.

Tonelli, Giorgio, "La formazione del testo della *Kritik der Urteilskraft*," *Revue Internationale de Philosophie*, 30, no. 8, 1954, pp. 423–48.

———, "Von den verschiedenen Bedeutungen des Wortes Zeckmässigkeit in der Kritik der Urteilskraft," *Kant-Studien*, 49, no. 2, 1957–58, pp. 154–66.

Trebels, Andreas Heinrich, *Einbildungskraft und Spiel. Untersuchungen zur Kantischen Aesthetik*, Bonn: Bouvier, 1967.

Uehling, Theodor Edward, *The Notion of Form in Kant's "Critique of Aesthetic Judgment,"* The Hague: Mouton, 1971.
Weber, Samuel, *Mass Mediauras: Form, Technics, Media,* ed. A. Cholodenko, Sydney: Power Publications, 1996.
Zelle, Carsten, *Die doppelte Ästhetik der Moderne. Revisionen des Schönen von Boileau bis Nietzsche,* Stuttgart: Metzler, 1995.

Index

Addison, Joseph, 242n2
Adelung, Johann Christoph, 21, 24, 28
Adorno, Theodor W., 221n1
aesthetics, 2, 90; double, 6, 237n1; formalist, 60; Kant's, 3, 5–6, 8, 10, 60, 90, 156–57, 178–80, 221n4, 221n5, 230n2, 237n1, 241n2, 243n3
analogy, 212–13
a priori, transcendental, 11, 27, 37, 54, 56, 58–59, 78, 230n18
Aquinas, Thomas, 217
architype (*Urbild*), 118
Ariadne, 28
Aristotle, 8, 61, 74, 205, 207, 216
art, 5, 14, 34, 62, 75, 80, 180; beautiful, 106, 108, 116, 169, 183–95, 199, 203, 206, 236n20; end of, 243n3; of genius, 113, 170, 178, 186, 191, 194–96, 199, 201; in Kant's aesthetics, 8, 11, 199; and nature, 181–82; work of, 181, 185–86, 221n1, 231n8
apprehension, mere, 127
attributes, aesthetic, 115, 195–96

Baeumler, Alfred, 218
Baumgarten, Alexander Gottlieb, 2, 5, 218
Beaufret, Jean, 209, 217
beauty, 56; beauty, artificial, 12, 75, 80–81, 88, 90, 174, 177–78, 181, 193, 198–200, 244n7, 244n8; ideal of, 7, 104, 243n2; intellectual, 159, 167–68, 177; and morality, 157, 160; natural, 1–3, 12, 70, 75, 80–81, 90, 96, 126, 170, 174–78, 181, 192–93, 198, 200, 221n1, 227n54, 235n20, 244n7, 244n8; wild, 66–67, 110
Bernstein, Jay M., 226n43
Biemel, Walter, 68–70, 231n3
Boehm, Rudolf, 207
Burke, Edmund, 45, 241n21, 242n2

Campe, Rüdiger, 235n7
Cassirer, Ernst, 5, 30, 120, 221n4, 225n42
Chédin, Olivier, 18, 222n8, 236n24, 237n27, 243n2
Cicero, 205, 207, 214, 218
cognition in general, 4, 10, 39–40, 46–55, 69, 80, 82, 98–99, 103, 129, 175, 177, 183, 186–88, 194, 203–4, 239n11, 242n6, 243n3
Crawford, Donald W., 208, 223n6

Deleuze, Gilles, 53
de Man, Paul, 232n22, 237n1, 242n5
Derrida, Jacques, 110, 224n22, 230n2, 237n26
Descartes, René, 217
disgust (*Ekel*), 200–201, 229n15, 234n46, 244n7
disinterestedness, 3, 156–58, 161–62, 164–65, 167–70, 177, 199, 241n2
Du Marsais, 207, 214

Epicurus, 45
Escoubas, Eliane, 246n17
Euler, Leonard, 63, 231n3
experience, condition of possibility of, 15–16, 37, 41; empirical, 38; mere, 38–39; unity of, 24, 31, 36

feeling, moral, 158–59, 160–62, 164–65, 173–75, 239n10
Fontanier, Pierre, 207
form, 3, 6, 12, 37, 60–64, 68, 71, 81–83, 86–87, 110, 176, 179, 186, 192, 200, 222n7, 232n11; aesthetics of, 10, 230n2; beautiful, 6–8, 65–67, 71, 85; indeterminateness of, 185–88, 190–91, 195–96, 198–99, 236n20; inner form, 62; and matter, 61, 74, 189, 197, 244n6; mere, 8–10, 62, 66, 70, 72–73, 79, 82, 85–88, 91, 93, 97–98, 101, 103–6, 118, 128, 133, 135, 157, 185, 189, 191, 224n18, 239n12; natural, 80–81, 175–77, 179, 240n14; of the schools, 185–86, 189–91, 244n5
formalism, 10, 61, 63–65, 68, 82, 87, 106, 109, 186, 192, 230n2
formlessness, 3–4, 6, 60, 123–28, 130, 134, 136, 149, 152, 165, 233n30, 234n46, 235n15
Förster, Eckart, 231n4

genius, 107–9, 116–17, 185–90, 192, 195, 197–98, 203, 233n32, 243n3, 244n4, 244n5, 245n9
Grassi, Ernesto, 246n19
Gregor, Mary J., 232n15
Grimm, Jacob and Wilhelm, 22
guideline (*Leitfaden*), 28–29
Guillermit, Louis, 69, 223n15, 232n21, 238n2, 239n10, 240n14, 243n3

Hegel, Georg Wilhelm Friedrich, 2, 20, 221n1, 231n8, 240n14, 243n3
Heidegger, Martin, 68, 70, 225n25, 231n3, 244n6

Helfer, Martha B., 234n4
Henrich, Dieter, 81, 92, 228n5, 232n20
Husserl, Edmund, 20
Hutcheson, Francis, 242n2
hypotyposis, 12, 35, 89, 102, 206–11, 215–18, 234n7, 246n13

Ibanez-Noé, Javier, 95
idea, 12, 101, 107, 109, 115, 117, 235n17; aesthetic, 106–16, 118, 189, 194–99, 203, 206, 227n55, 236n20, 236n25, 244n8, 245n9; mere, 34, 102–3, 105, 117
ideal, 101, 103, 105–6, 114, 117, 235n17
imagination, 76, 93–95, 99, 104, 106, 109, 113, 116, 138–39, 141, 149, 218, 241n20, 242n4; productive, 110–11, 113, 117, 195–96, 217; and understanding, 46, 55, 75, 242n6; and reason, 101, 107, 114, 144–46, 149, 162–64, 166–67, 242n6
interest, 155, 157, 158, 161, 164–65, 167–70, 177, 181, 199–201; empirical, 171–72; intellectual, 171–75, 181
intuition, mere, 84, 137

judgment, aesthetic (or of taste), 2–10, 19, 27, 32, 35, 42–47, 52–57, 60–63, 65–66, 72–88, 97–102, 104, 108, 117, 124, 130, 134, 155–56, 173, 191, 221n4, 226n43, 226n44, 228n10, 228n12; upon the beautiful, 122, 153–54; cognitive, or determining 4–5, 11, 13–18, 23, 27, 54–55, 57, 75, 93, 226n52; infinite, 69–70; upon magnitude, 134–36, 139–40; merely reflective, 13–18, 22–28, 37–40, 53, 93; moral, 5–6, 10; power of, 13–15, 23–27, 36–37, 40, 94–95, 103, 215, 226n51, 228n10; reflective, 4–7, 10–19, 24, 29, 34, 37, 39, 66, 71, 73–76, 96, 226n52; standard for, 100–102, 105, 114, 134–35, 139–41; upon the sublime, 121, 124,

127–29, 133–34, 136–137, 141–43, 146, 148, 152–54, 161, 237n1, 238n7, 239n14, 242n6; teleological, 4, 27–28, 30–32, 35, 62, 74, 78, 221n4, 226n44, 238n7

Klopstock, Friedrich Gottlieb, 91
Krüger, Gerhard, 241n19
Kulenkampff, Jens, 108

La Rocca, Claudio, 70, 84
laughter, 45
Lévi-Strauss, Claude, 31
life, 58; life, feeling of, 44–45, 50, 52, 56–57, 228n10; of the mind, 44–45, 204, 206, 209–11, 216–18, 228n5
Longinus, 236n25
Longuenesse, Béatrice, 223n13
Lyotard, Jean-François, 26, 120, 144, 222n8, 223n8, 225n31, 235n17, 237n1, 239n10, 242n5, 245n11

magnitude (or size), aesthetic estimation of, 137, 139, 141–43; mere, 96, 135, 239n12
Makkreel, Rudolf A., 44, 48, 217, 225n37
Marsden, William, 65–66
Menninghaus, Winfried, 229n15, 231n6
mere, or merely (*bloss*), 18–24, 41, 97, 133, 224n16, 224n21, 224n22, 225n25, 232n21
mind (*Gemüt*), 108; mind, state of (*Stimmung*), 47–49, 52, 228n5
morality, symbol of, 6, 106, 208–9
Morier, Henri, 208
Mülder-Bach, Inka, 234n4

nature, 2, 15, 17, 36, 229n15; formal, 233n28; other, 111, 227n55; purposiveness of, 5, 34; second-order, 36, 227n55; wild, 1–2, 5–6, 67, 231n8
Newton, Isaac, 243n3
Nietzsche, Friedrich, 3

observation, mere, 72, 79

pain, feeling of, 143–45, 147, 149
Patočka, Jan, 239n9
perfection, 2, 62–63, 67, 100, 180, 182
Pippin, Robert B., 221n5, 222n7, 228n11
Plato, 238n9
play of the faculties, free, 10, 26, 39, 45–46, 48–51, 53–57, 59, 82–83, 187, 204, 228n5, 228n12, 229n15, 243n3
pleasure, feeling of, 2–4, 7, 9, 38, 44, 50–53, 77, 79, 98, 106, 125–26, 156, 171, 223n6
presentation (*Darstellung*), 9, 73, 75–76, 81, 83, 89–99, 101–3, 109–10, 163, 169, 193, 195, 206, 208, 234n4, 234n7, 235n15; schematic, 12, 102, 114, 117–18, 210–11, 213–15, 246n17; symbolic, 12, 103–5, 111–14, 118, 210–11, 213–15, 246n13, 246n17
purity, 19–20, 22, 34, 39–41, 224n17, 224n18, 225n25, 230n2
purpose, natural, 31–32
purposiveness, formal, 24, 34–36, 39–40, 74, 76–77, 80, 129, 225n37, 225n41, 233n30; inner and relative, 84, 121, 238n7; subjective and objective, 84; without purpose, 99, 235n18, 237n26

Quintillian, 207, 214, 218

reason, 4, 7, 10, 94, 107–8, 116, 125, 130, 132, 147, 149, 153–54, 221n5; and form, 12, 91; maximum of, 9, 101–4, 106, 112–13, 116, 138–40, 235n17, 240n15; and poetry, 204
reflection, 17, 95, 223n8, 225n42, 228n11; mere, 30, 36–37, 41; principle of, 24, 27, 29, 31, 33–36; task of, 31
regularity, 65–66, 231n5
representation (*Vorstellung*), 8, 25, 35, 47, 86–87, 91–92, 96, 115–16, 118, 193, 209; mere, 97–98, 118

resistance, intellectual power of, 151–52, 166
rhetoric, 202–3, 205, 208, 216, 218; philosophical appropriation of, 202, 218, 234n7; and poetry, 203, 205–6
Riedel, Friedrich Justus, 242n2
Riedel, Manfred, 226n42, 235n16
Rivelaygue, Jacques, 233n28

Saussure, H. Bénédict de, 231n7
schema, 214, 216, 217
Schiller, Friedrich, 221n1, 237n1
Schlenstedt, Dieter, 234n4
Schopenhauer, Arthur, 3
Seel, Martin, 221n1
Sextus Empiricus, 206
Shaftesbury, Earl of, 242n2
Socrates, 216
spirit (*Geist*), 46, 108, 110–11, 117, 194, 196–97
standard, intellectual, 140–41, 143–44, 152–153; aesthetic, 137, 139–41, 145, 148
Stolnitz, Jerome, 242n2
Strube, Werner, 242n2
sublime, the, 1–2, 4, 56, 107, 169, 222n8; aesthetics of, 119–20; dynamically, 131–32, 151, 223n7; feeling of, 120, 126, 131–32, 138, 141, 143, 145–47, 165, 169, 239n10, 240n16; intellectual, 159, 167–68; mathematically, 131–32, 151, 223n7, 237n28
symbol, 213–16

taste, 113–14, 190–192, 194; archetype, 101–3, 105, 107, 113–15, 117–18; mere, 190–91, 198
Theseus, 28
Tonelli, Giorgio, 9, 120–21, 225n41, 237n2
Trebels, Andreas Heinrich, 42, 48–49

Uehling, Theodor Edward, 230n3

violence, 126, 138, 144, 147–48, 164, 169

Weber, Samuel, 231n11
Winckelmann, Johann Joachim, 68
Wolff, Christian, 91

Zelle, Carsten, 222n6, 237n1
Zweckwidridkeit, 124, 126

Cultural Memory in the Present

Jean-Luc Nancy, *Finite Thinking*, edited by Simon Sparks

Theodor W. Adorno, *Can One Live after Auschwitz?: A Philosophical Reader*, edited by Rolf Tiedemann

Patricia Pisters, *The Matrix of Visual Culture: Working with Deleuze in Film Theory*

Talal Asad, *Formations of the Secular: Christianity, Islam, Modernity*

Dorothea von Mücke, *The Rise of the Fantastic Tale*

Eric Michaud, *An Art for Eternity: The Cult of Art in Nazi Germany*

Marc Redfield, *The Politics of Aesthetics: Nationalism, Gender, Romanticism*

Emmanuel Levinas, *On Escape*

Dan Zahavi, *Husserl's Phenomenology*

Rodolphe Gasché, *The Idea of Form: Rethinking Kant's Aesthetics*

Michael Naas, *Taking on the Tradition: Jacques Derrida and the Legacies of Deconstruction*

Herlinde Pauer-Studer, ed., *Constructions of Practical Reason: Interviews on Moral and Political Philosophy*

Jean-Luc Marion, *Being Given: Toward a Phenomenology of Givenness*

Theodor W. Adorno and Max Horkheimer, *Dialectic of Enlightenment*

Ian Balfour, *The Rhetoric of Romantic Prophecy*

Martin Stokhof, *World and Life as One: Ethics and Ontology in Wittgenstein's Early Thought*

Gianni Vattimo, *Nietzsche: An Introduction*

Jacques Derrida, *Negotiations: Interventions and Interviews, 1971–1998*, ed. Elizabeth Rottenberg

Brett Levinson, *The Ends of Literature: Post-transition and Neoliberalism in the Wake of the "Boom"*

Timothy J. Reiss, *Against Autonomy: Global Dialectics of Cultural Exchange*

Hent de Vries and Samuel Weber, eds., *Religion and Media*

Niklas Luhmann, *Theories of Distinction: Redescribing the Descriptions of Modernity*, ed. and introd. William Rasch

Johannes Fabian, *Anthropology with an Attitude: Critical Essays*

Michel Henry, *I Am the Truth: Toward a Philosophy of Christianity*

Gil Anidjar, *"Our Place in Al-Andalus": Kabbalah, Philosophy, Literature in Arab-Jewish Letters*

Hélène Cixous and Jacques Derrida, *Veils*

F. R. Ankersmit, *Historical Representation*

F. R. Ankersmit, *Political Representation*

Elissa Marder, *Dead Time: Temporal Disorders in the Wake of Modernity (Baudelaire and Flaubert)*

Reinhart Koselleck, *The Practice of Conceptual History: Timing History, Spacing Concepts*

Niklas Luhmann, *The Reality of the Mass Media*

Hubert Damisch, *A Childhood Memory by Piero della Francesca*

Hubert Damisch, *A Theory of /Cloud/: Toward a History of Painting*

Jean-Luc Nancy, *The Speculative Remark (One of Hegel's Bons Mots)*

Jean-François Lyotard, *Soundproof Room: Malraux's Anti-Aesthetics*

Jan Patočka, *Plato and Europe*

Hubert Damisch, *Skyline: The Narcissistic City*

Isabel Hoving, *In Praise of New Travelers: Reading Caribbean Migrant Women Writers*

Richard Rand, ed., *Futures: Of Derrida*

William Rasch, *Niklas Luhmann's Modernity: The Paradox of System Differentiation*

Jacques Derrida and Anne Dufourmantelle, *Of Hospitality*

Jean-François Lyotard, *The Confession of Augustine*

Kaja Silverman, *World Spectators*

Samuel Weber, *Institution and Interpretation: Expanded Edition*

Jeffrey S. Librett, *The Rhetoric of Cultural Dialogue: Jews and Germans in the Epoch of Emancipation*

Ulrich Baer, *Remnants of Song: Trauma and the Experience of Modernity in Charles Baudelaire and Paul Celan*

Samuel C. Wheeler III, *Deconstruction as Analytic Philosophy*

David S. Ferris, *Silent Urns: Romanticism, Hellenism, Modernity*

Rodolphe Gasché, *Of Minimal Things: Studies on the Notion of Relation*

Sarah Winter, *Freud and the Institution of Psychoanalytic Knowledge*

Samuel Weber, *The Legend of Freud: Expanded Edition*

Aris Fioretos, ed., *The Solid Letter: Readings of Friedrich Hölderlin*

J. Hillis Miller / Manuel Asensi, *Black Holes / J. Hillis Miller; or, Boustrophedonic Reading*

Miryam Sas, *Fault Lines: Cultural Memory and Japanese Surrealism*

Peter Schwenger, *Fantasm and Fiction: On Textual Envisioning*

Didier Maleuvre, *Museum Memories: History, Technology, Art*

Jacques Derrida, *Monolingualism of the Other; or, The Prosthesis of Origin*

Andrew Baruch Wachtel, *Making a Nation, Breaking a Nation: Literature and Cultural Politics in Yugoslavia*

Niklas Luhmann, *Love as Passion: The Codification of Intimacy*

Mieke Bal, ed., *The Practice of Cultural Analysis: Exposing Interdisciplinary Interpretation*

Jacques Derrida and Gianni Vattimo, eds., *Religion*

if the symbol is not in (pure) time 2, 14 + elsewhere
+ if Tr Ego is (only) in time
   does the Tr Ego attenuate in Symbolism's timelessness